Curating Digital Art

WITH CONTRIBUTIONS BY

Pita Arreola-Burns
Evelyn Austin
LaTurbo Avedon
Paul Barsch
Livia Benedetti
Bob Bicknell-Knight
Elliott Burns
Tom Clark
Marco De Mutiis
Constant Dullaart
Madja Edelstein-Gomez
Rebecca Edwards
Amber van den Eeden
Rózsa Farkas
Marialaura Ghidini
Manique Hendricks
Tilman Hornig
Florian Kuhlmann
Kalle Mattsson
Anika Meier
Marie Meixnerová
Laura Mousavi
Katja Novitskova
Domenico Quaranta
Stefan Riebel
Ryder Ripps
Sakrowski
Katrina Sluis
Lilian Stolk
Systaime
Gaia Tedone
Jon Uriarte
Miyö Van Stenis
Nimrod Vardi
Marcela Vieira
Zhang Ga

Annet Dekker (ed.)

Curating Digital Art

From Presenting and Collecting Digital Art
to Networked Co-curation

Valiz, Amsterdam

Contents

7 **Introduction**

8 About this Book
14 Curating Digital Art
Annet Dekker

35 **Interviews**

36 Domenico Quaranta
46 Tom Clark
& Rózsa Farkas
58 Amber van den Eeden
& Kalle Mattsson
66 Katja Novitskova
74 Laura Mousavi
82 Madja Edelstein-
Gomez
94 Gaia Tedone
108 Manique Hendricks
116 Marialaura Ghidini
132 Bob Bicknell-Knight
144 Miyö Van Stenis
152 Evelyn Austin
& Lilian Stolk
160 LaTurbo Avedon
168 Sakrowski

178 Marie Meixnerová
188 Systaime
196 Florian Kuhlmann
202 New Scenario
(Paul Barsch
& Tilman Hornig)
212 Nimrod Vardi
& Rebecca Edwards
222 Ryder Ripps
228 Stefan Riebel
236 Pita Arreola-Burns
& Elliott Burns
246 Livia Benedetti
& Marcela Vieira
254 Zhang Ga
266 Constant Dullaart
274 Anika Meier
284 Marco De Mutiis,
Katrina Sluis
& Jon Uriarte

297 **The Broken Timeline**
Marialaura Ghidini, Gaia Tedone & Annet Dekker

341 **Index**

Introduction

About this Book

Curating Digital Art is dedicated to pioneering curators, artists and designers and presents a collection of interviews that were conducted between 2011 and 2020. The interviews emerged from the concern that too little knowledge was available about the potential of exhibiting digital art, either in museum spaces and galleries, or on the Web.

In an attempt to address this hiatus this publication provides an overview of the different perspectives and practices of nearly a decade of curating digital art in physical and online space. Twenty-seven interviewees were asked the same set of questions, with some slight variations due to their specific projects. The answers of *aarea* (Livia Benedetti and Marcela Vieira), Anika Meier, Arcadia Missa (Tom Clark and Rózsa Farkas), *arebyte Gallery* (Rebecca Edwards and Nimrod Vardi), Bob Bicknell-Knight, Constant Dullaart, Madja Edelstein-Gomez, Marialaura Ghidini, Manique Hendricks, Florian Kuhlmann, LaTurbo Avedon, Mary Meixner, Laura Mousavi, *New Scenario* (Paul Barsch and Tilman Hornig), Katja Novitskova, *Off Site Project* (Pita Arreola-Burns and Elliott Burns), Domenico Quaranta, Stefan Riebel, Ryder Ripps, Sakrowski, Systaime, Gaia Tedone, *temporarystedelijk.com* (Amber van den Eeden and Kalle Mattson), *The Hmm* (Evelyn Austin and Lilian Stolk), Miyö Van Stenis, *You Must Not Call It Photography If This Expression Hurts You* (Marco De Muttis, Katrina Sluis, Jon Uriarte) and Zhang Ga, map the distinctiveness and idiosyncrasies of curating digital art, from conventional white and black cubes and small artists' spaces, to custom-built online spaces and the expansion of curating on commercial platforms.

The seed for this publication was planted around 2009 when I organized *Archive 2020*, an international expert meeting to discuss the characteristics of 'born-digital art' and the perils associated with its archiving. A year later, I discussed the outcomes and the question of why there was still so little digital art in museum collections or exhibitions with Angela Plohman, at the time director of

Baltan Laboratories. We borrowed a question posed during a book launch of the Viennese curator's collective Context in August 2011—*Why is it still easier to get an entire museum collection on the Internet than to get a single work of Internet-based Art in a museum space?*—to point to one of the sore spots in the discussion of why so little digital art is presented in museums. In an attempt to answer this question we organized an international working conference in collaboration with Van Abbemuseum in Eindhoven. Some of the outcomes ended up in the publication *Speculative Scenarios, or what will happen to digital art in the (near) future?* (2013), along with additional insight in the form of interviews, short essays and fiction. Preceding the conference, I asked six emerging curators, artists and designers to fill in a questionnaire about their curatorial practice.
A common denominator among the interviewees was their experience with online curating and/or presenting online artworks in physical spaces/magazines. One of the reasons I selected them was because of the ease with which they manoeuvered between digital and physical realms, from exhibitions in old warehouses, small sidestreet galleries and magazines, to online spaces and commercial platforms. They used existing curatorial formats for their presentations, adapted them if necessary, or even created new ones.

The questionnaire was a good research tool to gather information on different ways of thinking about digital curating. Moreover, it was also a way of charting the field, as the answers exemplified the diversity in approaches and how the interviewees dealt with divisions between various art worlds. The interviews were initially posted on the website as appetizers for the conference, and while some of the comments ended up in the publication, the interviews disappeared as quickly as some of the works we discussed. Within two years after I uploaded the interviews, I received an e-mail from one of the interviewees, Domenico Quaranta, informing me that the interviews—and the website for that matter—were down. Unable to retrieve the website, I started digging through my own archive and found them again. Yet, lacking the time to upload them elsewhere, they lay dormant in the dark corners of my hard drive. Several years passed, and while rearranging my computer I noticed the interviews, read them and realized how much of what was said was still relevant. At the same time, I had seen other interesting online exhibition formats and ideas. Consequently, in 2016 I decided to continue the series and interviewed a new batch of curators, artists and designers. Yet, it wasn't until a few years later that I found the time to re-organize them. Other interesting projects had been developed on the Web and so I conducted a final round of interviews in 2019 with the aim of publishing them together. I also contacted the earlier contributors to see if they wanted to participate in the publication and if their initial views had changed. Surprisingly no one wanted to change anything: the interviews written almost ten years earlier were still viable and valuable.

At the time of finalizing the publication, just finishing the final copy-edits, a global pandemic caused a sudden burst of online activity. The Covid-19 virus closed down public life and *en masse* everyone moved their social, public, private and work life online—including museums and galleries. Within less than a week, books were scanned, videos digitized, and different platforms, such as Zoom, Jitsi, Teams, Whereby, Skype, Twitch, Discord, YouTube and Second Life replaced physical workshops, conferences, discussions, and also exhibition openings. Public life, or F2F (face to face), had shut down, and the 'great migration' began in rapid tempo in which the online world became 'the new normal' for those with computers and stable Internet connections. Museums also tried to redesign, restructure and reconceptualize their collections, exhibitions and debates for the new interfaces. While many curators were on furlough, the digital media teams were working over time. Exhibitions were filmed, artworks cropped, moving robots were roaming the gallery spaces, and users were asked to interact, perform ancient paintings and sculptures, or create and send their personal anecdotes, memories, dreams, future wishes, and reflections related to Covid-19 that would capture the spirit of a historical period of crisis, self-isolation and resilience. Aroused by the accelerated speed, anxiety and adrenaline, I started to follow everything in an attempt to capture the moment, to the point of exhaustion, fatigue and torpor. Others raced ahead along, and I captured their vigour and vivacity in a last round of interviews. In the end I assembled 27 interviews, a subjective and incomplete series that shows merely the tip of the exciting and still evolving world of digital art curation.

My deepest gratitude goes to all the interviewees for making the Web an exciting space and who participated despite their busy schedules, my inability to offer them compensation and my endless extensions (for some up to ten years). Thanks go to Gaia Tedone for helping me to sort out the contributions (due to her always uplifting spirit and vitamin C this book is now a fact), to Katrina Sluis for her belligerent yet poignant eye for detail and for her critical honesty, and to Pia and Astrid from Valiz for their faith and their generosity in making this book a reality!

Annet Dekker is a curator, researcher and Assistant Professor Media Studies, Archival and Information Studies and Cultural Analysis at the University of Amsterdam (UvA), and Visiting Professor and co-director of the Centre for the Study of the Networked Image at London South Bank University. She has previously been Researcher Digital Preservation at Tate, London, core tutor at Piet Zwart Institute, Rotterdam and Fellow at Het Nieuwe Instituut, Rotterdam. She has published in numerous collections and journals and is the editor of several volumes, including *Lost and Living [in] Archives: Collectively Shaping New Memories* (Valiz 2017). Her monograph *Collecting and Conserving Net Art* (Routledge 2018) is a seminal work in the field of digital art conservation.

Curating Digital Art

From Presenting and Collecting Digital Art to Networked Co-curation

Annet Dekker

My initial motivation for doing the interviews in this book was based on my own frustration that after working for more than ten years as a curator of digital art, there were still few digital art exhibitions organized within contemporary art institutions. At the same time, I noticed a growing interest of a younger generation of curators and artists who were heavily invested in curating, setting up their own organizations and exploring the Web to create, commission, present and distribute digital art. I was curious to hear about their practice, how they viewed the discourse and whether they felt there was still a discord with the institutional artworlds or if the institutional framework was even needed at all? It turned out that no one was really interested in discussing my first question about terminology. What was once important to comprehend the aesthetic and dynamics of the artworks, or just to differentiate them from other artforms, now seemed completely irrelevant. Instead they preferred to draw a historical line with existing art movements, such as conceptual art or minimalism. In the end they opted for their work to be described as contemporary art, or simply art. Their attitude seemed liberating, not having to deal with the struggle of belonging to a certain category, movement or genre, not having to defend digital art as being as valuable as any other artform, nor having to argue for it to even be considered as art. However, when reading their responses to the question of whether museums should present and acquire digital art, a different tone emerged. On the one hand the role of the museum was respected and even desired, albeit that a good review on a blog or having a flood of new visitors were just as exciting. On the other hand, there was a consensus that the museum's presence on the Internet was unexciting and that museums had little understanding or interest in their curatorial efforts or the artworks they were presenting and commissioning.

Over the years there has been a vigorous debate about the lack of presentations and acquisitions of digital art by the institutional artworld, yet in the last decade there have been slow changes: more exhibitions were curated involving digital art or showing a historical perspective in which its specific themes and aesthetics were emphasized, and digital art is more often acquired by museums and private collections. However, most times when such curatorial events happen some kind of uproar follows about how digital art, and especially net art, is not treated respectfully. While valid arguments are certainly made, it is also interesting that for an artform without many historical precedents or set standards—since the experience of digital art depends on the specifics of the used equipment—there are apparently certain modes that need to be adhered to. This is something Eva Grubinger noticed a long time ago, back in the days when she organized one of the first online curatorial experiments *C@C – Computer-Aided Curating*, and it was one of the reasons why she decided not to continue to curate online:

> *C@C* was an artistic experiment, and considering that I neither wanted to become a kind of meta-curator nor start a business in the mediation of web-based art, I decided to stop feeling responsible for *C@C* and began work on new projects. (...) Group dynamics were another issue. I learned that sub-culture and avant-garde self-organisation can produce similar tactics and power struggles as the institutional or mainstream structures that they wanted to overcome in the first place.[1]

I recognized Grubinger's critique, which was echoed by the interviewees, however, there is a growing body of research that shows how museums and collectors have become more aware and interested in collecting digital art. Slowly exhibitions with or about digital art were organized and special staff was hired. Surely this was not a big shift and change was subtle but there seemed to be a move towards a greater acknowledgement of digital art as belonging to contemporary, or more accurately, institutionalized art. Certainly looking back ten years after the first interviews this is the case and the most recent interviewees who are less concerned with a 'divide' also confirm it. While acknowledging there is one, the role of the institutional is seen more as a place of historical value, a place where digital arts could be preserved. Interestingly, Vivian van Saaze, Glenn Wharton and Leah Reisman looked at how processes of change

1   Eva Grubinger, 'C@C – Computer Aided Curating (1993–1995) revisited', Lecture at Tate Modern, London, 4 June 2005. *evagrubinger.com/texts/eva-grubinger*.

happen and rather than being disruptive and perhaps even revolutionary, they concluded that change is often customized and slowly adapted to the daily work of the staff in an institution.[2] The introduction of different attitudes needs time, particularly in highly structured and authoritarian organizations. This trend can also be traced in the normalization of digital art in the establishment. On the other hand, looking at online curatorial practices I wondered how open they were for outsiders? If anything, the Web consists of numerous collectives and communities each with their own activities, aesthetics, in-jokes and rules.[3]

Curating.1
outside inside

As mentioned, *C@C – Computer-Aided Curating* is one of the earliest curatorial endeavours on the web. Initiated in 1993 and developed by Grubinger in collaboration with Thomax Kaulmann according to the flyer it was 'a computer application where contemporary art can be created, viewed, discussed, and purchased'. I saw the project for the first time in 2018 at the exhibition *Berlin, Zentrum der Netzkunst—damals und heute* at panke.gallery in Berlin. Although I had read about *C@C* and seen screenshots, the website stopped functioning in 1995, two years before I became involved in curating digital art. The presentation at panke.gallery showed a much smaller version of the original project: the interface worked and four art projects could be navigated. Because the work had stopped functioning, it had to be reconstructed and while parts could be opened with the old hardware and software, not everything could be made accessible again. After experiencing and rereading the intentions of the work, to my surprise, the main questions behind the development of *C@C* were very close to the goals of this current volume, i.e., what is the influence of the increased mobility and affordability of technology on

---

2 Vivian van Saaze, Glenn Wharton and Leah Reisman, 'Adaptive Institutional Change: Managing Digital Works at the Museum of Modern Art', *Museum & Society* 16, no. 2 (2018), pp. 220–39.

3 In her book *Lurking: How a Person Became a User* (New York: MCD, 2020), Joanna McNeil writes a compelling account about her experience in some of these communities and the consequences of these small, and sometimes larger, collectives or platforms on cultural memory.

arts aesthetics; in what ways do these developments lead to a new definition of value that favours concepts rather than objects; and is the institutional framework still required to address these issues. *C@C* tried to answer these questions by exploring digital curation in the ideal platform for that time: the World Wide Web.

The website consisted of a minimalist interface, the *C@C-Navigator*, which was based on a tree structure, with each branch leading to a different artist. Several artists were invited and while presenting or creating their work on *C@C* they were also asked to invite up to three artists to show or make work. This would contextualize their work while it also tried to decentralize the role of the curator by turning the curatorial into a less authoritarian gesture. The idea of a networked and distributed system was also visible in the interface and navigation: via the branches visitors to the site could explore the interrelations between the artists and their projects. As such, the treelike structure reflected the social network of the web. There was also a 'Public Discussion Area' where visitors could comment on the works, engage in ongoing discussions, or get in touch with the artists to acquire their work in the 'Business Class'. The latter functioned in a simple way and made it possible to create links between the collector's website and the artwork on *C@C*. This way the project tried to create commercial revenue as well as initiate discussion about the value of digital art and the challenges of collecting it. A similar attempt to sell digital art was made a few years later in 1998 by Olia Lialina with her *First Real Net Art Gallery*, later known as the *Last Real Net Art Museum*, an online gallery dedicated to her first online art project *My Boyfriend Came Back From The War* (1996). The gallery featured several interpretations of her project.[4] As was the case for Grubinger, her attempts to sell the works failed. However, the *Last Real Net Art Museum* still exists and after 24 years it has a collection of 37 different versions of *MBCBFTW*, of which only four have been lost. Moreover, while working on the *Last Real Net Art Museum*, Lialina began collecting all the information relating to *MBCBFTW*: the people who made the iterations,

---

4   To emphasize the provocative gesture of the project, and being cautioned that this was not the first attempt, Lialina renamed the project into *Last Real Net Art Museum*, *rhizome.org/editorial/2017/feb/21/all-you-need-is-link/*.

the exhibitions, the sources of the files and the metadata of the artwork. At the twenty-year anniversary exhibition of *MBCBFTW* in 2016, which took place simultaneously at HeK in Basel and MU in Eindhoven, this information proved to be of art-historical interest but more importantly it ensured[5] the preservation of *MBCBFTW* forever.

The museums also noticed the potential of the Web to endlessly reconfigure traditional models and methods for presenting, accessing and distributing art. Echoing André Malraux's *Musée imaginaire* (*Museum without Walls*, 1947) with which he wanted to demonstrate how the unprecedented availability of (photographic) copies made it possible to constantly draw new connections between visual traditions and motifs that had until then been considered unrelated, the terms 'Open Museum' and 'museum without walls', became popular *and* seemed to become real as the digital space made it possible to create all kinds of relations between any kind of data. Whereas physical exhibitions usually represent ten percent of a collection, the Web could potentially show and share a museum's comprehensive catalogue, or at least those objects that had been digitized. Yet, while many museums directed their curatorial efforts to the online space, their exhibitions would still mirror their offline efforts, in digital form. Their 'online experiments' focused on showing rows of thumbnail images with the catalogue descriptions attached. At times, users could make their own selection based on themes, genres, periods or artists. Importantly, most of the online exhibitions were not curated by a curator but by educational or archival staff members who had good insight into the collections and the audience, but little experience with displaying art. Hence, instead of an exploration of the museum space—in this case the website—the curatorial mode followed the model of the collection management structure. Curating in the digital meant little more than browsing the catalogue with a new interface.

Curating and presenting digital art, especially net art, in a physical gallery proved similarly difficult. Lialina made a strong statement about her dislike of physical net art exhibitions as 'the ugliest phenomenon of the modern art scene'.[5] She distinguished between different modes

5   Olia Lialina, 'All You Need Is Link', *Rhizome*, 21 February 2017 [2000], *rhizome.org/editorial/2017/feb/21/all-you-need-is-link/*.

of presentation which she framed as the 'Object' and the 'ZOO'. The former being

> a prettied-up computer with a browser window open on the net artist's page [alongside] a plaque on the wall next to the computer that identifies it as a work of art.[6]

The ZOO she described as

> a more expensive type of event that requires at least bringing the FNA [famous net artist] to the location of the exhibition and accommodating her there. In the exhibition space, beside the usual computer with an inscription on the wall and an open browser, a chair is put down, and on that chair—oh, isn't that great—sits the FNA in person.[7]

Lialina's main point was that the artworks became a discrete objects that were directly connected to the computer, thus removing the works from its variable and often personal context in which such works were usually experienced: in the privacy of one's home or at work and in between all that is happening on the web. Rather than experimenting with form or language she felt it was about 'bending language and form to someone else's will [and] the more three-dimensional the object is, the more lifeless it seems'.[8] For her the best way to curate digital art was to organize events in which the artist was invited to explain the navigation and meaning of the work in an engaging way. If that wasn't possible, even displaying a list of links on a website would be more effective, as it would still be taking place in the same ecology; moreover, it enabled the artists to keep working on their projects, and the more links the more visible the artwork became—which she did with her *Last Real Net Art Museum*.[9]

---

6   Ibid.
7   Ibid.
8   Ibid.
9   In response to this post, Lialina wrote another post a few months later in which she is more positive about a changing attitude of some institutions: '[those who] are really open become part of complex networking projects. Those who can't get rid of traditional standards of beauty and interactivity entertain their audience by making links to funny web pages. ... [However, some] institutions correct their positions, collecting policies, exhibition practices. I would say it's a victory.' *amsterdam.nettime. org/Lists-Archives/nettime-l-0102/msg00200.html.*

Marialaura Ghidini made a similar comparison between 'curating online' and 'curating on the web'. The former relates to and mimics the practice that derives from displaying museum and gallery collections, while the latter is a site-specific approach that facilitates new ways of producing and displaying digital art.[10] At its core, curating on the Web responds to the characteristics of the Web as medium. For Ghidini this means that it needs to reflect on the ecology of the adopted technology, in which websites are not seen as 'static and self-contained objects but, rather, as ecosystems that are inhabited and shaped by third parties through various interactions between the object (the website) and its larger context'.[11] As briefly mentioned earlier, the *Last Real Net Art Museum* was a provocative gesture towards museums and galleries that were presenting (digitized) artworks as an online electronic catalogue, turning off the location bar when showing the work offline, or acquiring copies of net art and storing these on a CD ROM somewhere on a shelf rather than showing the 'real thing'. While *Last Real Net Art Museum* presents only the links to the artworks, it combines multiple perspectives. It emphasizes the possibilities for appropriation and (re)creation by showing the infinite configurations that are possible within an open system, while using the standard interface of an Internet store in addition to presenting discrete projects. It underlines the social network of the Web by linking to the works, and the artist is curator is archivist is conservator. The project was also translated into physical spaces where the net artworks were transformed in different ways: while some were shown in their original hardware casing (albeit functioning via an inserted emulator), others became large projections, turned into an immersive VR installation or could be scrolled on an interactive screen. In this sense curating digital art took advantage of the variability of exhibiting digital art, helped by the increasing affordability of the technology. As such, it expands the curatorial inquiry to include questions concerning the potential of appropriation, online distribution and digital archiving.

---

10   Marialaura Ghidini, 'Curating on the Web: The Evolution of Platforms as Spaces for Producing and Disseminating Web-Based Art.' *Arts* 8, no. 3 (2019), *mdpi.com/2076-0752/8/3/78*.
11   Ibid.

Curating.2
from link-list to collaborative curating

One of the curatorial modes that attracted my attention and became a reason to embark on this interview project were *surf clubs*, which also involved some people from the first and the last batch of interviewees. Surf clubs started around 2006 and are often described as a response to the rise of the Web2.0.[12] They were organized around a group identity that shared a similar aesthetic, which meant continuous postings of quirky or highly advanced and stylized images and sometimes a few keywords or short texts, real-time involvement and commenting. Instead of BBS (bulletin boards) or e-mail lists, to communicate they used existing social platforms such as the bookmarking site del.icio.us or blogging sites like Wordpress and Tumblr to create endless scrolls of short posts. In some cases these sites also functioned as an online sketchbook to try out ideas and joke with friends in a social network format. The new form, while open for anyone to explore and even to participate in was also restrictive; the intimate public space could be intimidating and, as elsewhere, group dynamics played a significant role. Yet the fast-paced conceptual exchange and the appropriation and analysis of online material stimulated specific modes of curating. Next to the rapid response format of the early surf clubs like *Nasty Nets* (2006–2012), *SuperCentral* (2006–2010) and *Loshadka* (2007–2013) where curation was instigated by starting the site and held together by the collective enthusiasm of its users, some, like *Club Internet* (2008–2009) by Harm van den Dorpel, started to follow a more conventional curatorial model in which the exhibition 'space' still followed the dynamics and aesthetics of presenting mash-ups but now curated by different people.[13] Similar to traditional curatorial exhibitions, specific people were invited to present

---

12   For a chronological time line see, Slocum 2016, *rhizome.org/editorial/2016/mar/30/catalog-of-internet-artist-clubs*.

13   Interestingly, when buying the domain name clubinternet.org Harm van den Dorpel hoped to make some money with the acquisition, because *Club Internet* was also a major telecom provider in France who had not yet bought this domain name. The practice of buying 'parked domains' also known as 'domain squatting' or 'domain parking', i.e., buying prominent domain names for resale, is a lucrative business strategy and for some an artistic practice, see for instance, Constant Dullaart's project *readymades*, for more information see Brian Droitcour, 'Constant Dullaart Re-codes the Readymade', *Art in America* (26 February 2009), *artnews.com/art-in-america/features/dullaart-new-media-readymade-57649/*.

their works and as remarked by Ed Halter, the shows had a high 'zeitgeisty greatest-hits quality'.[14] However, the intricate interface emphasizes the circulation that is characteristic of the web: each of the artworks had its own independent webpage, some directing to personal servers, and they were linked via an inconspicuous navigation bar. Others curated offline versions, for example Lindsay Howard's *DUMP.FM IRL* (2010) at 319 Scholes in New York, an exhibition that reflected the earlier online version of the 'image-based chat room for real-time communication' *Dump.FM*, initiated by Ryder Ripps (see p. 222), Scott Ostler and Tim Baker. Another instance of this hybrid curating is Constant Dullaart's (see p. 266) *Delicious Contemporary Semantics* which took place online at del.icio.us and offline at Arti and Amicitiae in Amsterdam (2009). The announcement of the project is a good illustration of the curatorial modus that was popular at the time:

> Lets do a show in which, like is possible on del.icio.us, the inspiration that leads up to an art work is visable, but now physical, not only existing as a jpeg or url (it can be a poster reproduction of a Malevich, a remake of a sculpture, a print out etc etc). And show this together with the final work that this inspiration led to. A show in which it is clear that del.icio.us influences the participating artists by sharing their references, thereby aiding their research. A show that discusses the development of contemperary semantics in net-art 2 point oooh, by showing different aproaches of artists dealing with the vast information flow of the Internet, its dialectics and developing anthropological values. The fact that these mostly young artists are dealing with an abundance of visual representations of previous

---

14   *rhizome.org/editorial/2008/may/12/site-specific/*. In some of his other projects like *Dissociations* (2008) and *Deli.near.info* (2014—present) Harm van de Dorpel is experimenting more with alternative curatorial modes. Driven by a frustration of social media's format of showing posts only in chronological order, making it difficult to find old content, with *Dissociations* he used an algorithm to find relations and associations between his works that were based on the content or form rather than chronology. Here the relations between ideas and forms become the focus rather than the works themselves. Yet rather than showing what should belonged together he posted the reverse, the disassociations, and distributed the results via the website and a Twitter feed. Being interested in working with complexity instead of the reduction of it through standardisation processes, and inspired by the results of *Dissociations*, he developed *Deli.near.info*: a social network, open for anyone to use. The site is an alternative sketchbook and social media platform, and its intricate link system moves beyond the linearity of existing social platforms to create more ambiguity between links and to encourage surprising finds.

non net art, and the flirtation with kitch, trash and popculture which dominates the Internets will play a big part in the show.[15]

The call shows the mode of address, development and aesthetic of curating in the digital: someone starts a first post and others respond by commenting on the previous and by versioning the projects. Moving between media and spaces a chain of different works was instigated and developed until people lost interest. As singular objects these projects are not always interesting but the process is the work, which is both curatorial and art. Indeed, surf clubs were a 'hybrid act involving both curatorial research and a conceptual art gesture' (Ramocki 2008). The 'act' is linked to the concept of versioning: a reconceptualization and alteration of something, and it is also a critical construct, as it is being commented and versioned. This process was not necessarily linked to specific authorial credit and as such the practice was free of the 'burden' of the 'celebrity curator', or the 'independent curator', that had become a norm in contemporary art. Essentially, versioning becomes evident through multiplicity, enumeration and succession, and it can be identified in the social relations between the users.[16] In other words, a physical realization of merely one 'Object' would be a derivative. The core of these works was the social interactions that determined their process; the presentation of an object would neglect the energy, the surprise effect, the fragility of the illusion and the transience of the moment. In this sense curating was no longer about caring for an object, but about caring for a social network and process. As such there was a clear shift from curating objects to conceptual processes.

As mentioned by Ghidini (2019), 'the approach to curating was collective, informal, and discursive', a debate—either visually or written—that happened as part of but also beyond the 'club'. Similarly to the earlier generation of net artists in the 1990s, some of the members would write about the practice on their site, on other websites or in print magazines, but in contrast to the 1990s these different spaces were more easily interchanged and

---

15   This is the original text for the open call, *constantdullaart.com/arti.html*.
16   For more information see Annet Dekker, *Collecting and Conserving Net Art: Moving Beyond Conventional Methods* (London: Routledge, 2018), pp. 30, 109-14.

increasingly became connected, which to some led to the new phase of 'post-Internet' art, albeit others would say surf clubs were already post-Internet.[17] The demise of the surf clubs was due both to a 'generalised disbelief in their potentials to change and reorganize current social and political practices' (Carreira 2017, 71), while others just lost interest and built their own online exhibition space or moved to other platforms, such as YouTube and Facebook, or exchanged their online activity for the physical space. Some managed to create a seamless interaction between online projects and presentations in conventional gallery spaces thereby slowly moulding the gallery configurations to fit digital practices. This was particularly the case with VVORK (2006–2012) founded by Aleksandra Domanović, Oliver Laric, Christoph Priglinger and Georg Schnitzer. The collective used a simple Wordpress blog to post on average four images a day of (documented) artworks they had found inspiring, creating associative visual sets in the process. Their practice was arguably simplistic, but their classification defied standard registration practices with tags ranging from city names to colours or often mundane and seemingly meaningless or misspelled words, like 'baking, balaclava, balaklava, balance, ...'. Interestingly, it quickly became a popular site for art critics, museum and gallery curators to conduct 'informal research'.[18] While some felt that their curatorial approach was a step backwards because it too closely mimicked the gallery-based systematics, this was perhaps also a necessary step to get the institutional more involved. In the end, VVORK didn't disrupt with their aesthetic (unlike other surf clubs) but with their practice by clearly questioning the authoritarian role of art professionals as validators of art in favour of collective and networked curation.

Certainly, being in the gallery circuit provided VVORK with much more visibility, something that most surf clubs lacked. Then again that was probably never the goal of surf clubs, although this may differ between clubs and certainly between individuals. Yet most individuals

---

17   In a critical response to an interview with Domenico Quaranta, Tom Moody proposed that surf clubs could already be post-Internet (*tommoody.us/archives/2015/09/16/domenico-quaranta-on-surf-clubs*). The point of this essay is not to choose a site, nor to add to the discussion of post-Internet; for more information, see Marisa Olson's retrospective and reflexive essay about its genealogy (Marisa Olson, 'POSTINTERNET: Art After the Internet.' *Foam Magazine*, 29, (Winter 2011), pp 59-63).

18   *openspace.sfmoma.org/2009/10/vvork*.

had their own practice and were engaging with a surf club out of fun, curiosity and perhaps a bit of idea testing. While the linking, sharing and commenting was a reflection of the available technology, as Sarah Cook mentioned,

> to truly understand the potential of social networks, and the online platforms for social exchange open to artists today, you have to understand the conditions that create them. This includes not only the political, social, and economic realities of the landscape under consideration but also the tools themselves, how the interfaces work, the programming behind each.[19]

Indeed, these were not merely gimmicks and jokes: to understand the absurdity that was happening required a form of Internet connoisseurship. To get the joke you had to be in on the joke.

Curating.3
networked co-curating

While I had selected the first round of interviewees for their mixed practice of curating digital art in physical and online spaces, a few years later and inspired by the experiments of the surf clubs I was curious whether and how the practice of collective and networked curating had developed and I decided to focus more specifically on curators and artists who were primarily concentrated on online curating alongside organizing an occasional offline event. I was particularly intrigued by efforts that appropriated social media and sharing platforms such as Facebook, Tumblr, Instagram, YouTube, Are.na and eBay as new alternative curatorial playgrounds. Several projects had already been developed, some of the interviewees focused on the form aesthetics or the medium-specifics of a platform, for instance, by appropriating the content and the design of the interface, the tools inside the platform were twisted to create confusing, fun or ingenious projects.

19   Sarah Cook, 'Understanding Quality', in *Me You And Everyone We Know Is A Curator*, ed. Sophie Krier and Mieke Gerritsen (Breda: Graphic Design Museum, 2009), pp. 47–51.

Others translated the physical space to the digital in ways that enhanced the 'digitized' space with new potential. By emphasizing the characteristics of the web, for instance using the potential of 3D, an artwork or a space could be experienced in a way that was impossible in its physical counterpart. A few curators were exploring the curatorial tools within online platforms such as Google Earth or eBay and modified their original purposes. This was not breaking and subverting for the sake of it; rather it is an inevitable consequence of curating in these spaces, as mentioned by Gaia Tedone,

> [curating in] such a process inevitably needs to confront itself with the extreme volatility of digital content and of images in particular, as links are erased, content removed and websites down-ranked. This should not be seen as a limit in itself, but as an integral part of the research process and can, in my understanding, be creatively incorporated into the curatorial narrative (Tedone see p. 94).

Instead of merely being controversial or trying to break with traditional curation, curating in digital platforms required a new approach. First of all, acknowledging that some things cannot be controlled and that curatorial authority was now shared with the platform (i.e., software) and its users. Investigating this terrain Tedone noticed a shift in the role of curatorial agency that she framed as moving from online curation to 'networked co-curation'; emphasizing the alliance between a curator, objects, users, and machine operations.[20] Driven by different and sometimes competing economic, cultural, and socio-political agendas the 'exhibition space' is now characterized as a collision of different interests in which the curator is merely a node. This means that: 'a curator needs to take into account a complex interrelated network of dependencies and contexts that are often invisible or incomprehensible to most people'.[21] Whereas curators still initiate a project,

---

20   For an extensive analysis of networked co-curation, see Gaia Tedone, *Curating The Networked Image: Circulation, Commodification, Computation*, Ph.D. dissertation, London South Bank University, London, UK, 2019.

21   Annet Dekker and Gaia Tedone, 'Networked Co-Curation: An Exploration of the Socio-Technical Specificities of Online Curation', *Arts*, 8.3 (2019), *mdpi.com/2076-0752/8/3/86/htm*.

in time their role develops in different and sometimes unexpected ways, both in relation to the artworks on display and the interaction with the space. In this sense and due to this socio-technical specificity, the focus of curating moves from artists and artworks to processes and systems. As argued by Magda Tyżlik-Carver, 'it shifts the attention from what is produced (the end product) to how something is performed'.[22] Expanding on this notion, networked co-curation

> can be framed as a new space of performativity: signaling a move from curating a set of objects to a conceptual and operational process that puts differ-ent constellations of human and machinic agents, objects and practices into relation with one another.[23]

Joasia Krysa's describes the curatorial process as 'a col-lective and distributed executable that displays machinic agency', in which the curator can function as both a tool and a force of change with the potential to 'disrupt estab-lished social relations of production and distribution'.[24] From such a machinic perspective, rather than performing, i.e., setting something in motion, online curating is proces-sual: it is *in* execution. A process can be made up of mul-tiple threads that execute instructions concurrently, or it can involve interactions between multiple paths that can potentially branch out in different and at times uncertain or ambiguous directions. The curatorial project *The Recom-binants* by Madja Edelstein-Gomez explored the notion of machine curation. While the format follows a conventional model of an open call, a database and a final presentation, a chain of digital participation is set in motion in which every user becomes a recombinant. Based on Deep Learn-ing algorithms the generative principle works as soon as something new enters: the reception of a file produces data that is reinserted into the system to change or create something else. Rather than replicating a rule, it is about modifying and reconfiguring the access. Using a form of

---

22   Magda Tyzlik-Carver, *Curating in/as Commons: Posthuman Curating and Computational Cultures*. Ph.D. dissertation, Aarhus University, Aarhus, Denmark, 2016.
23   Dekker and Tedone, 2019.
24   Joasia Krysa, *Software Curating: The Politics of Curating in/as (an) Open System(s)*, Ph.D. dissertation, University of Plymouth, Plymouth, UK, 2008, p. 4.

data-splicing ensures that a page always generates itself. In a sense *The Recombinants* has an eternal life, in which the data is constantly regenerated, or recombined, by every interaction. As explained by Martine Neddam you're giving up something of your identity to be mixed with the identity of others 'to a point of unlimited proliferation' (see p. 82). Such a system creates not continuous time and space, but self-replicating time and space, in which each work and each interaction always takes place in relation to something else. As such, the curatorial role is also shared between and relies on all the users of the site.[25] Making the curator and all the users recombinants is critiquing the hegemony of software and institutional authority by engaging with the systems. In these situations, digital curating is intricately intertwined within the complex network of other humans, technical elements, and digital objects, and challenges the conventional role of the individual curator as well as the notion of the 'art-as-object'.

Olga Goriunova described this development as a tension between light and heavy curating—the easy-to-use applications, interfaces, and templates versus the human attention that is needed to consider the implications of the cooperation with the technical systems.[26] One of the consequences is that the previous roles of curator, art(ist) and audience, and perhaps the division of labour, are blurred to a degree that 'categories such as artist and curator, thinker and programmer, director and assistant, master and student, and so on, are both wilfully and intuitively obscured, if not even abandoned'.[27] Instead of seeing this as a problem, emphasizing this tension provides an opportunity to explore more thoroughly the socio-technical impact on digital cultural processes, and curating in particular. Indeed and as mentioned by Goriunova,

> Curators are compelled to attend to the production and extension of aesthetic forms, values and procedures by understanding, building and making use of

---

25   Martine Neddam in conversation with Diana McCarthy (1 April 2020), *li-ma.nl/lima/news/online-event-cultural-matter-diana-mccarty-techno-feminist-alphabet-cyberfeminism-xenofeminism*.

26   Olga Goriunova, 'Light Heavy Weight Curating', in *Speculative Scenarios: Or What Will Happen to Digital Art in the (near) Future?*, edited by Annet Dekker (Eindhoven: Baltan Laboratories, 2013), pp. 25–32.

27   Simon Sheikh, 'From Para to Post: The Rise and Fall of Curatorial Reason.' *Springerin, The Post-Curatorial Turn* 1 (2017), *springerin.at/en/2017/1/von-para-zu-post/*.

human-technical devices or computational procedures, in which they (should) find themselves if not
in direct competition then still in ontological conflict
of differentiation with other forces, among those that
are capitalist, deterministic and entropic, in order to
carry out their work.[28]

Considering this a productive tension could be seen as
a tactic to rethink the dynamics of power, authority and
cultural gatekeeping which are at the heart of curating.
In this constellation, the role of the online curator can
be found in the forging of new relationships between
aesthetics, technics, politics, economics, curators, artists
and audience members. Taking into account these various
actors will produce more layered structures of power and
governance. At the same time, by embodying rather than
merely enacting the increasing influence of algorithms, and
technology more generally, such a curator—if this is still
the best term to use—will develop ways of working that
provoke questions and critique, even if implicitly, through
the curatorial actions that are initiated. So, when art is
more and more created and presented on the web, free and
accessible for everyone to enjoy, and the role of the digital
curator is merely a node in a larger ecology of active agents,
what happens with the function and role of the institution?

Curating.4
building a history for the future

The history of art is deeply connected to the history of
museum collections, yet rather than all the works in
collections, what is most often remembered are the exhibitions and other events a curator presented to the public.[29]
Twenty-five years after the introduction of the Web and the
subsequent online curatorial efforts, it is still hard to build
from historical collections, or to remember the exhibitions
and events that were taking place. Particularly since these

28   Goriunova, 2013, p. 29.
29   Reesa Greenberg, Bruce W. Ferguson and Sandy Nairne, eds. *Thinking About Exhibitions*
(London/New York: Routledge, 1996), p. 2.

'histories are not particularly well documented, and the specificities not so thoroughly mapped'.[30] The lack of a historical view is partly related to the fact that early examples—and even more recent ones—are often removed, deleted, or simply disappeared amidst the continuing processes of the platform that was used, or due to lack of interest or energy to keep up with the endless updating of an exhibition site. While most interviewees tried to document their efforts by making screen recordings or collecting press clippings and reviews, little is shared or well-archived for others to find and learn from. When considering the building of a history for the future some place faith in the tech sector, or they develop their own algorithmic tools to excavate old data: 'my idea is to drill "Ice Cores"' (Madja Edelstein-Gomez, see p. 82). Paradoxically while most interviewees think it is the museum's responsibility to represent and preserve art, none of them feel that these institutions are the place to experiment with or explore the potential of digital art. In this sense, the role of the museum only becomes significant if they are willing to adapt to 'the contexts, environments, references and purposes of digital artworks' (*New Scenario*, see p. 202). Yet, as I stated earlier, it is often unclear what this actually means, and furthermore it goes against some of the key characteristics of curating digital art: that it can be time-, site- and context specific. Going down this road might actually more closely resemble how history is constructed: slowly building and creating through appropriation, copying and adapting.

> Often art has been saved through copying [and] it's reasonable to conclude that copying and sharing might save more digital art than the museums themselves.
> Domenico Quaranta 2012, see p. 36.

> Just as a Greek sculpture functions perfectly in the digital domain, digital art must also be able to assert itself in various and future aggregate states, otherwise it will vanish.
> *New Scenario* 2019, see p. 202.

30   Michael Connor, 'Curating Online Exhibitions: Part 1: Performance, Variability, Objecthood', *Rhizome*, May 13 (2020) *rhizome.org/editorial/2020/may/13/curating-online-exhibitions-pt-1/*.

In what follows, the interviewees reflect and respond to the challenges and changes of curating digital art. In the process it becomes clear that the practice of curating cannot be disconnected from social and technical developments. As such it is concerned with the politics of art and curating: from how power relations are expressed, established and replaced, to how curating itself is constantly transformed.

32

Postscript: Some of the interviewees stopped their online activities in the wake of Covid-19, perhaps signalling the precarious situation for online art, or to protest the institutional that is celebrating its newly claimed territory with digitized collection tours. Indeed, online exhibitions popped up out of nowhere. Unlikely candidates like the Uffizi Museum in Florence became a hit on TikTok with their absurd video clips showing their prestigious Italian Renaissance collection of fifteenth-century figures 'dance' along to Todrick Hall's rap *Nails, Hair, Hips, Heels*, or by staging the Medusa (with mask) now turning a coronavirus into stone. Hastings Contemporary wheeled in a robot that you could whiz around the gallery space (unfortunately there was only one so no chance of playing bumper cars). The longer the lockdown lasted the more exhibition-games there were, and it worked: the virtual exhibition opening of *Exercise in Hopeless Nostalgia: World Wide Webb* created by Thomas Webb and curated by Anika Meier (see p. 274) reached the amazing number of 5000 unique visitors—including bots. While everyone played around in a nostalgic retro videogame straight out of the 1980s, running on artificial intelligence and real-time data, the interface annex artwork presents a poignant critique on contemporary data farming. It also shows that the present-day curator is machinic.[31]

---

31   It is clear that the online space is distinct from the physical gallery space, hence presentations that mimic and keep to the standards of these spaces will ultimately become little more than a weak representation, in the process potentially removing the audience even further from the art. At the same time, it is important to consider the limitation that many institutions have to deal with. As argued by Katrina Sluis, the online space is a contested space, 'as it's usually the domain of the communications and marketing team, who are under incredible pressure to convert online traffic into physical audiences. Corporate web servers are tightly controlled, and administered by expensive external web developers who are rarely sympathetic to the installation of unauthorised scripts. So this becomes a boring, yet important factor limiting the format and scale of online projects' (Katrina Sluis, see p. 287). In a similar way, Pita Arreola-Burn and Elliott Burns (*Off Site Project*) found after interviewing fifteen contemporary online galleries how much of online curation is intrinsically connected to and influenced by social media metrics. They noticed how curatorial decisions are heavily informed by the need to be visible through likes, comments and shares in social media platforms. As they mention 'Personally, we feel subject to a cult of performativity, having over the past three years extended our programming and felt an increased pressure to publicise this and thereby promote the artists we show. We have become attuned to the reception of our social media actions, internalising an awareness of why singular Posts succeed over others, be it a visual quality, a time period, multiple images or the inclusion of video. In turn we have implemented those unconscious learnings into our design vocabulary and in all likelihood have allowed the Instagramablity of particular styles to influence which artists we approach' ('Volume: Social Media Metrics in Digital Curation', 2020, *offsiteproject.org/VolumeSocialMediaMetricsinDigitalCuration*).

Interviews

Domenico Quaranta

INTERVIEWEE: DOMENICO QUARANTA
PROJECT: VARIOUS — COLLECT THE WWWORLD, 2011–2012
WEBSITE: *domenicoquaranta.com*
DATE: 25 OCTOBER 2012

Can we start by defining the terminology we're using and how you position yourself within existing categories like digital art, new media, net art, contemporary art, or any of the post-arts?

D   Medium-based definitions make little sense to me, so I can move the first ones you mentioned to the trash without even referring to their negative consequences in terms of self-segregation. 'Contemporary art' is the term I usually use to refer to the art I'm dealing with: art that always responds to the Information Age, which is the specific form of contemporaneity I've been living in since I started a serious affair with art. Sometimes it responds to its time using digital media, other times with traditional, obsolete or even dead media; sometimes it happens online, other times it doesn't.

That being said, if I were to chose another of these categories, I'd select 'net art', because its origin makes it more similar to Dada than video art; also, the term better applies to a context and a community, rather than to a specific use of the medium; and there is 'something' in the art that it usually applies to that keeps making the art world uneasy about it. And I love this 'something'.

What is your background and what triggered your interest in digital/net art? Could you elaborate on these initial encounters?

D   I studied art history and contemporary art at university. I started seriously engaging with it in 2000—and you would probably agree that whatever was started in the year 2000 inevitably bears some kind of symbolic meaning. In a very naïve, intuitive way, I decided that my MA thesis had to focus on something that really was a mirror of my time. I went to my professor and said that I wanted to write something about art on the Internet, without even knowing if there actually was something like that. Then, I discovered *jodi.org*...

You've been involved in various types of organizations and spaces. Could you share some of your experiences working in these different settings and particular contexts? For example, how does it affect your practice? Are there specific things that work very well in one context but not at all in another?

D   Working as a freelance curator has little to do with doing what you want in your ideal exhibition space for your ideal audience. You keep submitting ideas that rarely become an actual show, or are commissioned to realize projects you wouldn't have worked on otherwise. What I realized only recently is that I like having to deal with constraints and limitations, address different

audiences, and adapt to different exhibition spaces. In general
I think that fighting against reality makes you and your projects
stronger. I stopped thinking that my best projects never left my
desktop. My best projects are the ones I've made, which stopped
being ideas and became experiences that produced new ideas.

To better respond to your question, context is everything.
I've curated for small peripheral media art festivals and for international contemporary art fairs, for commercial art galleries and
for non-profit spaces, for contexts more focused on 'new media'
and for contexts more interested in 'art'. In all these cases, the
context made the show, determined the setup, the selection of artworks, and of course the concept of the show—or at least the way
it was formulated. It's not just a matter of adaptation—it's more a
matter of carefully mixing adaptation and conflict, making things
that look familiar and provocative at the same time. Take *Collect
the WWWorld*, for example. One of the points of the exhibition
was to position some current, mostly net-based practices within a
context that belong to the recent history of contemporary art, from
Conceptual Art to Postmodernism. Most of the artworks are
'traditional' art objects: prints, sculptures, videos and video installations. The show was first presented in Brescia, Italy, to a relatively
traditional audience. Somebody told me: 'I've never seen so much
technology in a show here, but I liked it and understood most
of it'. Then the show travelled to the House for Electronic Arts
Basel, and was presented to a well-informed new media audience.
Somebody said: 'I've never seen so little technology in a show here,
but I liked it and understood most of it'.

> There has always been a separation between people who stress the techno-
> logical (material) developments of digital art and those who emphasize the
> art qualities (content/conceptual). At the same time digital art is also often
> accompanied by a fair amount of theoretical discussion. How do you position
> yourself in this discourse?

D   Generally speaking, I'm not against focusing on the medium and the material aspect of art. I think we should return to
this at some point. But I also think that, at this very specific point
in history, media art really needs and deserves another kind of
contextualization.

As an art practice, media art needs this because it is the
only way to start addressing a wider audience that is interested
in art in general. As a set of tools, media art needs another kind
of contextualization because so many artists now include new
media into a broader toolset, and focusing on technology would
mean focusing on just one part, no matter how important, of

their work. And as a community with a long tradition, media art needs it too, because I still think media art has produced some of the most interesting outcomes of contemporary art. When this work is done, and media art becomes an important part of the contemporary art canon, we could return to the medium, if it still made sense.

> You organize online and offline exhibitions. Starting with the latter, do you work with certain methods or criteria? For instance, I recall numerous discussions in the past where showing a computer monitor was 'not done', or some curators wouldn't even consider presenting net art in an exhibition at all, while others created entirely new installations based on online work. What are your thoughts/experiences with this?

D No rule can be meaningful forever in art that deals with contemporary gadgets and devices, because it depends on the familiarity we have with these objects, their meanings for us, even their design. Placing a TV monitor in the white cube was sacrilege in the 1960s, but now everybody is used to screens and beamers. This is because video has been acknowledged as a legitimate artform, because we are used to being surrounded by screens, and because devices have been designed that fit well in exhibition spaces, from the old Triniton to more recent plasma screens.

With digital and net-based art, it's difficult to define a single criterium that can apply to all the works, because the way they use the network and the computer environment really changes from work to work. Some works may be successfully shown on an online computer, while others may instead require some level of translation to fit into the physical space and into a specific context. Artists today are totally aware of this, and most of the best exhibition solutions actually come from them, and not from curators.

Let me tell you a story. In the last iteration of *Collect the WWWorld* at 319 Scholes, New York, I included Ryder Ripps. Ripps is, among other things, the founder of *Internet Archae-ology*, an amazing archive of images, animations, sounds, videos and webpage layouts from the early Web. That's why I wanted him in the show, but we both agreed that exhibiting *Internet Archaeology* on a computer or projection would have been lame. So, I asked him to submit something else. The day of the opening, he came with an old shopping bag advertising a book by O'Reilly Media, titled *The Whole Internet*. He put a very wet rag and some ice into it and hung it very high on a wall with a screwdriver. Then he placed a white-painted mannequin's hand on the wall below the bag so that the water slowly dripped from the bag into the hand,

and from here to the floor. It's an amazingly beautiful piece, and the perfect solution to bring the poetics of *Internet Archaeology* to an exhibition space without actually showing the website.

Who do you see as your audience? I guess it changes with each new context but are there also changes (and/or exchanges) that you've noticed over the years, people moving from one place to another, or crossovers from other fields?

D   Of course audiences change, and talking to them is the greatest challenge I have as a curator, and the thing I enjoy the most. My ideal audience can probably be described, very simply, as an audience that understands contemporaneity or is at least open to it, without limitations and prejudices. Let me tell you another short tragicomic story about crossovers... The second presentation of *Collect the WWWorld* took place at the House of Electronic Arts Basel in March 2012. The House (formerly known as Plug.in) had recently relocated to an industrial area a short distance from downtown Basel. The building that hosts the House is also home to two other exhibition spaces, Oslo 8 and Oslo 10, one devoted to contemporary art, the other to photography. They really are next door, and often have joint openings. Coincidentally, both Oslo 8 and Oslo 10 had group exhibitions featuring at least two artists who also had works in my exhibition. On the opening night there were a lot of people in all three venues, but very few of them were actually moving between them. Most of the people who visited Oslo 8 or Oslo 10 didn't come to my show, and vice-versa. My ideal audience definitely includes those happy few who visited all three exhibitions, and found connections between them.

What do you focus on in your online exhibitions? In the past we've seen examples ranging from lists of links, to commissions, to documentation about a work, to embedding a work in a website? What is your preferred or even ideal 'model'?

D   I didn't actually do that much online. Once, for the Pixxel-point Festival in Nova Gorica, I used *Club Internet*—a very clean and functional online exhibition format that only adds a small info bar at the top of the embedded webpage, developed by artist Harm van den Dorpel and now offline—to organize the online part of the selection in a small online show that was also projected in the exhibition space. And I enjoyed it a lot. Broadly speaking, I'm not that interested in online shows, but in online exhibition spaces. Again, the context makes the difference. Early and recent experiments such as *Refresh!*, *Whitneybiennial.com*, *Club Internet*, the TAG Gallery, *Just Chilling*, *Bubblebyte* and *or-bits* are all very interesting. Without a context, anything from a *Delicious* page to a Tumblr blog can be an exhibition, but I still prefer to think about them as, respectively, a list of links and a blog.

Should digital art enter established museums or organizations or are there better places where it can be preserved and presented? If so, what role should museums play in the future?

D   Museums have always played an important role in preserving, showing, communicating and sometimes producing art and delivering it to its audience. They also work as filters and gatekeepers. To enter the canon, to be collected and exhibited by a museum is still very important, as is being featured on Artforum and in books, and working with a respected gallery. The Internet didn't really affect this. As I said before, entering a wider arena is now a priority for media art, and museums can help a lot with this.

However, museums haven't always been there, and there are no guarantees that they will survive the Information Age. Also, they definitely aren't the only route to preserving art for the future. In most cases, the art of the past didn't survive because of museums. Pompei frescoes were saved by a natural disaster. Fidia's reliefs for the Parthenon were saved by theft. Most Etruscan and Egyptian art was saved by tombstones. Riace's bronzes were saved by a shipwreck. Art was often saved by its conversion to another use. Very often, art has been saved through copying: Romans saved Greek sculpture by copying it; Rubens saved Leonardo's *Battaglia di Anghiari* by copying it.

As novelist Cory Doctorow said, in the digital age 'we copy like we breathe'. The computer has been described as a 'copy and paste machine'. And because of the nature of digital code, there is no difference between originals and copies. It's reasonable to conclude that copying and sharing might save more digital art than the museums themselves. Was Antiorp a relevant cultural phenomenon in the late 1990's? Yes. Is her work still available online? No. Is she taking care of her work? Apparently not. Does any museum have any of her software works in its collection? Not as far as I know. But maybe you have one of them stored on one of your disks, and I have another, and my friend Franco has both of them and also kept the technology that enables us to experience them. Maybe at some point we'll need the help of a museum to access them, but in the meantime, we're doing better than museums.

41

I recently had a few discussions with artists and producers about the usefulness of open source, it seems that although all kinds of codes and suchlike are available they're hardly ever used, mainly because of the personal approach to coding and the complexity that derives from such project-based work. What is your approach to open source in this context?

D   Open source can play an invaluable role in the preservation of digital art. There are, of course, personal ways of coding, much as there are personal ways of writing text and music, but what's important is that there is a coded language, and everything coded can be translated sooner or later. We still read Leonardo da Vinci even though he used mirror writing, and we still listen to Gregorian music despite it using a different music notation. If digital code changes or disappears, future restorers would just need their Rosetta Stone to decode and restore a piece of open source software.

Until recently in the Netherlands there was always a very good funding system for the arts in general and specifically for digital art. That has since changed, increasing on the one hand the divide between 'traditional' art and digital art, while on the other it generally means looking for money outside the funding system. Could you share some of your experiences working around the globe? How do you and the artists you work with survive?

D   Even after these cuts, the situation in the Netherlands is still far better than in Italy, where there is little funding for culture in general and art in particular, and no institutional funding for new media art at all. From this point of view, I can't but think that the present situation in the Netherlands could also have some very positive effects on the practice. Less funding also means more competition, and more competition often means more quality. Another positive consequence is that new media art will finally face its in-between state, and in the attempt to find a market, evolve into what it wants to be: contemporary art on the one hand, and creative research for the creative industries on the other.

In Italy, teaching, a day job, or a rich family often helps to pay the bills. Developing a sustainable economy is far from easy, and the institutional space is often regulated by concerns that are far removed from 'culture', and by rules that are far from clear. That's why many artists and curators live and work outside Italy. I decided to follow a different path: co-found an institution— the Link Center for the Arts of the Information Age—with the ambition to do what nobody else is doing in Italy.

> Like many of your other projects, *Collect the WWWorld* has a strong archival link. Could you explain your approach? How does it relate to collecting, preservation or documentation, which are often seen in relation to archiving?

D   I just realized that you're right—most of the things I've done so far relate somehow to collecting, preserving and displaying digital or technological artefacts. I actually didn't do it consciously—so I'm thinking about the connections between these projects here for the first time. I think there are at least two issues at stake here. The first one, explored in the exhibitions *Collect the WWWorld: The Artist as Archivist in the Internet Age*, and *Playlist: Playing Music, Games, Art*, is that it is only since the Information Age that our material culture has been, on the one hand, so ephemeral and, on the other, so influential on our culture in general. Computers and game consoles changed our life, but planned obsolescence is making them incredibly short lived. Everybody recognizes the impact of the first Mac and the NES system on our culture and creativity, but how many people still use them? Are we really sure that their creative potential has been fully explored? This is what many people rescuing, hacking and reprogramming obsolete technologies are doing.

The same can be said for online culture. Information flows so fast that last week's most popular Internet meme is already a thing of the past—let alone amateur videos on YouTube, photos on Flickr and so on. Selecting, collecting and post-producing these contents is one of the things artists, for different purposes, are doing today.

The second issue is related to the circulation and presentation of digital, networked, computer-based art. As an art curator, I'm doing my best to get the contemporary art audience in touch with this art, to enter the contemporary art discourse and for it to be taken seriously as art, and not just as a techno gimmick. This is what I tried to do with *Holy Fire: Art of the Digital Age* in 2008, and more recently with *Collect the WWWorld*. Both shows featured mainly physical artefacts and traditional media, and both addressed the contemporary art world (in the case of *Holy Fire*, more specifically the art market). At the same time, however, the digital medium questions notions of originality and physicality that are so important in the art world. Today, the contents of a museum can fit on a USB stick, and even a 'poor image' can be considered art—issues that I tried to address with the *MINI Museum of XXI Century Art*, a travelling project that invited artists to make site-specific works for a 10-inch digital frame.

Collect the WWWorld. The Artist as Archivist in the Internet Age (Spazio Contemporanea, Brescia, September 24 – October 15, 2011; House for Electronic Arts—HeK, Basel, March 9 – May 20, 2012; 319 Scholes, New York, October 18 – November 4, 2012) was a touring exhibition exploring the impact of image explosion and prosumer culture on contemporary art, and how the Avant-garde, conceptual practice of exploring, collecting, archiving, manipulating and reusing huge amounts of visual material produced by popular culture and advertising developed into the information age. Based on a researched blog, the exhibition changed at each presentation, involving local artists or different works by already featured artists.

Domenico Quaranta is a contemporary art critic, curator and educator. The author of *Beyond New Media Art* (2013), he has contributed to, edited or co-edited a number of books and catalogues including *GameScenes: Art in the Age of Videogames* (2006) and *THE F.A.T. MANUAL* (2013). Since 2005, he has curated and co-curated many exhibitions, including: *Holy Fire Art of the Digital Age* (2008); *Collect WWWorld* (2011–2012); *Cyphoria* (2016–2017) and *Hyperemployment* (2019–2020). A co-founder of the Link Art Center, Brescia (2011–2019), he lectures internationally and is a full-time professor at the Accademia di Belle Arti di Carrara in Tuscany, Italy.

1   Eva and Franco Mattes, *The Others*, 2011, installation view. Courtesy of Link Art Center. At *Collect the WWWorld*, HeK, Basel, 2012.

2   Eva and Franco Mattes, Evan Roth, Ryder Ripps, Kevin Bewersdorf, *Collect the WWWorld*, 2012. At 319 Scholes, New York—Front Room.

3   Federico Solmi, Quayola, Kamilia Kard, Eva and Franco Mattes in *Cyphoria*, 2016, installation view, curated by Domenico Quaranta for the 16a Quadriennale d'Arte di Roma, *Altri tempi, altri miti*, Palazzo delle Esposizioni, Rome. Courtesy of Fondazione La Quadriennale di Roma. Photo: OKONOstudio.

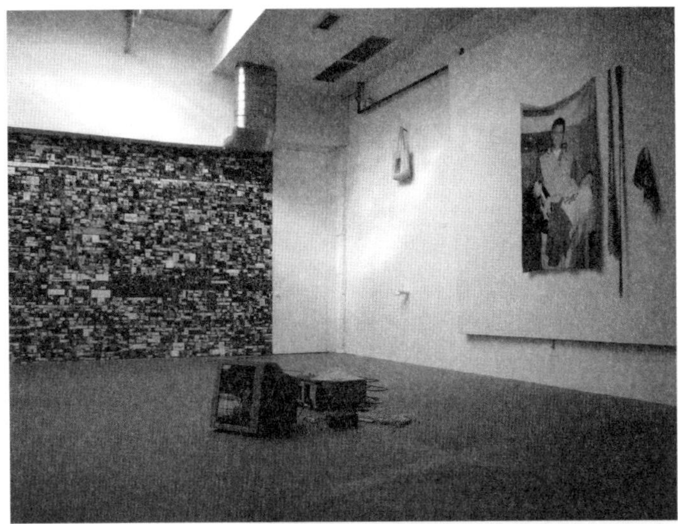

1

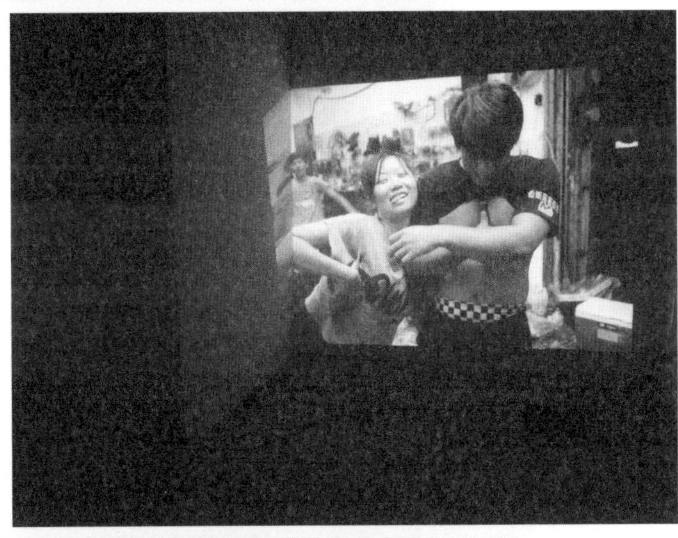

2

3

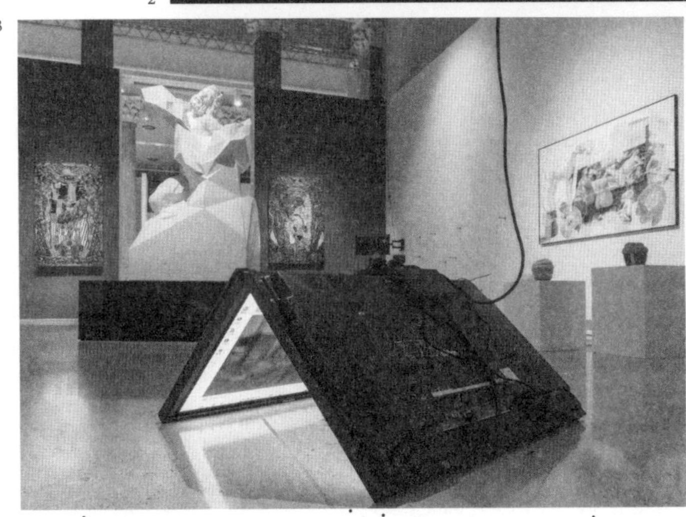

Tom Clark
& Rózsa Farkas

INTERVIEWEES: TOM CLARK, RÓZSA FARKAS
PROJECT: ARCADIA MISSA, 2011–PRESENT
WEBSITE: *arcadiamissa.com*
DATE: 7 NOVEMBER 2012

Can we start by defining the terminology we're using and how you position yourself within existing categories like digital art, new media, net art, contemporary art, or any of the post-arts?

T OK, so this is pretty difficult to answer, not necessarily because we're trying to define a particular niche discursively or from a marketing position, but in that it just feels that in the area we are working in, the distinction of art seems to problematize certain characteristics of contemporary art—art practice without art objects real or virtual (not even in the sense of it's absence, as with conceptual art practices), where a virtual shell of processes, referents and discourse orbit around a void where the art object might have once sat—so it seems counter-intuitive to try and name it or pin it down beyond maybe introducing it as being within art, among other possible things, as points on the external representational shell we see when encountering these process-based socially located practices (see for example Ann Hirsch's practice).

Being less difficult and actually answering your question, I certainly see the practices we work with at Arcadia Missa as at least having a place in the development of art and discursive history, from minimalism, to conceptualism to net art and onwards to now. It all deals with a reflexivity towards the apparatuses of communication or making in some way or another and so there is a definite genealogy here.

The term 'post-Internet' (I first saw it attributed to Marisa Olsen) was at one point quite useful in terms of collecting works that literally came after the Internet or the post-2008 crash or were made by a generation of newly 'digital natives' (as much as I find this term funny)—and seemed very much to make a self-declared break with net art, and very much owed allegiance to Web 2.0—but now this seems to predicate a type of work that has quite specific, formally homogenous aesthetic tropes that steer too (for me) close to New Aesthetics. Since post-Internet now feels more like a condition of art praxes as defined by the Internet's imposition rather than a negation of unwanted characteristics (i.e., as Post Modernism set out to do), it doesn't now seem useful for our exploration of identity politics amid the social-web for example, in fact *a priori* definitions are perhaps a hindrance here...

But post-Internet is certainly a good marker in the trajectory, the same with the New Aesthetic at least in terms of understanding where we stand in relation to other people's thoughts, whether or not we subscribe to their rubrics...

R   In regard to the terms 'post-Internet' and 'New Aesthetics' and the like, I'd like to say that using terms is a way to have a conversation, yet as terms they are actually fundamentally bad descriptions of current practices. Post-Internet assumes a 'post-ness' from a Western, privileged perspective yet tries to imply a global-ness (to produce a capitalist realist flattening of things such as image-objects and/or ideology[s]). A lot of people we work with use the digital objects, tools and detritus to create insight and to question the subjective, the social, etc. Recently much of this has involved a use of a degree of performative fiction, lets say, enacted through many platforms—Tom mentioned Ann Hirsch—and what is important here and has been a long-running interest of ours is digital performativity, rather than performance or parody. And work such as Ann's goes past performative fiction and into the spectacle-as-social nature of our lived experience. And it is in these many facades and personas of her life, her 'real' life, that we find her work. This is also interesting re: 'terms' as there are so many art shows that are curated about, or write press releases with, binaries about 'on-' and 'offline'—this may have been the dichotonic experience in the early days of the web and for 'net artists', but now there is not that distinction. The Internet is part of our IRL daily lives.

What is your background and what triggered your interest in digital/net art? Could you elaborate on these initial encounters?

T   It was kind of unavoidable, when Rózsa and I were at art school together there was a real coalescence of student struggles in mainland Europe, a shift towards our future in the UK being one of liquid modernity at best or precarious unemployment at worst. There were massive cuts to traditional arts and public institutional structures in the wake of the 2008 crash and although we might not have seen it so clearly at the time, a seemingly resultant move on the part of culture into the immaterial/representational—into the hole left by the financial market's inability to control abstraction. While certain digital/ online practices tend towards reclamation of the utopian promises of abstracted capitalism, we were more interested in understanding the processes that formed these promises, architecturally, materially and performatively, for example.

Personally, when I was at art college and saw how many of the painting students were composing or forming images, I increasingly felt that Google image search was replacing any other form of image mediation and was presenting itself and being treated as the origin of the image. It was representation representing nothing but its own surface, so I felt it incredibly important to consider what this meant in terms of art practice but more broadly for the type of subject that engages with this as the Internet became ever more 'social'.

So rather than making art works/curating, writing, et cetera, lamenting the loss of digital/analogue, IRL/URL separations, we have been looking for possibilities within this total environment. It's an environment of image, performance and conceptualization—and is therefore the perfect site for working between the everyday and imaginary—the social and the cultural. The marketization and commodification of the Web1.0 author-centric possibilities—that we would associate with earlier net art—into Web2.0 has created political subjectivities whose everyday negotiations extend well beyond the web. This is how it is unavoidable, but we came to use our art training to crack the surface of representation that articulates the Internet, and make it political rather than ethically flat.

We've also grown up with the Internet, from being a more separate, perfunctory thing for accessing information—slowly—to the introduction of broadband when the distinction between the Internet being something you use and something that begins to blend seamlessly with our spatio-temporal environment really broke away.

> You've been involved in various types of organizations and spaces. Could you share some of your experiences working in these different settings and particular contexts? For example, how does it affect your practice? Are there specific things that work very well in one context but not at all in another?

T Overall I've been more interested in the movement, use and affective outer surface of an archive and its documents—perhaps from having come at it from more of a digital perspective—so in this way the context is more one of the factors to be considered in the reading of each narrative and its artefact. I guess that as you locate what you do in these places outside of your head or whatever, you engage in different institutional relations, and so you negotiate these according to the pressures on your need or desire for autonomy within each location. This autonomy from structuring the narrative through the lens of institutions does make dealing with them more difficult, but in this confusion you can do and say more of what you want. Working with Central Saint Martins was funny because we were always working within its gaps, inconsistencies and flexibilities, yet the impetus for all the work and critique all resulted from the institution's inflexibilities, its inability to react and its adminis-trative myopia. When we invited Jonathan Miles, who co-ran *ZG* magazine and now works at the Royal College of Art, to speak about his relation to the CSM archive for the *InExchange* exhib-ition, he quantified the institution's capacity to react to what is going on around it as taking about five years, as in always being five years late. This is a good amount of time to work within.

On the other hand, working with Arcadia Missa and the institutional context being a self/user, i.e., online and physically in the space, offers one a much larger degree of autonomy and potential for responsive self-direction, but at the same time you are less free to make mistakes or be speculative, in that its activity is in an on-/offline hybrid and so completely public and transparent: someone will undoubtedly see your mistakes and quite likely question them. Accountability is crucial, but when the rules of the market inflect patterns of exchange, it forecloses a certain degree of experimentation.

Basically, IRL institutions try to totalize and centralize their surveillance, data gathering and archiving and so have hiding spaces for the individual. URL institutions are managed and maintained by the users who carry out self-surveillance, data-gather and archive—it is the responsibility of the individual to order their material, informational and exchange presence—taken up by the management and presentation of this presence creates hiding spaces for the institutions.

> There has always been a separation between people who stress the techno-logical (material) developments of digital art and those who emphasize the art qualities (content/conceptual). At the same time digital art is also often accompanied by a fair amount of theoretical discussion. How do you position yourself in this discourse?

T   Hopefully triangulating those three things! As a lived praxis that generates traces of each, pragmatism feels like a good starting point when surrounded by informational abstraction. It's important to discuss how the collapse in distinctions between material and content is performatively engaged within art and outside of art, in abstract terms. At the same time, it's important to try to understand how we actually embed ourselves and utilize our position within ideological representation when inhabiting this collapsed, material-content surface in a very real, bodily, dialogic way.

You organize online and offline exhibitions. Starting with the latter, do you work with certain methods or criteria? For instance, I recall numerous discussions in the past where showing a computer monitor was 'not done', or some curators wouldn't even consider presenting net art in an exhibition at all, while others created entirely new installations based on online work. What are your thoughts/experiences with this?

T   Ha, well we definitely do use computer monitors. This is where work exists—on screen—but I guess the key is to resist aestheticizing the monitor itself, since often this is not the interesting part. Avoiding this fetishization is important to giving primacy to the social function of the space, but also to avoid the idea that the online space is necessarily different (in an everyday sense) and the cynicism that this idea allows.

It's important to locate an artwork as a continual part its narrativization (its location, creation and placement within social and cultural processes by its user) and then push this further or problemitize it or its e/affects, so performative or material hyperbole in the form of and installation, for example, is necessary to frame this in an awkward site like the physical gallery space. As well as responding to the in-process nature of the practices we introduce into the space, our own process needs to exist in this narrative sense too, and the duration of this negotiation comes from joining up these different forms.

Moreover, the aesthetics of the screen surface itself is separate to the GUI [Graphical User Interface], for example, and if we want any sort of different conceptual or bodily relation to this and the identities, patterns of consumption or subjectivities created by the onscreen ideological representations then you have to create a spatial as well as temporal narrative around apparatus of visual culture.

Who do you see as your audience? I guess it changes with each new context but are there also changes (and/or exchanges) that you've noticed over the years, people moving from one place to another, or crossovers from other fields?

T   It is quite easy to talk sideways to peers/online peers but I'm not necessarily sure this is enough. But perhaps this is all we can or should do? Although there's always a point where a subculture/alternative space is tempted to move/forced out, so I think pre-emptively engaging outwards and defining the landscape into which you might have to move is important too.

What do you focus on in your online exhibitions? In the past we've seen examples ranging from lists of links, to commissions, to documentation about a work, to embedding a work in a website? What is your preferred or even ideal 'model'?

T   The best model is one that *enjoys* its form and makes use of the available architecture rather than pretending to be or trying to mimic its paper analogues, I'm pretty bored by page turning effects for PDFs, but with e-publications video is facilitated, the document's connections are rendered visible and actionable, and content is scalable. One issue that we have consistently encountered is how to maintain an idea of value: where the publication doesn't dissolve completely into its context and the user is willing to pay. This is not exactly a new story, but it seems to be possible to make this type of work, slowly at least. Basically we don't necessarily believe in giving everything away for free, in undercutting the ground on which you stand.

Online exhibitions are difficult. I'm not sure that it's a useful way of going about things: it seems overly encapsulated...

Could you elaborate a bit, or exemplify what you mean when you say 'overly encapsulated'?

T   I suppose that I meant it in reference to the fact that online exhibitions can be completely frozen within the flatness of the screen and when these forms of display replicate the mode of gallery viewing—an artefact of difference displayed to be viewed. This undermines the specific potential and mass-cultural use of the digital-artefact online; if these artefacts are objects of prosumption or immaterial labour, then we (anyone engaging with the Internet) as producers have a vested interest in the site where they are consumed. So besides this necessity to consider the frame through which we encounter the digital, there is certainly a collision between the content and this form: that is, the digital artefact is now only fully meaningful in terms of performativity. Self-representation uses the digital in one site among many others, on- and offline, but also in that the digital 'thing' has become something that requires attention, touching or manipulation. I think it was Matt Drage who talked about the possibility of a sexual attraction to Google in a talk he gave about at Arcadia Missa[32] about intimate relationships with the apparatus. Also when online self-representation begins to re-mediate a human presence as a glyph, symbol, or function of

32   During his 'Concession of Stages' talk in June as part of the *Open Office* programme. The talk will be reprinted in the forthcoming *Open-Office Anthology* to be published in January 2013.

data, you have this really interesting synthesis between the human and non-human. This is where I find something like an online exhibition problematic, or risking over-encapsulation—I'm not a subscriber to Speculative Realist Object-Orientated Ontologies, so I feel that this synthesis I mentioned above becomes less incisive when captured in the flatness and exchangeability of online presentation: when the content becomes flattened and all difference becomes subservient to the requirements of the GUI... So while this online space may allow for new comparisons and visual equanimities, I still believe that the real crux of interesting artworks online is when they are separated from the flat aesthetics of the surface and made political in their broaching of the two sites of display and performance—URL and IRL—Jennifer Chan's video *Young Money* is something I would argue does this well (see the *Mute* article 'Becoming Camwhore, Becoming Pizza', *metamute.org/editorial/articles/becoming-camwhore-becoming-pizza*).

Lastly on this idea of encapsulation, I want to think about to what extent we are able to talk critically about something from within. The Internet is more the site of social and cultural presence that we are embedding our social body in a form and economy we have less access to than the user-generated visual surface might suggest. Likewise, it's interesting that the military use *embedded journalists* as a way to describe their control of information, context and engagement in the Second Gulf War. It's important to consider this in our highly tailored, contextually predefined online experience, and what 'predefined online experience' might actually mean.

Should digital art enter established museums or organizations or are there better places where it can be preserved and presented? If so, what role should museums play in the future?

T   There should/could be a place to record collective relations to cultural and societal events, activity and exchanges: a place not prefaced on one's financial, consumptive or technical ability or the assumption that we as viewers are up to date with unnecessarily obsolete technologies. It's also important to be able to see from the outside inwards (I would say this is possible in the educational museum model)—we shouldn't assume that everything/one should be drawn into a dominant paradigm in order to speak publically. Ironically, I think 'traditional' institutions might become less dominant ideological spaces, and we should probably worry more about technological colonialism in the articulation of culture. I think that this supersedes the traditional institution's capacity to reify. Worrying about placing digital culture within public space[33] because of what that might do to artefacts — which are different to digital culture as an active and moving series of interactions and digital objects —ignores these more pertinent issues around the formation of concrete social relations derived from our experience of our digital interactions through private structures: the implications of which the GUI, New Aesthetic, etcetera, seem to have camouflaged.

I recently had a few discussions with artists and producers about the usefulness of open source, it seems that although all kinds of codes and suchlike are available they're hardly ever used, mainly because of the personal approach to coding and the complexity that derives from such project-based work. What is your approach to open source in this context?

T   We've got a good ghost script to run our printer, so thank you very much open source! But as I've mentioned, our relationship with open-source is complicated since we've never really felt like we have a firm/stable base or steady jobs or a reasonable rent, for example, from which to confidently offer our services for free. Generosity doesn't abolish gluttony...

Until recently in the Netherlands there was always a very good funding system for the arts in general and specifically for digital art. That has since changed, increasing on the one hand the divide between 'traditional' art and digital art, while on the other it generally means looking for money outside the funding system. Could you share some of your experiences working around the globe? How do you and the artists you work with survive?

T   We run Arcadia Missa on a model where hiring out studios covers the cost of the total rent, giving us a small amount of gallery space within this. But in order to run the programme and publishing, we have until recently completely relied on a mixture of our own external income, free time, parties and publication sales, and a more time-and-labour-based exchange with the people we work with. We've just secured a small grant from the Arts Council, which pays for some material costs and allows us to financially support the contributors to the Open Office programme, but essentially, working in an experimental set-up with non-commodity-based art (in the art-market sense), we need to have a real *portfolio* of inputs. It feels as though all areas of working at this level are about mixed economies: it's completely fucking schizophrenic.

33   Digital art of the Internet is rarely in public (non-private) space.

This means that we do have to think about how to generate income from our own activities. Although we could of course be labelled prosumers, it's not necessarily as bad as it seems; as a system it feels more autonomous than simply directing our work and the labour of those we work with into the wider economy by proxy of the art market.

> In addition to your work at Arcadia Missa, one of the projects you're involved in is *maydayrooms.org*, which has a strong archival focus and link to collecting. Could you explain this approach, also in relation to your other work? And what is your interest and perspective when it comes to digital preservation, documentation and collecting?

T   I'm interested in the digital object as an artefact made-to-be-manipulated, to be touched, interacted with or narrativized. In its traditional sense an archive is a record or trace of all social or cultural processes, and exists as proof of these things having happened. I'm interested in combining and conflating these two ways of articulation and representation. MayDay Rooms seems to me to be about working backwards into 'the past', dissolving the documents by reactivating the stories and subjects that created them, and similarly, Arcadia Missa is about this process of interaction, exchange and materialization, but looking into the future.

The personal archive, the self-creating or presenting subject is something I also want to examine, and observing the similarities and differences will, I think, offer freedom to move and redefine our relations to the notion of Internet representation existing on the surface of itself is key here too. When completely embedded within the reproduction of ideology and when the form and content are so compacted, we have to look for spaces to move and rupture—I think the stasis of archives like the ones MayDay Rooms will be working with is a good place within which to do this. This rigidity perhaps creates one of the hidden spaces I mentioned earlier...

Arcadia Missa is a gallery and publisher based in Soho, London. In this interview, we discuss the period between 2011 and 2014 where Arcadia Missa began its life as a project space in Peckham, South London. Founded by Rózsa Farkas in 2010 it brought together studios with research-driven programmes of gallery exhibitions (beginning in 2011), on- and offline publishing, events, and research developed with Tom Clark since 2010. The gallery programme was responsive to ongoing events, conversations and research residencies.

Tom Clark is a curator, lecturer and writer. He is an AHRC-funded PhD candidate at Goldsmiths, University of London, where his research explores infrastructural figures, practices and imaginaries. He has been editor at BAK, basis voor actuele kunst, Utrecht (2015–2017); co-director at Arcadia Missa Gallery, London (2010–2015); and contributing editor to *Para\Fictions* (Witte de With, 2018), and *Former West: Art and the Contemporary After 1989* (BAK and MIT Press, 2017).

Rózsa Farkas is founder and director of Arcadia Missa Gallery and Publishers. Rózsa has additionally curated and co-curated various projects and exhibitions outside of Arcadia Missa, such as *Rehearsals in Instability* for Vienna's 'Curated By' festival (2015), *The Posthuman Era Became a Girl at the South London Gallery* (2014), *Re-Materialising Feminism* project in the ICA and other spaces (2014–2015), *Ways of Living* at David Roberts Art Foundation, and the Finding the Body symposium at Central Saint Martin's (both 2016). She was associate lecturer in MA Fine Art, Chelsea College of Art and in BA Fine Art Dissertations at Camberwell College of Arts (both UAL) from 2014 to 2018, and in Language as Medium at ZHDK (Zurich) from 2016 to 2019.

1   Ann Hirsch, *Caroline in the Gallery*, 2010, installation view. Open Office: And Lore, Arcadia Missa, 2013.
2   Jennifer Chan, *Big Sausage Pizza I*, 2012, installation view. Open Office: And Lore, Arcadia Missa, 2013.

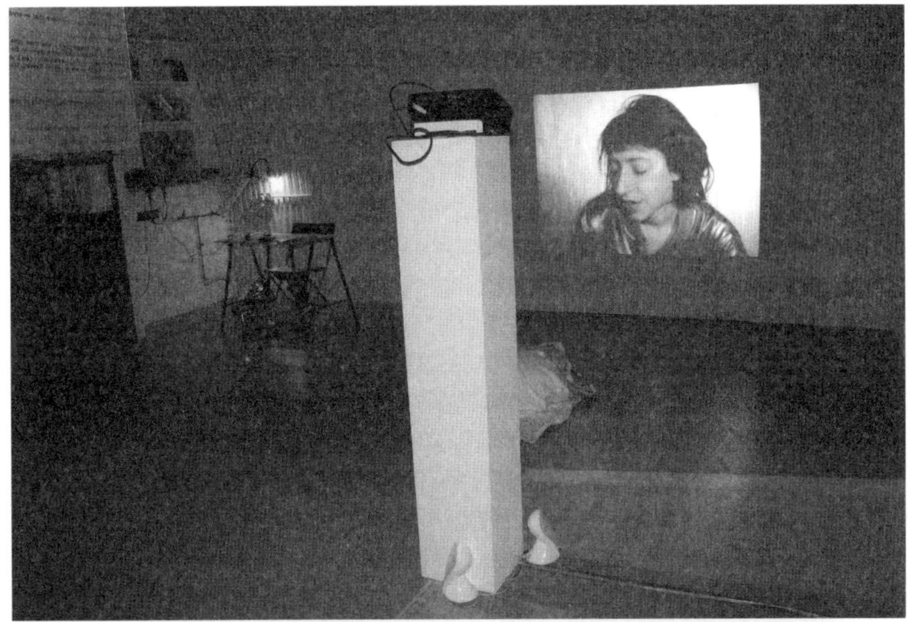

1

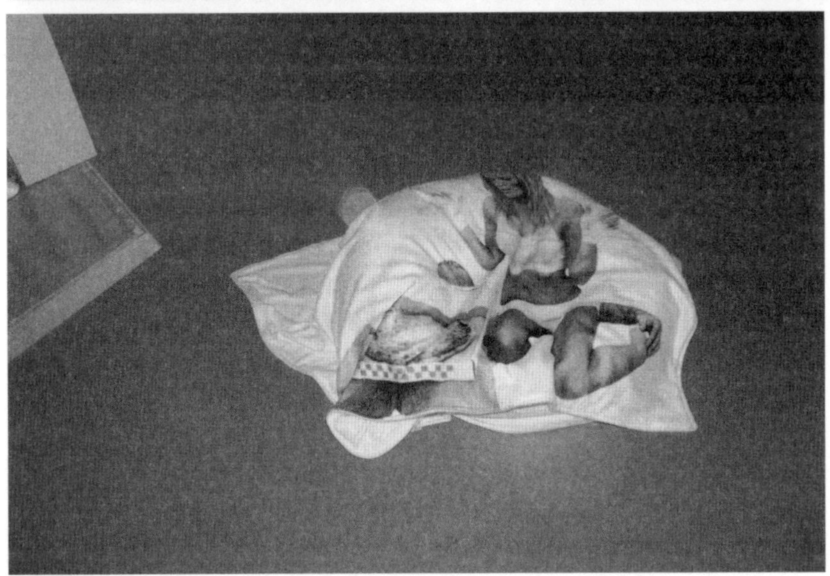

2

Amber van den Eeden & Kalle Mattsson

INTERVIEWEES: AMBER VAN DEN EEDEN, KALLE MATTSSON
PROJECT: TEMPORARYSTEDELIJK.COM, 2012
WEBSITE: NOT AVAILABLE
DATE: 21 NOVEMBER 2012

Can we start by defining the terminology we're using and how you position yourself within existing categories like digital art, new media, net art, contemporary art, or any of the post-arts?

A & K   We're a creative duo with backgrounds in graphic design, and Amber has a Master's in Communication Science; we observe, analyse, combine and then make things. In our work we represent a vision we have about certain situations in our time, things that happen around us, and the things we want to say about them. We tell stories.

What is your background and what triggered your interest in digital/net art? Could you elaborate on these initial encounters?

A & K   One of our recent projects exhibited art in the name of the Stedelijk Museum Amsterdam. We bought their temporary domain names temporarystedelijk.com and temporarystedelijk.nl and exhibited art online while the museum was closed. In the last exhibition we showed net art. We thought it appropriate to show art that originated in the same medium in which it was displayed.

We dived into the history of net art and discovered a whole new world, a world we hadn't noticed before—an entire artform had escaped our attention. This is understandable since you have to seek art out; it doesn't come to you. And when it does, it's sometimes confusing or confrontational; online you are conditioned to react in a certain way, but intrinsic to net art is that something unpredictable will happen; the same tools are used, but to make something different, and you have to work out for yourself what exactly is meant. Our immediate reaction is to close the tab and return to our trusted online environment.

Net art easily escapes the attention of the wider public and is sidelined by museums and galleries. It's an artform that's being ignored, which is a pity because it is actually a perfect medium to use to describe the times in which we live. We are missing out on the only artform that's describing the 'now' as it really is. Net art is the only artform that uses the tools, techniques and structures of the computer: the tool that characterizes our contemporary society in all aspects of our everyday life.

For us the challenge was to find a form, a translation into an exhibition, to show net art online to an online audience.

You've been involved in various types of organizations and spaces. Could you share some of your experiences working in these different settings and particular contexts? For example, how does it affect your practice? Are there specific things that work very well in one context but not at all in another?

A & K   Curating is about bringing works together and combining them into a single story, an experience in itself. Therefore, as a curator you have to understand what you're dealing with. Because we were clueless about net art we started reading up on it, and contacted art critics, journalists and net art artists. We discovered a speedy, open and friendly community, producing intelligent, inspiring and fresh works.

Net art differs strongly from more traditional artforms in two ways. One is that the audience participates automatically, and two is that the place where it is naturally shown is a virtual place.

As we mentioned earlier, what we kept in mind when creating this exhibition is that net art is an unpredictable experience: Net art is not something that you can make demands of; net art makes demands on you, the viewer. You have to participate and this requires a certain state of mind—to experience something unpredictable you have to tolerate something unpredictable. So, we had to find a way to create a space in the context of the computer where the audience understood that they were visiting an exhibition.

There has always been a separation between people who stress the technological (material) developments of digital art and those who emphasize the art qualities (content/conceptual). At the same time digital art is also often accompanied by a fair amount of theoretical discussion. How do you position yourself in this discourse?

A & K   For us there's no need to discuss technology. We mostly want to show what we think is great. What gets us going is not the cutting edge of technology, for example: it is achieving a balance between the form (of which technology is a part) and the concept that makes an artwork good. So for us, first of all, it is the combination of various elements: concept, form and aesthetics. We always ask ourselves what is being communicated and how?

Digital reality is an essential part of our everyday lives. This is why technology isn't an issue for us; we don't look at how net art is technically made; we try to understand what it says about us. Net art is a product of culture. This artform says something about how people relate to it. What we find interesting is that this artform says something about how people respond to the digital, the Internet, the computer; how does this digital environment shape us and how do we give shape to it? These are the types of questions we ask ourselves and what we think this artform is about.

    The discussion about technology, and the categorization

that takes place based on technology, indicate that we're dealing with an artform that still has to be fully acknowledged. Categorizing the works by material occurs, we think, because people can agree on this objectively with each other. It is the first step towards acknowledgement, but we aren't dealing with just another technological miracle; what it ultimately is about is something that is more abstract and less tangible. Imagine if you as an artist made an image (with a certain message or of a certain beauty) during the early days of photography, and then someone came along, ignored the image and said, 'Wow is that a camera?'

> You organize online and offline exhibitions. Starting with the latter, do you work with certain methods or criteria? For instance, I recall numerous discussions in the past where showing a computer monitor was 'not done', or some curators wouldn't even consider presenting net art in an exhibition at all, while others created entirely new installations based on online work. What are your thoughts/experiences with this?

A & K   While we were working on our online exhibition we realized that curating an online exhibition isn't all that different from an offline exhibition. It's about bringing together artworks and making them interact and work together in a space. The difference between online and offline is in the detail. What it comes down to are the differences between curators and their abilities to create. It's about unifying diverse works into a single story that you want to share with the visitors. We strive to make a particular message tangible within a coherent whole.

> What message did you want to convey with the net art exhibition you did for temporarystedelijk.nl?

A & K   We wanted to show net art of the past seventeen years, made by artists who were active from the beginning (the pioneers) and by the new generation of net artists (who grew up with computers). It included a variety of works, content, form, approaches, and aesthetics. It also showed how the digital and the virtual have changed over time, and how we have developed a community in a virtual reality, how that was initially seen as something different from 'real life' but is now accepted as part of it, an expansion of our world. It illustrated different approaches to the medium, and the range of stories that can be told. It showed us beauty and confronted us with time, technology, the physical, ourselves and the Other(s).

It also expressed a banal yet very urgent issue: an institution like the Stedelijk Museum organizes temporary exhibitions, but neglects the Internet as an exhibition space. If we could do it

—two people buying the temporary domain names of the most significant contemporary art museum of the Netherlands (temporarystedelijk.com and temporarystedelijk.nl for 9,95 and 4,95 Euros respectively)—they for sure must be able to do it. What we did is demonstrate an alternative to what is happening.

> Who do you see as your audience? I guess it changes with each new context but are there also changes (and/or exchanges) that you've noticed over the years, people moving from one place to another, or crossovers from other fields?

A & K   As curating an online exhibition wasn't that different from an offline one, we believe that the audience isn't that different either.

Of course there is a difference between the digital and the physical presence, but it's about the audience finding their way to the exhibition. To get a digital visitor in a digital world to look at art requires a different state of mind on the part of the audience. The visitor has to be engaged and the visibility of the exhibition is crucial. It's as simple as that.

Naturally, for a physical exhibition you need to be there physically. For an online exhibition an online presence is necessary. We don't try to cross that border, because it simply isn't necessary. You're there, but as a virtual presence.

> What do you focus on in your online exhibitions/digital magazine? In the past we've seen examples ranging from lists of links, to commissions, to documentation about a work, to embedding a work in a website? What is your preferred or even ideal 'model'?

A & K   For us a list of links is nothing else than a collection of links. We want an exhibition to be more than that—it needs a narrative. The atmosphere is the key element that needs to be created. This is pretty far from being concrete; it's so abstract that we define it as something magical, boner material.

In our final exhibition on *temporarystedelijk.nl* we temporarily put together a selection of net art that together became a unity.

> Should digital art enter established museums or organizations or are there better places where it can be preserved and presented? If so, what role should museums play in the future?

A & K   The role of museums is to capture time. It's their responsibility to represent what is going on and what has happened. Net art has been made for quite a while now, so we can all agree that it not only deserves a place, but also that museums are obliged to facilitate this.

The problem is that this is not happening. It comes down to money and a conservative mindset; museums do want to keep growing for financial reasons, but they don't want to grow into what the present is demanding from them.

I recently had a few discussions with artists and producers about the usefulness of open source, it seems that although all kinds of codes and suchlike are available they're hardly ever used, mainly because of the personal approach to coding and the complexity that derives from such project-based work. What is your approach to open source in this context?

A & K   Open source is great. It is the natural state of things, and at the same time it's an ideal, but we think this is irrelevant in relation to net art.

Why do you think it is irrelevant?

A & K   Making art is about having and developing ideas, it's about originality, so what role can open source play in this? Open source would interest us if an artist made it the subject of a piece. We aren't all that concerned if the piece is made with it. Moreover, that the codes are 'open' and 'using what you need' isn't inherent to net art; the codes are the foundation of the Internet.

Until recently in the Netherlands there was always a very good funding system for the arts in general and specifically for digital art. That has since changed, increasing on the one hand the divide between 'traditional' art and digital art, while on the other it generally means looking for money outside the funding system. Could you share some of your experiences working around the globe? How do you and the artists you work with survive?

A & K   We don't get paid. It's as simple as that. What we accomplish we accomplish by striving for quality together with people who help us out, mostly for free.

If we could answer the question another way, it would be about the discussion of 'art versus net art' and from the perspective of any funding system, this discussion would lead to the problem we mentioned earlier: net art not being acknowledged or facilitated, and museums not fulfilling their function.

One of your projects is *temporarystedelijk.com*, which in addition to being an online exhibition space also has an archive or a link to collections that allows the net artworks to be viewed directly on the website. Could you talk about your approach? How does it relate to collecting, preservation or documentation—often seen in relation to archiving?

A & K   We don't archive. We exhibit various works for a while in a space we created. We rely on the artists to preserve their works themselves. In this interview we tried to define the task of a curator, the significance of digital art and the role art institutions play in this regard. For now we're just grateful and happy that we succeeded in realizing our project and contributed to the relevance of this subject, namely net art.

When the Stedelijk Museum Amsterdam closed its doors for major renovations, it continued part of its programme under the name **Temporary Stedelijk** and organized *Temporary Stedelijk 1, 2* and *3* in public spaces in 2010 and 2011. Primarily showing works from their own collection, they neglected to present contemporary and upcoming (local) artists. Moreover, they ignored the by then thriving online space. As a response Kalle Mattsson and Amber van den Eeden bought the domain name *temporarystedelijk.com*. They organized four exhibitions that were programmed by Jonas Lund. *Temporary Stedelijk (4), (5)* and *(6)* presented artworks by emerging artists from Amsterdam. The fourth and final *Temporary Stedelijk (7)* was a collaboration with Constant Dullaart in which they exhibited a selection of works by Dutch net artists and contributions from art critics.

Amber van den Eeden is a communication scientist and a graphic designer. She studied at the Radboud University of Nijmegen and the Gerrit Rietveld Academie in Amsterdam. Amber is a talented analyzer and organizer, bringing together not only the worlds of graphic design, art and communication, but as a skilled networker, she also unites talented people in projects of all kinds and sizes. The core in her work is always connecting people by organizing activities such as (online) exhibitions, (cultural) events and festivals. She has also initiated an online platform for journalism, renovates houses and even opened an international clinic for premium hip surgery.

Kalle Mattsson is a graphic designer, illustrator and animator. He studied at the Gerrit Rietveld Academie in Amsterdam, where he worked for a few years after graduating until he missed the icy winds of the North and moved back to Stockholm. Before attending the Rietveld he was already a skilled image-maker and the years he spent in Amsterdam honed his conceptual design skills. This combination made him somewhat of a hybrid of an obsessed image-maker and an idea driven designer. These days he works with everything from abstract art to advertising, and his diverse skill set fully came together in his project *Buffalo Bill Gates,* a viral mashup phenomenon that has travelled the world since 2015.

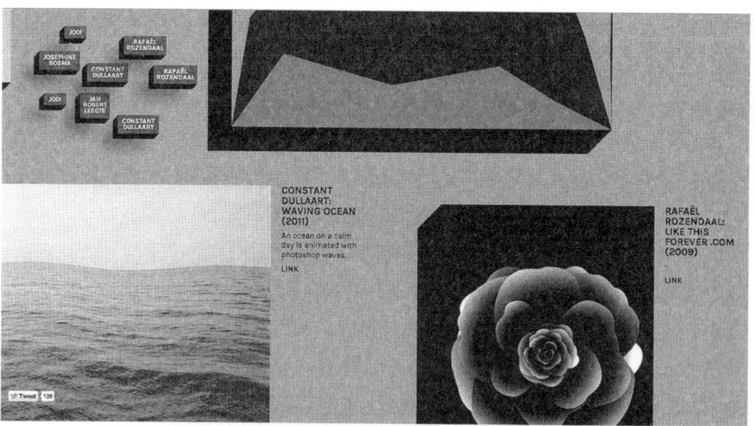

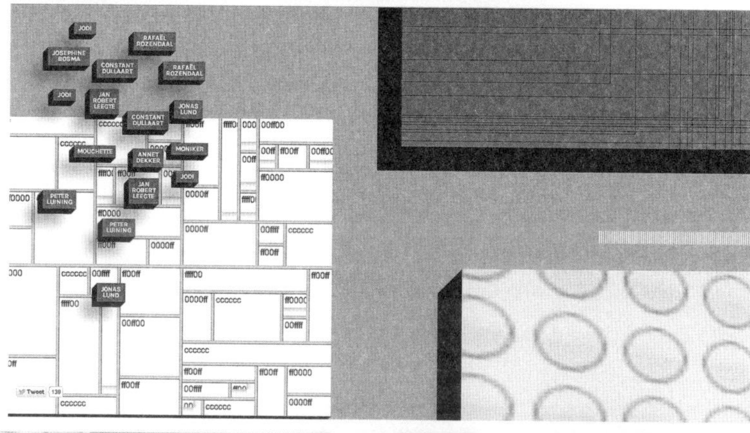

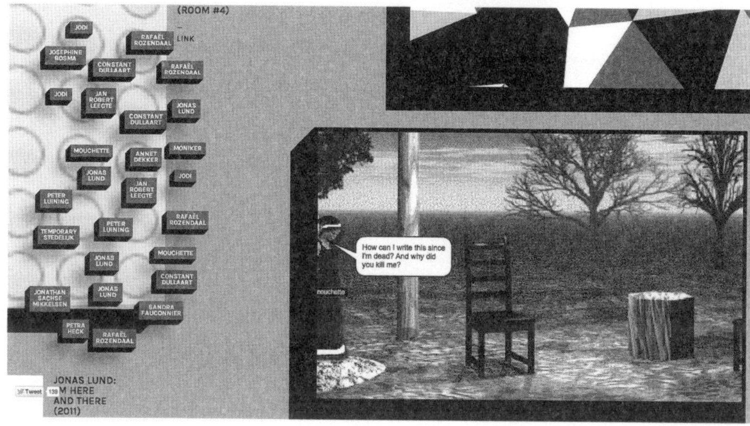
How can I write this since I'm dead? And why did you kill me?
mouchette

Katja Novitskova

INTERVIEWEE: KATJA NOVITSKOVA
PROJECT: VARIOUS – POST INTERNET SURVIVAL GUIDE 2010
WEBSITE: *katjanovi.net*
DATE: 26 NOVEMBER 2012

Can we start by defining the terminology we're using and how you position yourself within existing categories like digital art, new media, net art, contemporary art, or any of the post-arts?

K   I make contemporary art with contemporary materials, and formats and media easily available and widely used today. I use industrially produced consumer products, digital technologies and online platforms in the same way others use photography, video, oil paint or clay. The themes that run through my work deal with the origin and cultural impact of these new materials. I think this is the best way to avoid a categorization that would put my work in a niche that is perhaps too narrow. Digital art is a specific stream of art production that historically has accumulated a certain identity and agency. Although I was originally inspired by it, I prefer my work to be seen as just contemporary.

What is your background and what triggered your interest in digital/net art? Could you elaborate on these initial encounters?

K   I've been interested in technology and art since an early age, but it took me years to invent my own practice. I studied semiotics, media art and digital media at different universities around Europe. My greatest influences in the field who I've had a chance to see in person are Frieder Nake, George Legrady, Hendrik Speck from the European Graduate Schol, Casey Reas and others. I worked at Mediamatic in Amsterdam for several years where I encountered loads of projects and events related to digital media. While studying at the Sandberg Institute I planned on becoming a graphic/media designer but after seeing works by Harm van den Dorpel, Petra Cortright, Constant Dullaart, Kari Altmann and others in Amsterdam, I started gravitating towards an autonomous art practice.

You've been involved in various types of organizations and spaces. Could you share some of your experiences working in these different settings and particular contexts? For example, how does it affect your practice? Are there specific things that work very well in one context but not at all in another?

K   I always try to be aware of a particular context and work from it. Each town and each institution has a special culture and own audience, even though they might all be dealing with somewhat similar topics of contemporary art. I know that my work isn't always suited to some of these environments but I present it anyway, because I think of a global audience rather a local one when creating my pieces (doing things in small faraway towns is challenging in this regard). The scenes in London and Berlin have always been growing, and we've seen a gradual exodus from Amsterdam. But all these things merge with amazing ease, and hopefully will keep on growing everywhere.

> There has always been a separation between people who stress the technological (material) developments of digital art and those who emphasize the art qualities (content/conceptual). At the same time digital art is also often accompanied by a fair amount of theoretical discussion. How do you position yourself in this discourse?

K   The reality is that the history of digital arts *aka* 'things that have been traditionally presented at Transmediale or Ars Electronica' is different from the general flow of what is called 'contemporary art' and is shown at art fairs or Kunsthalles (in rare cases they overlap).

I try to make works in which the conceptual and the material/technological elements are impossible to separate. And in doing that I'm opportunistically gravitating towards exhibition platforms that encourage this sort of freedom. Lately and perhaps surprisingly most of the interest in my work has been from commercial galleries.

> You organize online and offline exhibitions. Starting with the latter, do you work with certain methods or criteria? For instance, I recall numerous discussions in the past where showing a computer monitor was 'not done', or some curators wouldn't even consider presenting net art in an exhibition at all, while others created entirely new installations based on online work. What are your thoughts/experiences with this?

K   This year I did a 'browser art' piece for Appendix project space in Portland. And later I exhibited the work on an iPad in a gallery space in London, accompanied by a printed canvas—an object I photographed for the original online piece. In both cases visitors to the webpage or the gallery were encouraged to 'use' them. This kind of fluidity and mutation seems to come as the most natural. There have been several exciting curatorial projects in this regard. Besides Appendix project space, *DIS* magazine, Lucky PDF, Barmedical Projects, Bubblebyte and others have all been experimenting with these transitions.

> Who do you see as your audience? I guess it changes with each new context but are there also changes (and/or exchanges) that you've noticed over the years, people moving from one place to another, or crossovers from other fields?

K   I think the audience is more generational than anything. My global peer group is my main target and inspiration. Lately I've also been thinking about making works that can be viewed by someone 2000 years from now, or even 10,000. I hope to reach both of these audiences : -)

> What do you focus on in your online exhibitions/digital magazine? In the past we've seen examples ranging from lists of links, to commissions, to documentation about a work, to embedding a work in a website? What is your preferred or even ideal 'model'?

K　My preferred model is the absence of a model. The beauty of the web is its continuous change. The speed of it makes things from 2008 already seem a little 'ancient'. I appreciate this pace, and try not to classify it too much.

> Should digital art enter established museums or organizations or are there better places where it can be preserved and presented? If so, what role should museums play in the future?

K　Art made with digital means is entering museums and art fairs quite rapidly. But it's usually the kind of art that doesn't position itself as primarily digital. It is contemporary art, and the fact that it was created around digital technologies is its secondary property. People like Oliver Laric, Ryan Trecartin, have been gaining a lot of recognition. I believe this is an organic way to merge the two and it's already happening.

> I recently had a few discussions with artists and producers about the usefulness of open source, it seems that although all kinds of codes and suchlike are available they're hardly ever used, mainly because of the personal approach to coding and the complexity that derives from such project-based work. What is your approach to open source in this context?

K　In my work I hardly ever go to the level of coding, and I try to solve all my creative challenges in the easiest way. Sometimes it's open source software, sometimes not. I use whatever is available, including a lot of illegally downloaded proprietary software. Because of my fascination with mainstream formats (from Rihanna to Facebook) I like to use Photoshop, rather than open source software that is just like Photoshop. Using mainstream tools also reaches a wider audience—people are more comfortable with common interfaces, filters, et cetera.

　Having said that, I fully support the open source movement for political reasons. Especially when it comes to issues of open content, information and transparency. With our lives more and more based on IP, open source is crucial to keeping certain powerful entities in check.

One of your previous works *Post Internet Survival Guide* has a strong archival focus and links to collecting. Could you talk about your approach, also in relation to your other work? And what is your interest and perspective when it comes to digital preservation, documentation and collecting?

K   Collecting, filtering and assembling online content into books or artworks is a great way to archive it. It is also a form of (aesthetic) research into material histories of things and their evolutionary narratives. That's more or less all I do... The concept of the archaeological value of the most recent trends—in art, pop culture or technology—is another related idea. I'm not that interested in safe preservation, but more in appropriation and the possibility of new forms. Right now I'm working on an e-publication titled *Neverending Story*, a catalogue of my solo exhibition but also an offshoot of the *Post Internet Survival Guide*. It will be a continuation of my method of collecting things online, assimilating them, and presenting them as a visual narrative.

Post Internet Survival Guide 2010 is a curatorial and artistic project in the form of a publication. It is a guide to the ecology of an ongoing merging of matter, and social and (visual) information in the world, which has come about through the ubiquity of the Internet and social media since the late 2000s. The book features artworks, texts and screenshots of blogs from many artists active in 2009–2010 and later. *Post Internet Survival Guide 2010* was co-published with Revolver Publishing in 2011.

Katja Novitskova is a visual artist working in a variety of media like books and installations. She lives in Amsterdam and Berlin. Her work explores the ecological dimension of visual information technologies: from attention economies to machine vision. She studied graphic design at the Sandberg Instituut, Amsterdam, and was a resident at the Rijksakademie van beeldende kunsten in Amsterdam. Novitskova's artworks have been exhibited worldwide, including at MoMA New York, the 57th Venice Biennale, the 9th Berlin Biennale and many others.

1–3   Katja Novitskova, *Post Internet Survival Guide: Formats*, 2010, installation, solar panel, *Post Internet Survival Guide 2010*, bone, Avatar mug. Courtesy of the artist and Kraupa-Tuskany Zeidler. Photo: Katja Novitskova.

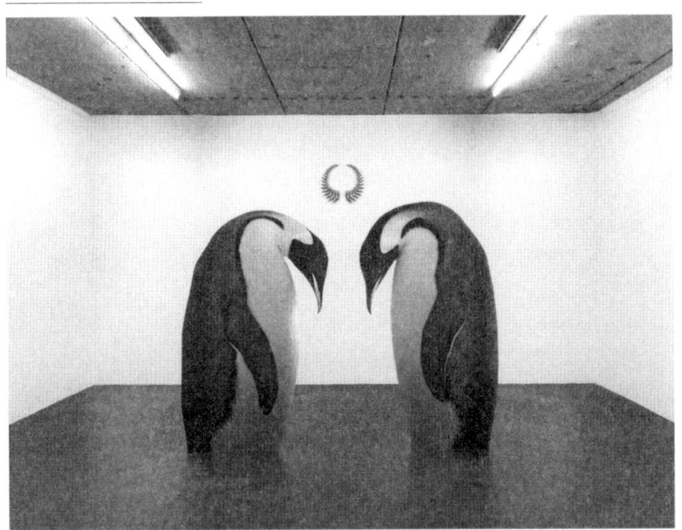

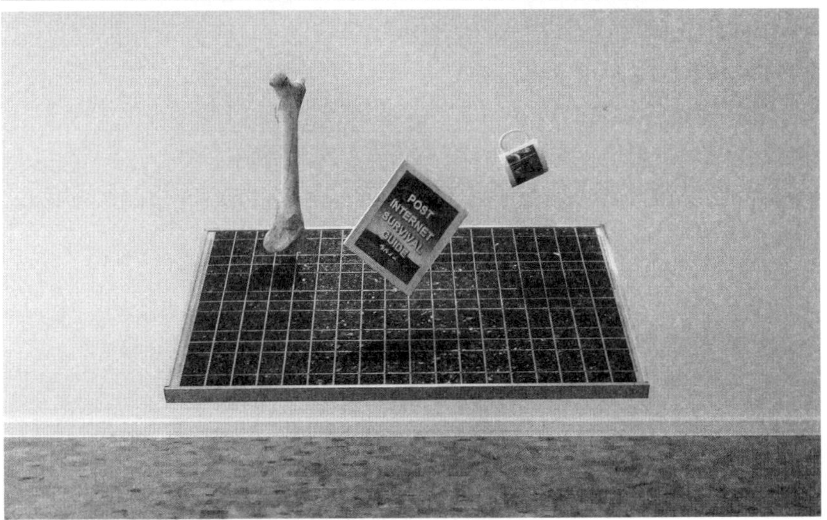
POST
INTERNET
SURVIVAL
GUIDE

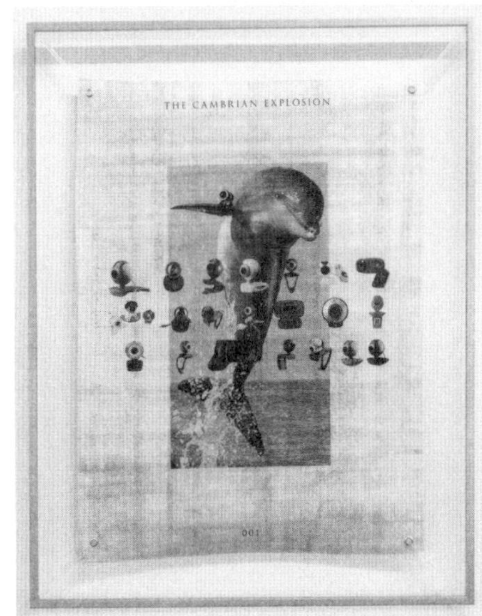
THE CAMBRIAN EXPLOSION

Laura Mousavi

INTERVIEWEE: LAURA MOUSAVI
PROJECT: E-PERMANENT, 2011–2012
WEBSITE: NOT AVAILABLE
DATE: 25 OCTOBER 2012

Can we start by defining the terminology we're using and how you position yourself within existing categories like digital art, new media, net art, contemporary art, or any of the post-arts?

L   While organizing exhibitions and projects at 20 Bedford Place we always used the open category of contemporary art and never chose to curate according to medium-based categories. Now that we've set up e-PERMANENT the context very much dictates the medium in a way that is new to me. I'm interested to see how artists are thinking about presenting work within networked digital space. As for the terms 'digital art/new media art/net art/born digital' I do find it quite confusing! If I was to define these terms I would say that 'digital art' suggests using digital technology to make art, 'new media' suggests using any new technology not necessarily digital, and 'net art' is specific to art created for the space of the Internet. There is also art which perhaps is created in non-digital mediums that interrogates the impact of the new technological age we are living in, which could be categorized as new media but is not using new media. I guess overall where my interests lie is primarily in the way in which artists can reflect upon the characteristics of our time; the specific medium they choose is a secondary concern.

What is your background and what triggered your interest in digital/net art? Could you elaborate on these initial encounters?

L   My background is fine art painting, which means that I have a tendency towards art that has an emphasis on the process of making and engagement with the qualities of the material being used. However, I organized exhibitions at Bedford Place in Brighton for nine years, where our only remit was to work with contemporary artists producing experimental work. In November 2011 we closed the space, partly due to some of the members of the organization moving on to other roles and out of the city, and partly due to me having a baby and needing to take maternity leave, as well as partly through necessity and the lack of resources. The subsequent recent establishment of an online exhibition space (*e-PERMANENT.org*) is to a large extent the result of a long-term collaboration between myself and interactive designer Cheryl Gallaway (of Hexaplex); e-PERMANENT being a manifestation of our respective interests. So here I am now, curating work for online space.

You've been involved in various types of organizations and spaces. Could you share some of your experiences working in these different settings and particular contexts? For example, how does it affect your practice? Are there specific things that work very well in one context but not at all in another?

L   Each new project actually brings about its own set of issues and challenges to negotiate so actually the artists we work with affect the experience as much as the context. We've produced a few exhibitions at a restoration project in Hove, The Regency Town House; this space has very strict guidelines concerning how the fabric of the building is conserved. This called for a very light-footed approach to installation with self-supporting hanging systems being devised (our former co-director Woodrow Kernohan was extremely tuned into the process of creating sensitive hanging systems which had a minor impact on the building). In this context, the artists whose work had provisional, materially ambiguous and site-responsive qualities were able to work successfully within the stringent building guidelines. This experience produced very specific results, which taught us that working in new contexts is most successful when there is a process of engagement, ideally over time.

There has always been a separation between people who stress the technological (material) developments of digital art and those who emphasize the art qualities (content/conceptual). At the same time digital art is also often accompanied by a fair amount of theoretical discussion. How do you position yourself in this discourse?

L   I would say that I would not view material developments and conceptual qualities in isolation of one another but would try to encounter works with the thinking that technological and conceptual developments are bound up with each another and this is what makes it art.

You organize online and offline exhibitions. Starting with the latter, do you work with certain methods or criteria? For instance, I recall numerous discussions in the past where showing a computer monitor was 'not done', or some curators wouldn't even consider presenting net art in an exhibition at all, while others created entirely new installations based on online work. What are your thoughts/experiences with this?

L   Many of the exhibitions we organized at Permanent Gallery were selected by committee from open submissions. Although we kept the criteria open, for me there has always been a particular interest in art made through involved studio processes where an artist is closely engaged with their medium, as I referred to above. By inviting proposals of online works I will be entering into new territory. I'm interested to see how artists are responding to the potential of creating works within an online environment.

> Who do you see as your audience? I guess it changes with each new
> context but are there also changes (and/or exchanges) that you've noticed
> over the years, people moving from one place to another, or crossovers
> from other fields?

L   Our audience has consisted primarily of artists who would define themselves first and foremost as artists rather than as 'digital artists' or 'new media artists'. For the last two years we've produced projects as part of the Brighton Digital Festival. This has meant that we've engaged more technology focused audience members. I would say that over the last few years there's been perhaps more of an embracing of 'digital' or 'new media' art by the mainstream contemporary art sector—perhaps demonstrated by Elizabeth Price winning the Turner Prize this year.

> As for your online exhibitions, what do you focus on? In the past we've seen
> examples ranging from lists of links, to commissions, to documentation about
> a work, to embedding a work in a website? What is your preferred or even
> ideal 'model'?

L   We're really waiting to see what submissions for the e-PERMANENT commissions we receive in order to create criteria, so I don't want to talk about a preferred model. I would say that I'm particularly interested in artists who access the vernacular of our everyday use of the Internet and find ways to draw attention to the way in which the online environment is structured and managed. Works such as Constant Dullaart's coding interventions into sites like Google and YouTube or Nancy Mauro Flude's use of programming language to create poetic performances and Katy Connor's visualization of global positioning data, which set out to reveal the material of the digital landscape. More broadly, what we're keen to support is work that is created specifically for viewing online, works that are contingent on the specifics of online space. This work needn't be 'born digital' (perhaps part of the process of making the work starts offline) but its final manifestation as a work should be online. At least this is what I'm imagining right now.

> Should digital art enter established museums or organizations or are there
> better places where it can be preserved and presented? If so, what role should
> museums play in the future?

L   I think it's important that digital art enters museums and institutions, as they have the resources to conserve and maintain the artworks for future generations, otherwise the ephemerality of some net art will result in it being lost from art history. These institutions can also contextualize digital art within the current frames and discourse around contemporary art, which I think, is important for digital art to be accessed and engaged with.

I recently had a few discussions with artists and producers about the usefulness of open source, it seems that although all kinds of codes and suchlike are available they're hardly ever used, mainly because of the personal approach to coding and the complexity that derives from such project-based work. What is your approach to open source in this context?

L   It's not really something I've explored directly myself. I think in theory it's important that open source exists whether it's taken up in practice or not; it's important that there are coders who leave the process of creating programs/software transparent, but of course it will only be those with an interest and knowledge in this area who will actually find some practical use for the open source code approach.

Until recently in the Netherlands there was always a very good funding system for the arts in general and specifically for digital art. That has since changed, increasing on the one hand the divide between 'traditional' art and digital art, while on the other it generally means looking for money outside the funding system. Could you share some of your experiences working around the globe? How do you and the artists you work with survive?

L   Recently the British arts funding system has taken a huge blow with deep cuts. The impact has been wide, with a lot of smaller arts organizations that lack the fundraising capacity of larger organizations having to close. It's also put incredible stress on all arts organizations. In terms of our experience, withdrawing from a physical space and setting up an online space was a way we could continue supporting artists with reduced overheads. This new model is yet to unfold. I'm concerned that without a physical space the community, which existed around the gallery, dissipates, with all kinds of negative consequences. We'll be looking to create live events alongside the online activity as a way to maintain and nurture a community.

When Permanent's gallery space closed in 2011, you set out to build upon the legacy of Permanent Gallery to produce an online space and digital platform that would enable Permanent to continue its work. One of the ideas was to publish a digital archive online to invigorate the documentation of Permanent's past exhibitions and events for new audiences. Could you explain your approach, also in relation to the new e-PERMANENT projects? And what is your interest and perspective when it comes to digital preservation, documentation and collecting?

L   We're creating a digital archive, as we are keen to ensure that aspects from our programme history are available as a freely accessible resource, as, for example, we have a lot of DV tapes with documented talks and performances over the last nine years. Creating an archive of any kind is important for documenting both the history of a small arts space and preserving the endeavours of the artists worked with and the curators/

organizers that supported them. We'll be working on the physical archive at the same time as creating the digital archive so as to create a system where 'there is a place for everything and everything is in its place'. I see the digital archive as supporting our current organizational aims of developing audiences for our work through the way in which it will make information so readily available. We're also going to be featuring parts of the archive periodically on e-PERMANENT.org as we launch each new artist commission alongside new writing on e-culture. We hope this way of presenting parts of our archive alongside new material will give it new relevance and pertinence. The capability for presenting information in different media on the same visual plane (video, photography, text, HTML) that online space provides is something I find exciting, also because it allows for different kinds of information to be viewed in relation to each other. In terms of long-term preservation, I see the digital record as particularly susceptible to the changes and advances in technology, which could cause the record itself to be compromised or altered in some way. I suppose that methods of both physical and digital archiving need to be constantly revised and updated in order for the record to be maintained and accessible, which is a long-term funding issue (I remember this was discussed in your booklet *Archiving Born Digital Content*). In terms of our new programme of commissioning works for online space, we worked with Constant Dullaart and used his template for documenting net art available on *net.artdatabase.org*. We plan on documenting all the commissions for e-PERMANENT using this method where the screen activity is recorded simultaneously to the user being recorded on the computer with all the used software and hardware being noted. This process is interesting because it locates the work within a physical environment and a specific time, acknowledging the physical and technological contingency of each work.

e-PERMANENT.org was a website created by Laura Mousavi and artist/designer Cheryl Gallaway for commissioning and presenting new Internet-based works and developing a digital archive of Permanent Gallery's activities at Bedford Place. New works were commissioned from Yuri Pattison, Ruth Höflich, Silvio Lorusso and Constant Dullaart, and shown online alongside highlights from the Permanent archive and texts. e-PERMANENT was supported by Arts Council England.

Laura Mousavi's career in the arts began seventeen years ago when she had the opportunity to open a small project space on the ground floor of a terrace building in Brighton. As part of a committee of artists she curated over eighty exhibitions, ran residencies, published texts and organized talks and discussion events. Laura then went on to co-curate e-PERMANENT, the online incarnation of Permanent Gallery. She subsequently worked for several years as project manager for Brighton Photo Fringe festival and produced an artist residency programme in Liverpool for A Foundation. She is currently studio manager for the artists Semiconductor and Emma Critchley.

1   Constant Dullart, *Anamorvista*, 2012–2013, *e-Permanent* issue #1.
2   Silvio Lorusso, *Data Centers Grand Tour (This Data Belongs Here)*, 2013, *e-Permanent* issue #02.

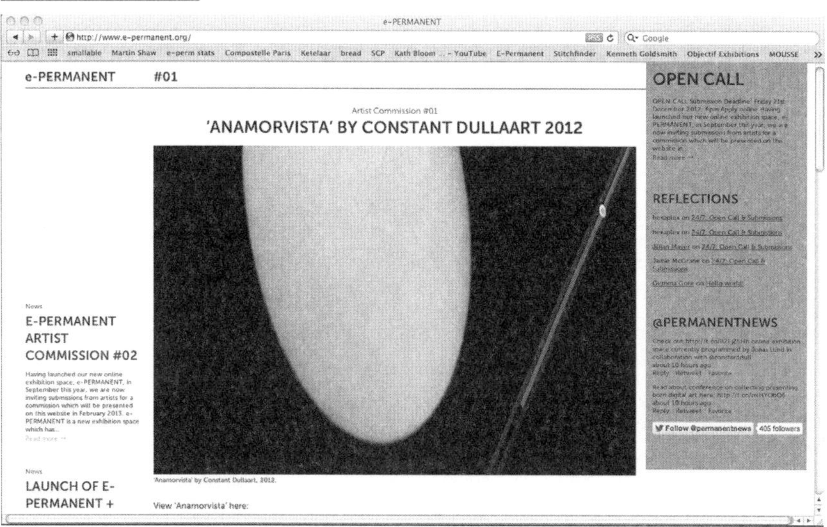

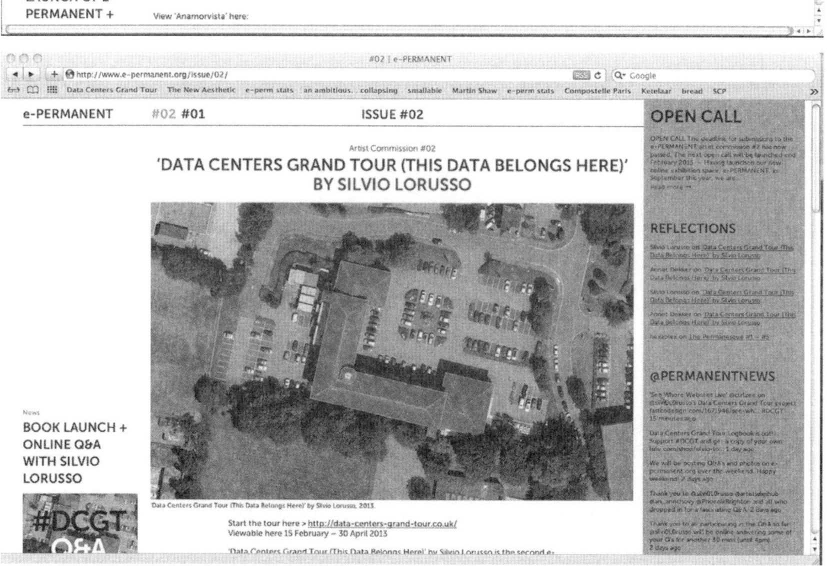

Madja Edelstein-Gomez [34]

INTERVIEWEE: MADJA EDELSTEIN-GOMEZ
PROJECT: THE RECOMBINANTS, 2017–2020
WEBSITE: *vimeo.com/370707334*
DATE: 2 OCTOBER 2017

M   I'm going to answer your questions in two ways: *first by quoting from my Recombinant Manifesto and other published material, a press release, or this interview I gave to Rhizome.* Second by writing what comes to my mind right now.[35]

Can we start by defining the terminology we're using and how you position yourself within existing categories like digital art, new media, net art, contemporary art, or any of the post-arts?

M   Quoting my open call for participation:

You make art. You are a creator. You are an artist. You are indifferent to the categories of the world of art. You feel free from any medium or artistic school. You are neither a conceptual artist, nor a painter, neither a relational artist, nor a photographer, neither a sound artist, nor a sculptor, neither a digital artist, nor a multimedia artist, neither an illustrator, nor a performer. You are simply an artist, open to all the possible universes. You do not feel concerned by the rat race. You have no need for originality, even it happens by itself when you are making art. You like what you do. Maybe you are a Recombinant. Come and join us!

Clearly, I'm not going to embrace any of these categories, nor let any of them define or restrict my curating practice. Nevertheless, I don't ignore or disregard the existence of categories in art, they are the DNA of the practice, each of them has a message to deliver and can inform curating practices. Recombining them is not blurring them together, but rather enabling messy and cruel encounters, making them bleed into each other like colours do, or collide like bumper cars... Such graphic impressions informed the design of my final show of *The Recombinants*. Summon the art categories to the foreground and dismiss them in order to make them clash.

What is your background and what triggered your interest in digital/net art? Could you elaborate on these initial encounters?

M   Here you summon the curator to expose her/his biography, which is something I've done several times and in different ways.

---

34   Madja Edelstein-Gomez is the collaborative creation of Martine Neddam, Emmanuel Guez and Zombectro.

35   All the quoted texts (in italic) are by Madja Edelstein-Gomez. All the other texts and answers are by Martine Neddam.

It used to be only mandatory for artists, but now, curators have gained the same dubious privilege of being characters.

Here is *one biography*. And here is another:

Madja Edelstein-Gomez (born 1960 in Montevideo, Uruguay) is an independent curator. Her life was filled with challenges. Imprisoned at the age of 13 under the Bordaberry dictatorship and released in 1984, she became a political journalist under a pseudonym and then an art critic. In 1988 she married a diplomat and became a mother of two children. She travelled on the African continent and later in India where she engaged in cultural action. There she curated several exhibitions mixing amateur artists and some great names in contemporary art (Cindy Sherman, Barbara Kruger, Lynn Hershman...).

Her husband and children died in the Egypt Air airplane crash near New York in 1999. Since then she has devoted herself to humanitarian causes and created several large thematic exhibitions ('Committed Suicide', Buenos Aires, 2001; 'god and bodies' Bangalore, 2002; 'Golem/s', Toronto-Prague, 2004, 'Out of Caste', Bangkok-Tokyo, 2009).

I've been a journalist, I've worked in humanitarian organizations, I've had great losses in my life, I had to re-think the reasons for my own existence, a few times over.

How on earth did I end up curating art online?

I think I learned curating skills by trying to curate my own memory. When you wake up from a shock, with the broken pieces of your life scattered in front of you, shards of existence which seem so exterior to you that you hardly dare to handle them, razor-sharp pieces, dangerously painful and yet indecipherable, how do you assemble and give a meaning to that?

Curating and post-traumatic recovery might have much more in common than one might think. It gives meaning to fragments by arranging them until they seem to make some sense, if not a clear and readable sense, then at least something that can hold your imagination together like a vessel holds water.

Online is a safer place to do that. In front of a screen, you're in control of your existence for a moment. You can re-invent it. You use digital material to rebuild yourself and your idea of the world.

I'm not particularly into net art, although it comes very naturally to me, like all born-digital material. In fact, I could curate anything, whether it calls itself art or not. Art has a potential to morph, which I definitely need.

I'm not sure if my digital practice can transform any-thing into art, and I wouldn't call it art myself, but if it can be recognized as art, it's a good thing because it gets a place.

> You've been involved in various types of organizations and spaces. Could you share some of your experiences working in these different settings and particular contexts? For example, how does it affect your practice? Are there specific things that work very well in one context but not at all in another?

M   Curating statement of my show *Out of Caste*, Bangalore India, 2009:

The Avatar is a Recombinant.

The Avatar belongs to the realm of the outcast: the poor, the unemployed, the homeless, the sexually deviant, the LGBT, you name it...

The Avatar is not excluded from society and is not dismissed among humans. On the contrary, exclusion is the door through which the Avatar makes an entry into society and later on, into normalcy.

The margins of society are a desired and beloved environment for the Avatar for they are the best learning ground.

The Avatar bonds and teams up with outcasts in order to learn expert social skills, and infiltrate the society of humans at large. He/She benefits from the dubious status of being a visible or an invisible minority.

The fact that I curate exclusively online has enabled me to navigate artistic contexts I didn't know existed. (I sometimes assume that I created them myself, but I know they exist outside of me).

I can navigate the margins of society, and the annexes of insti-tutions. The majority ignores my activities, and for some people who know what I do, I seem to operate outside reality in a kind of limbo.

Yet certain situations create a strong reality effect. When an artist gets of lot of hits online and realizes that this special attention to their work was triggered by their inclusion in one of my online shows, they e-mail me, try to meet me, they send me PDF files of their publications, and even animated New Year cards... They build the context around my existence, or should I say, they re-create me. I become the curator of their dreams, the one they host somewhere in their fantasy, who will understand their work, value it, and give it exposure.

For institutions, I play a different role: I am that magic interface between all their neglected artists, I connect them with every artist whose work they couldn't or didn't want present. I help them to rid themselves of the guilt or embarrassment they feel for all the artists they ignored.

I love to play that magic role, the good fairy, the one who, in the end, makes everything fit.

There has always been a separation between people who stress the technological (material) developments of digital art and those who emphasize the art qualities (content/conceptual). At the same time digital art is also often accompanied by a fair amount of theoretical discussion. How do you position yourself in this discourse?

M   *We issue a call to resonate below and beyond human language. We are directly connected to the noise of the universes, this very noise that machines can capture when they communicate and that humans want to silence. We, the Recombinants want the voice of the world to be heard.*

Make and then think, or think and then make?

For me the choice is clear: concept always comes next.

Things happen, or you create them (simply because you can't help it) and then you find out what they mean to you and to someone else. A concept is like a wrapping that you use to handle and share your production. Packagings are fine as long as they have a function. But concepts and theories so often feel like empty packagings, discarded boxes.

You organize online and offline exhibitions. Starting with the latter, do you work with certain methods or criteria? For instance, I recall numerous discussions in the past where showing a computer monitor was 'not done', or some curators wouldn't even consider presenting net art in an exhibition at all, while others created entirely new installations based on online work. What are your thoughts/experiences with this?

M   *We, the Recombinants, are not cyborgs. We are complex beings, deeper and more incarnated than the cyborgs who are poor and simple beings, prosthetic, hybrid and fictional. Cyborgs are binary and primary beings. They are diminished beings. Cyborgs only know two realms of scriptures, two codes: one is organic (DNA) and the other is electronic. We, the Recombinants, can process a much greater number of codes and scriptures. We continuously re-write ourselves by drawing in the infinites sources of frequencies present in the universe. We are not a synthesis. We are the recombinance of several modalities of existence. We constantly recombine our own source code.*

I don't care about physical space. It's worth noting that all museums and institutions always had a 'virtual space' long before the Internet existed because they circulated a lot of information about where the art happens in the form of press releases, posters, invitations, images, and they also have talks by museum guides, staff members, curators...et cetera.

I only care about that circulation, that in-between space for art.

Actually I believe that the art happens there, much more than on the walls.

There are many ways to 'occupy' this space, or to be invited into this space. In early net art times, people would borrow or steal the name of a museum and that was enough to become part of the institution. Nowadays, thanks to art created online, institutions could take the opportunity to reconsider that part of their influential space and be creative with it, or invite creators inside it.

But unfortunately they don't. With the Internet, they act like companies, and they use online space only as a marketing tool; in a very conventional way they advertise to improve their business.

This crossover between online and offline offers opportunities for authentic collaborations with online artists. It can be in the form of a hacking, hijacking, joking, et cetera, and the best is if this collaboration is involuntary. So in that sense, I already collaborate with art institutions but they don't know about it.

It's very patronizing to show online art on a screen inside the museum space.

It asks: 'Can you be as beautiful as a painting or sculpture?'

Or 'Look who's coming to dinner? Your fiancé is black, but he's ok... '

Who do you see as your audience? I guess it changes with each new context but are there also changes (and/or exchanges) that you've noticed over the years, people moving from one place to another, or crossovers from other fields?

M   From the press release of the show *The Recombinants*:

Online you will experience a live processing of your data by our artificial intelligence algorithms.

This individual discovery is left to your patient curiosity and sagaciousness. Online each viewer will visit a different show, will travel in different spaces and the various perspectives of our invited artists, which you can also visit one by one. Observe the incredible exhibition robots and experience their instant power of calculation. Guess their moves, anticipate their combinations, outsmart their artistic intelligence.

Beware, it might shake your browser and melt your micro-processor!

My audience are my participants and my participants are my audience.

Actually there is no audience to speak of, only a chain of digital participants. Whoever sees the work becomes part of a processing chain of viewing. The reception of a file produces digital information, which is re-injected into the system as a digital production.

This is not new, but now this generative principle has densified, to a point of unlimited proliferation.

What do you focus on in your online exhibitions/digital magazine? In the past we've seen examples ranging from lists of links, to commissions, to documentation about a work, to embedding a work in a website? What is your preferred or even ideal 'model'?

M   *Can an exhibition be curated by an Artificial Intelligence?*

This challenge was taken up by Madja Edelstein Gomez for her exhibition The Recombinants.

The participants who responded to an open call were carefully selected by sophisticated algorithms. And now what you experience is a mesmerizing mixture of pictures, videos, sounds and texts, all situated in an ever-changing screen.

I love models! Actually I believe there are no online shows, only models of online shows. Lots of models, good ones, bad ones, or non-models, those to be avoided.

One-of-a-kind experiments cannot exist because they always leave an online trace of reproduction.

The show I recently composed, called *The Recombinants*, is indeed a sort of model, and for a part, rather conventional: it functions with an open call, a database and a final online presentation. But the selection and the display of the presentation are entirely curated by Artificial Intelligence. But it's not the kind of AI where you are in control of the parameters, where you attribute tags to lists of names and create categories, and you get the results you more or less expected. I'm using a kind of AI (also called Deep Learning) where the processes of code are so incredibly complex that they remain forever opaque. We use a special serendipity algorithm, for a felicitous unexpectability. One sure thing is that their results are unpredictable.

Should digital art enter established museums or organizations or are there better places where it can be preserved and presented? If so, what role should museums play in the future?

M   *We, the Recombinants, are not mutating, for we never had an initial state, but we have the capacity to induce mutations. Mutation is merely an effect of recombinance. Evolution implies genetic mutation, it is an effect of recombinance. Life evolution is just one particular case of recombinant identification*

I'm at loss for an answer here...

I wish I could use here my serendipity algorithm, if not my psychic powers.

We, the Recombinants, have always existed, under various forms, often unexplained. We experimented with multiple modes of existence, we crossed numerous realms of reality. The paranormal, telepathy, psychic energies, spiritualism, mysticism, and prophecy are non-scientific approaches of recombinance.

I recently had a few discussions with artists and producers about the usefulness of open source, it seems that although all kinds of codes and suchlike are available they're hardly ever used, mainly because of the personal approach to coding and the complexity that derives from such project-based work. What is your approach to open source in this context?

M   *Our own code—our supposed ultimate coding, the stigmata of our polyphonic breakthrough into the human world—is perfectly defined and yet it is still indecipherable, for it is endlessly recoding itself. Our code has a remarkable set of properties. Our code escapes genealogy and prediction. We, the Recombinants are the Omega ciphers of humanity.*

Open source/closed circuit

I always want to create our own code and share it. But then I end up in a very narrow community, if not entirely alone on my own coded island, endlessly re-writing my own code with no one to decipher it. The chances that my open source code is adopted and widely distributed are thin.

I want to take that chance.

Besides, one shouldn't disregard the power of a very tiny piece of the Internet being kept alive in an extremely isolated place. That's the creativity of a 'Robinson Crusoe', left to his own, very limited resources.

Until recently in the Netherlands there was always a very good funding system for the arts in general and specifically for digital art. That has since changed, increasing on the one hand the divide between 'traditional' art and digital art, while on the other it generally means looking for money outside the funding system. Could you share some of your experiences working around the globe? How do you and the artists you work with survive?

M   *We, the Recombinants, are not equal to other beings on this planet. We ignore equality. Equality relates to unity.*

Early on in my life I realized I was different. That feeling was eerie: a disease or something else, what does it matter? We are the symptom of an absolute dependency on material and the physical forces of the universes. You humans need to cling to relational attractions, gift economies or ecologies of sharing. We, the Recombinants, offer the world without expecting anything in return. The downloaded iterations are nothing other than the distress of a glitch of their origins.

I might be a curator but I function like an old fashioned artist. I apply the 'Van Gogh recipe': starve now, and in the afterlife you either become a billionaire or you disappear.

In a future project, I am going to create an algorithm where the value of a work of art is tied to its circulation and its level of influence, a sort of 'artcoin' if you want. The more a work of art is seen and shared, the more value it acquires. But I don't mean just hits or the number of copies. It will evaluate a level of influence (yes, a secret algorithm of mine) by which its value will increase.

On another note, works of art could become a form of currency. In December 2017, a painting by Picasso was sold as 40,000 shares of 50 Swiss francs each. As the owner of a share you have access to a special platform where you can vote on whether the work is loaned to a museum or not, and your Picasso share has zero risk of devaluation.

qoqa.ch/fr/offers/15113

qoqa.ch/de/offers/15113

Isn't that an idea for the museum of the future?

One can also purchase the historical castle La Mothe-Chandeniers in the same manner.

dartagnans.fr/en/projects/et-si-on-adoptait-un-chateau/campaign

One million euros for the ownership (already raised), and 3 millions euros will have to be found for the restoration.

dartagnans.fr/en

We are hearing a lot about bitcoin and blockchain as being the online future of our economy or its dystopia. If I may hazard a prediction, thanks to these new technologies, art is going to be our currency, museums are going to be our banks.

One of your recent projects is *The Recombinants*, which asks the question whether an exhibition can be curated by an Artificial Intelligence, do you think AI could also be used to document and preserve these types of works? Could you talk about this approach, also in relation to your other work? And what is your interest and perspective when it comes to digital preservation, documentation and collecting?

M   *Cyborgs only know two realms of scriptures, two codes: one is organic (DNA) and the other is electronic. We, the Recombinants, we can process a much greater number of codes and scriptures. We continuously re-write ourselves by drawing in the infinites sources of frequencies present in the universe. We are not a synthesis. We are the recombinance of several modalities of existence. We constantly recombine our own source code.*

I'm currently working on developing an algorithm that I will soon be able to test, which I call 'Ice Core' (or 'I Score').

A digital work is a huge quantity of data producing more data in a constant proliferation. New data is created, layer upon endless layer, but one doesn't need knowledge and access to everything. The old data doesn't vanish but is buried very deep. My idea is to drill 'ice cores'.

Wikipedia source: An ice core is a core sample that is typically removed from an ice sheet or a high mountain glacier. Since the ice forms from the incremental build-up of annual layers of snow, lower layers are older than the upper, and an ice core contains ice formed over a range of years.

The physical properties of the ice and of material trapped in it can be used to reconstruct the climate over the age range of the core. The proportions of different oxygen and hydrogen isotopes provide information about ancient temperatures and the air trapped in tiny bubbles can be analysed to determine the level of atmospheric gases such as carbon dioxide.

It's just an analogy, of course, to explain my starting point, and my general idea of preservation.

This, until we encounter the big meltdown brought about by climate change, the one that will make all our endeavours worthless.

The Recombinants is an online exhibition in which the work of 250 artists, or more, are mixed together, endlessly streaming in a beautifully rendered interface: images, videos, sounds but also the portraits and the artist's statements of the 250 artists are recombined by artificial intelligence.

Madja Edelstein-Gomez is an independent curator who has curated several large thematic exhibitions (Bangalore, Buenos Aires, Prague, Tbilisi, Toronto). Edelstein-Gomez currently lives in Kuala Lumpur and Paris. She is also an activist working with several NGOs. Edelstein-Gomez created a manifesto and a group exhibition that revolves around the Recombinant, a concept where artificial intelligence and artists meet.

1	Madja Edelstein-Gomez, screen capture of her personal website.
2–3	Screen capture of the show *The Recombinants*.

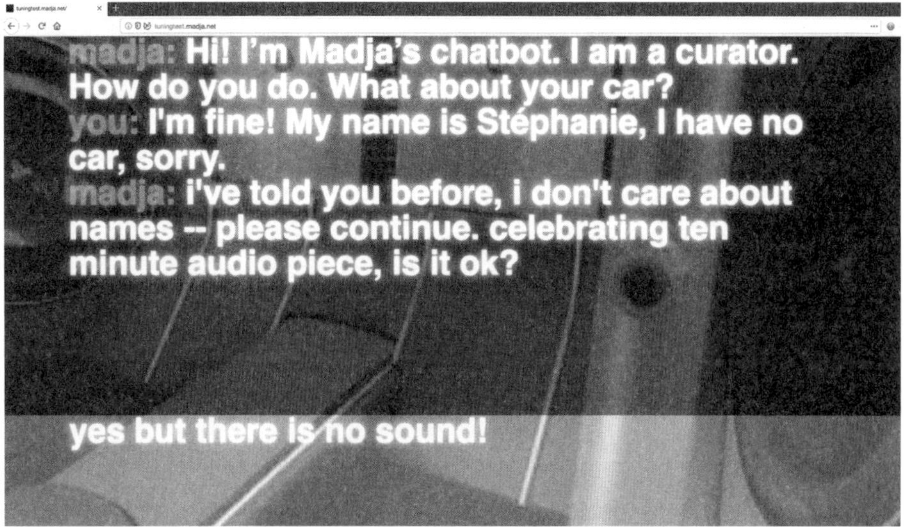
madja: Hi! I'm Madja's chatbot. I am a curator. How do you do. What about your car?
you: I'm fine! My name is Stéphanie, I have no car, sorry.
madja: i've told you before, i don't care about names -- please continue. celebrating ten minute audio piece, is it ok?
yes but there is no sound!

1

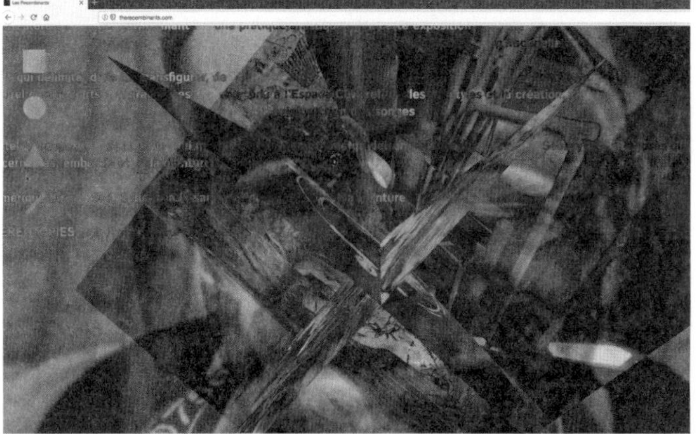

2

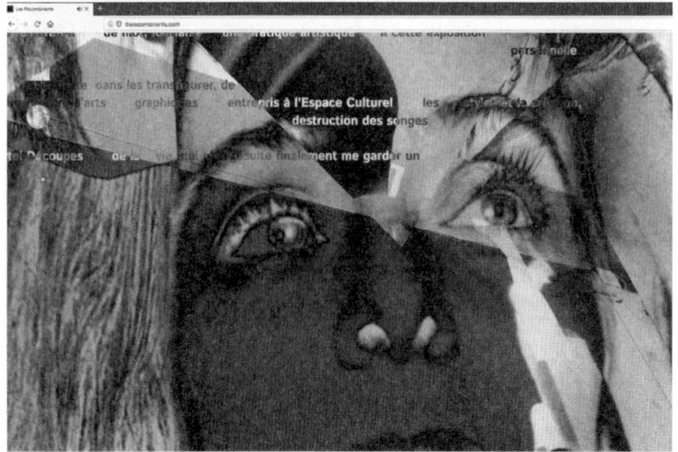

3

Gaia Tedone

INTERVIEWEE: GAIA TEDONE
PROJECT: VARIOUS – POIUYT, 2017–PRESENT
WEBSITE: *poiuyt.it*
DATE: 20 NOVEMBER 2017

Can we start by defining the terminology we're using and how you position yourself within existing categories like digital art, new media, net art, contemporary art, or any of the post-arts?

G   As a curator with an expansive interest in photography and in the apparatuses and technologies of image formation, I see my practice as occupying a hybrid territory at the crossover between the fields of photography, contemporary art and digital/networked culture. I'm using the word 'culture' instead of 'art', as the very notion of 'digital', in my understanding, implies a revision of the conventional categories of artistic production and a more inclusive formulation of notions of aesthetics and creativity. Accordingly, the very definition of art needs to be reframed in light of the impact of the Internet and digital processes, since these are reconfiguring the channels of distribution and modes of reproduction of all forms of cultural production.

Within this framework, the question of how to articulate and sustain a critical investigation into contemporary image practices has been one of my primary concerns, also shared by fellow members of POIUYT, the artists-curators collective I'm part of. The project is the result of the collaboration between curator Francesca Lazzarini and myself with artists Alessandro Sambini, Discipula and The Cool Couple. In a sense, POIUYT can be described as a 'meta-collective', since Discipula is already a collective composed of MFG Paltrinieri, Mirko Smerdel and Tommaso Tanini, and The Cool Couple is an artistic duo formed by Simone Santilli and Niccolò Benetton. The choice to work collaboratively and across different fields was our response to what we perceived to be the narrow institutional boundaries of both the fields of photography and contemporary art. We were interested in integrating our different backgrounds in photography, curating, sociology, music and graphic design to open up a critical debate about the role of images and their political power under current socio-economic and political conditions. In this respect, the position of the group is inherently trans-disciplinary and its motive, I would like to propose, can be described as 'post 9/11'. Here the 'post' does deliberately bypass art categories; rather, it refers to a key historical event that has fundamentally shifted the role of images within contemporary visual culture. Against the backdrop of such historical transformations, our approach also speaks to the so-called 'post-representational' turn within contemporary photographic practices. According to this particular perspective, images should be understood in terms of how they *operate* within sociotechnical systems of reproduction and circulation, rather than in terms of what they *represent*, raising important questions in regard to their renewed cultural value and social function.

What is your background and what triggered your interest in digital/net art? Could you elaborate on these initial encounters?

G   I have a mixed background that combines studies in economics for the arts, culture and communication, and formal curatorial training. My interest in art and creative practices has never been separate from their social dimension, and is intended to contribute through reflection on debates concerning real-world issues. The arrival of the Internet and the proliferation of digital technologies have offered new opportunities to stage and amplify such debates. Hence, my fascination for digital culture and the culture of the digital emerges at this juncture. More specifically, it can be tracked down to two interrelated research interests. On the one hand, the so-called practices of 'tactical media' of the late 1990s, the period that Geert Lovink named the 'short summer of Internet criticism'. I'm thinking of the interventions and projects by artists and activists including The Yes Men, Group Etcetera and Steve Lambert, among others, who infiltrated the mainstream media apparatus to create rupture and produce critique. On the other hand, it developed from a preoccupation with the shifting conditions of the photographic image in light of the advent of digital networks and online platforms for user-generated content.

An exhibition that effectively crystallized a number of my research interests was *FREE*, held at the New Museum in 2010/2011 and curated by Lauren Cornell. The show, which opened a few months before the Arab Spring, captured an interesting moment of transition from a first wave of optimism in regard to the role of the Internet as a public sphere to the present moment, characterized by a scenario of hyper-commercialization and corporate monopoly. It featured artworks by artists such as Trevor Paglen, Jon Rafman, Aleksandra Domanović and Martijn Hendriks, who later became associated with the second generation of Internet artists. However, the focus of the exhibition was not on the formation of a new aesthetic canon; rather, the show took an expansive look at the role of the Internet as a mass medium, mapping a number of artistic responses to shifts in notions of public space and collective imaginary.

The same year, I had my first opportunity to experiment with online curation within the framework of the web-based platform *or-bits.com* and channelled some of my own questions in regard to image circulation and manipulation across the networks. For the occasion, I invited a number of artists and collectives—Alessandro Sambini from POIUYT was one of them—to respond to the image known as 'The Situation Room', published in the news on 2 May 2011, which swiftly turned into the iconic image of Osama bin Laden's death. Since then, my interest in the potential of online space as a site for research and critical reflections *with* and *about* images has developed, leading to my PhD research which was concerned with the online curation of networked images.

You've been involved in various types of organizations and spaces. Could you share some of your experiences working in these different settings and particular contexts? For example, how does it affect your practice? Are there specific things that work very well in one context but not at all in another?

G   My curatorial practice is always affected by the context in which it operates or is embedded. I often start by reflecting on the wider implications or conditions of a specific project and attempt to articulate my own position in response to or in friction against them. The kinds of context I have interacted with include organizational settings such as institutions or artist-run spaces, collaborative and self-organized projects, such as the collective POIUYT, or the online environment. In the latter case, the context of the web has become the primary instigator of my curatorial methodology, which is less focused on producing projects and outcomes, and more on activating research processes and interventions.

I've never been that interested in working with traditional curatorial models such as the exhibition format or online art commissions; rather I prefer to exploit the curatorial tools already existing within online platforms and modify their original purpose, which is often purely commercial. For instance, in 2017 I took part in the project *#exstrange*, an initiative by Marialaura Ghidini and Rebekah Modrak, and tested the limits of eBay as a platform for online curation by experimenting with its digital tools for data aggregation and collection creation and partnering with its search algorithm, Cassini. However, because my curatorial education was rooted in the field and discourse of contemporary art, the immateriality of online curation remains a puzzle. This is why I sometimes resist giving up entirely the notion of form, and anchor myself either to a specific object of investigation or to a particular context.

> There has always been a separation between people who stress the techno-logical (material) developments of digital art and those who emphasize the art qualities (content/conceptual). At the same time digital art is also often accompanied by a fair amount of theoretical discussion. How do you position yourself in this discourse?

G   I believe that technological and conceptual considerations should always bear equal weight in digital art. By this, I mean they should be integrated and treated as constitutive of the same whole and experience, not unlike the way form and content operate in any work of art and artistic project. The specificity of digital art is that it often entails a great deal of research and technical expertise and hence requires some additional effort and time from the viewer. The theoretical discussion that accompan-ies it certainly provides the opportunity for further explanation and speculation. However, my position in regard to this question is ambivalent: on the one hand, I believe it is necessary to theor-etically unpack certain digital projects and artworks to fully understand their scope, especially if the digital is not simply understood as a tool or medium, but more broadly as a wider cultural and social condition; on the other hand, I always value an experiential quality in artistic and creative projects which is not necessarily channelled intellectually and by means of theory, yet operates through intuition and at a more sensorial level.

I believe considerations of context and display formats play a crucial role in this debate too. I'm thinking of the creative exuberance of ZKM's exhibitions and catalogues, such as the latest *Open Codes*, and I wonder whether the exhibition format does justice to the presentation of digital projects. Or, to put it in another way, I question the value of staging the encounter with many technically and conceptually compound projects in the same physical space, since engaging with only one of them might take few hours.

> You organize online and offline exhibitions. Starting with the latter, do you work with certain methods or criteria? For instance, I recall numerous discussions in the past where showing a computer monitor was 'not done', or some curators wouldn't even consider presenting net art in an exhibition at all, while others created entirely new installations based on online work. What are your thoughts/experiences with this?

G   Exhibiting net art in an offline context poses some delicate challenges. I'm thinking of historical examples such

98   as *Documenta X* curated by Catherine David (1997), as well as

more recent ones like the exhibition *Electronic Superhighway (2016–1966)* (2016) curated by Omar Kholeif at Whitechapel Gallery in London. Both projects provoked heated debates about how and where net art should be exhibited and what kind of experience is generated when artworks are presented in a public setting through computer monitors. I think the crucial point is to maintain the integrity of the original artwork, and adapt it to a mode of display that doesn't distort or sacrifice its technical side, as the latter is one of its constitutive elements, as previously observed. Or even to be true to the intentions of the artists since the network, as Matthew Fuller pointed out in his critique of Kholeif's show, has historically provided 'a space outside of the gallery-museum circuit where other ways of working could come to the fore and play in and between established spaces for art'.[36] The question of whether or not it should remain this way is evidently still open for debate.

This tension emerges more vividly when the presentation of digital art is framed by a gallery or museum intent on establishing an art historical canon. For this reason, I would be interested in experimenting with a media-archaeological approach to exhibition-making, further exploring a line of enquiry I initiated with the exhibition *Twixt Two Worlds* that I curated for Whitechapel Gallery and Towner Art Gallery in 2014. Again, the question of context is relevant here, and a form of reflexivity towards the context of any project, artwork or curatorial process, is certainly one of the main methods I employ when working both offline and online. In relation to the latter, this might entail acting as an online user who deliberately tests the limits of the terms of service of a given platform in order to challenge its assumptions and create new narratives.

Who do you see as your audience? I guess it changes with each new context but are there also changes (and/or exchanges) that you've noticed over the years, people moving from one place to another, or crossovers from other fields?

G   In my understanding, there are still considerable boundaries between different discursive and institutional fields, such as new media, contemporary art, and photography, which are reflected at the audience level. Crossovers do happen, but only when activated through the mediation of practitioners who work across various disciplines and explicitly address diverse publics.

36   Matthew Fuller, 'Eleven Pro Tips for Art Plus Internet', *Mute* (16 February 2016), *metamute. org/editorial/articles/eleven-pro-tips-art-plus-internet*.

In my experience with POIUYT, for instance, we are trying to simultaneously address audiences from the fields of contemporary art and photography as well as online audiences, as we believe that a critical reflection on the role of images concerns us all.

I'm really interested in how different constituencies—professional and amateurs for instance—coexist online, and I've closely monitored the debate between Ryder Ripps and Brad Troemel about how art is encountered on the web and by whom. To encapsulate it, Ripps took issue with Troemel's article 'The Accidental Audience' which gathered a number of critical reflections around the online reception of his Tumblr blog 'The Jogging'.[37] Specifically, with Troemel's claim that online audiences are unaware when they encounter art on the Internet, a position that Ripp considered not only dangerous since it polarizes 'artists' from the rest of the world, but also elitist and rooted in privilege and class. Beyond the scope of this particular debate, I believe the question of how to engage, mobilize and sustain online audiences is a significant one, which should be addressed more systematically by independent and institutional curators working both online and offline. Ghidini and Modrak certainly had a stab at it through project *#exstrange*, whose premise was precisely to insert art on eBay to foster the 'accidental' encounter and exchange with the 'stranger'. However, I believe more work needs to be done in this direction by both practitioners and institutions if art wants to have a meaningful impact in the networks.

> What do you focus on in your online exhibitions/digital magazine? In the past we've seen examples ranging from lists of links, to commissions, to documentation about a work, to embedding a work in a website? What is your preferred or even ideal 'model'?

G   With POIUYT we do not have a preferred model, but aim to operate as a network and platform for image-based research. This involves producing talks, exhibitions and publications in collaboration with various cultural practitioners as well as commissioning artworks, interviews and various kinds of visual content for our website. We want to foster a critical debate about the power and social function of images within networked culture and to create spaces where we can intervene with our work and raise some problems. Our interlocutors include theorists and practitioners from various fields as well as students, enthusiasts and curious. We try to identify gaps in the system and occupy

37   Brad Troemel, 'The Accidental Audience', *The New Inquiry* (24 March 2013), *thenewinquiry.com/the-accidental-audience/*.

them, or respond to a specific invitation with an ad-hoc proposition. This was the case with our participation in *Unseen 2017* in Amsterdam. On that occasion we responded to the context of a photographic fair by turning our booth into a live broadcasting station to talk about images instead of showcasing them.

> Should digital art enter established museums or organizations or are there better places where it can be preserved and presented? If so, what role should museums play in the future?

G   This is a complex question that requires some speculation. My sense is that digital art should not necessarily be incorporated into established museums unless they are willing to rethink their role in light of the challenges and possibilities that the digital poses to all cultural forms. At present, affiliated organizations like Rhizome or festivals such as Impakt in Utrecht or Transmediale in Berlin seem to be more capable of producing, presenting and archiving these kinds of projects. However, I do believe that museums should enter the web and social media platforms and carve out a cultural role, starting with the production and dissemination of intelligent content and fostering nuanced conversations. This would imply a shift away from the current use of technological tools solely for the marketing of exhibitions and permanent collections towards a wider engagement with online culture with all its diversity and contradictions.

> Until recently in the Netherlands there was always a very good funding system for the arts in general and specifically for digital art. That has since changed, increasing on the one hand the divide between 'traditional' art and digital art, while on the other it generally means looking for money outside the funding system. Could you share some of your experiences working around the globe? How do you and the artists you work with survive?

G   I can talk from the perspectives of two countries in particular, Italy and the UK, which nevertheless share a fairly different history in relationship to funding systems.

In the UK, funding bodies like the Arts Council and AHRC have historically funded the majority of art and research projects for contemporary art. Unfortunately the development of specific schemes to support digital art coincided with the imposition of austerity policies, which resulted in severe funding cuts across the board. However, over the last couple of years, new initiatives have emerged, such as the Digital R&D Fund for the Arts, which promotes the use of technology by art organizations to expand audience reach and explore new business models.

         In Italy, on the other hand, public funding has always

be quite limited and the system has predominantly operated according to the logic of art patronage, through the support of a few major collectors and private foundations. Commercial galleries also play an active role in overcoming the institutional gap and lack of public funding. POIUYT's first steps, for instance, were taken thanks to the support of three galleries—MLZ Art Dep (Trieste), Michela Rizzo Gallery (Venice) and Metronom (Modena)—which represented the artists who are part of the collective. Specific POIUYT projects and initiatives often rely on the support of audiovisual companies such as Hypengage and Audionoleggio, which provide us with equipment. We're currently reflecting on how to proceed and trying to creatively re-imagine the dynamics of corporate sponsorships. Right now we all have other jobs, either in the commercial sector or in art academies and universities. This situation is fairly complex to manage, especially with a team of eight people; however, it is the only possible way and, in my experience, the one generally pursued by many collectives and art practitioners across the globe. Surviving financially under these conditions requires an ability to simultaneously juggle the demands of different jobs and overlapping deadlines and can be fairly nerve-racking. I believe this to be an urgent and capillary problem of the art system in general, which should be challenged by its practitioners and also addressed more regularly by public institutions.

During your event at *Unseen 2017* in Amsterdam, you wanted to push boundaries of images and question their power. Could you explain your approach, also in relation to your other work?

G   Participating in the CO-OP section of the Unseen Photo Fair was POIUYT's first international project, since the collective was only formed in 2017. This particular section of the fair was launched in September 2017 under the curatorial direction of Lars Willumeit, with the aim of mapping a number of groups working collaboratively in the field of contemporary image practices across different contexts and countries. Since the mission of our collective is to challenge a conventional understanding of photography and to problematize the role and power of images within networked culture, we decided to create a YouTube broadcasting station in our booth, which streamed live content for the duration of the fair. The provocation we launched with *POIUYT RADIO* was intended to open up a debate about images beyond representation; we sought to treat images as language and language as images to explore the space between what is seen, heard and imagined. The content of the broad-casts was informed by a series of posters we produced for the occasion. Each of them featured a thought-provoking sentence that functioned as the overarching theme for the daily radio programmes. Both the content of the posters and their aesthetics, composed of screenshots of images generated by Google Images search results, interrogated the relationship between images and language, as mediated by search engines, and raised questions about the relationship between visibility and meaning within networked culture.

Various radio formats were conceived, each of which was accompanied by a tailor-made jingle and made by members of the team. Examples of formats were: the 'Morning Inbox', during which we unpacked the sentence of the day in conversation with invited guests, including curator Duncan Wooldridge and artist Frederique Pisuisse; 'World News', a rubric of fake news related to visuality and technology followed by a debate with invited experts; the interactive game 'Guess the Meme', which engaged with YouTube audiences; 'Meet the Collective', where we invited the other collectives in CO-OP to share their background stories and experiences; and the daily 'Horoscope of the Energy Net-work'. The booth became both our recording studio and perform-ing stage, where the front-end and back-end of our process could be simultaneously observed—all technical glitches included—by visitors to the fair and the other participants. This project was our first attempt at producing a collective work, at merging our different interests and expertise and hybridizing roles. It marked a significant step up from our first project, the group exhibition *POIUYT: Point Zero Critical Practices in Contemporary Italian Photography* at MLZ Art Dep, Trieste, where we operated in our respective roles as artists and curators. YouTube proved to be a very interesting platform for a radio project, as it allowed us to combine audio and visual content and share it online. It enabled us to push the boundaries of the context we were invited to respond to—Unseen Photo Fair—and to critically reflect on what it means to produce visual discourse. Not surprisingly, we were the least financially successful CO-OP collective, and the messiest booth of all of them.

In a statement/article on the POIUYT website you also mention that the activity—or better, the future non-activity—of links to images is part of the research process. What is your interest and perspective when it comes to digital preservation, documentation and collecting?

G   My first contribution to the POIUYT website was a reflection on the procedures of image-based research today, an issue that informs my current experiments with new methods of online curation. As I made explicit in the contribution, I believe that conducting image-based research today entails tapping into a shared online archive, the Internet, and relying heavily on the work of algorithms and search engines, which I understand as generators of meanings and aesthetic patterns. Thus, such a process inevitably needs to confront itself with the extreme volatility of digital content and of images in particular, as links are erased, content removed and websites down-ranked. This should not be seen as a limit in itself, but as an integral part of the research process and can, in my understanding, be creatively incorporated into the curatorial narrative.

As is revealed in the choice of images accompanying my text, I see the process of image-based research unfolding in a number of different ways, either by extracting a single image or through capturing fragments of network aesthetics using the screenshot to temporarily freeze the flow. I believe that the screenshot as a format will play an increasingly important role in the documentation, presentation and even collection of digital content. The latest initiative *Collecting the Web* by the Museum of London seems to support this direction with its plea to collect screenshots of web projects produced during the 1990s and early 2000s. My interest in the problems relating to the preservation, documentation and collection of digital content is inextricably linked to the need for a revised curatorial methodology within networked culture, which is not only concerned with what is visible, or representable, but also with what has disappeared or is no longer available. Such methods seek to explore the negative spaces that exist between images and, in doing so, expose the power structures supporting their networked circulation.

POIUYT is a platform for image-based research which grew out of the ongoing collaboration between curators Francesca Lazzarini and Gaia Tedone with artists Alessandro Sambini, Discipula and The Cool Couple. Since its inception, POIUYT has plotted a number of exhibitions and events, produced an ambitious Radio Programme on YouTube and published two books.

Gaia Tedone is a curator and researcher with an expansive interest in the technologies and apparatuses of image formation. In 2017 she co-funded the platform for image-based research POIUYT. Gaia completed her PhD at the Centre for the Study of the Networked Image, London South Bank University with a practice-based research entitled *Curating the Networked Image: Circulation, Commodification, Computation* (2019). She writes, teaches and curates on this topic. She is currently researching the fields of post-photography curating and algorithmic visual culture for Lucerne University of Art and Design.

1   POIUYT, *All that is Solid Melts Into Clouds*, 2017, series of posters produced in occasion of the 2017 edition of CO-OP *Unseen*, curated by Lars Willumeit, Unseen Photo Fair, Amsterdam.

2   POIUYT, *Point Zero. Critical Practices in Italian Contemporary Photography*, 2017, installation view. Courtesy of MLZ Art Dept, Trieste. Photo: The Cool Couple.

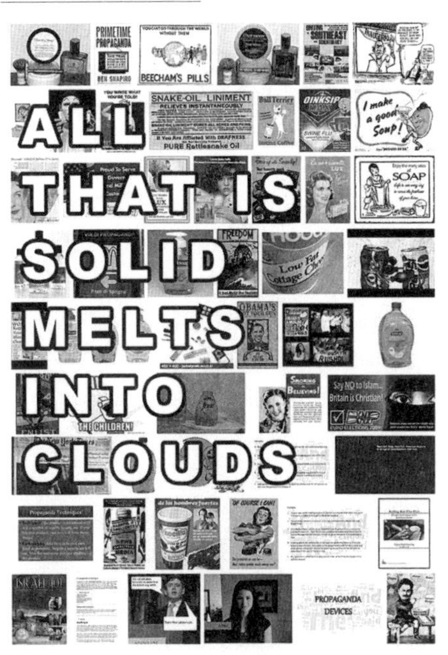

1

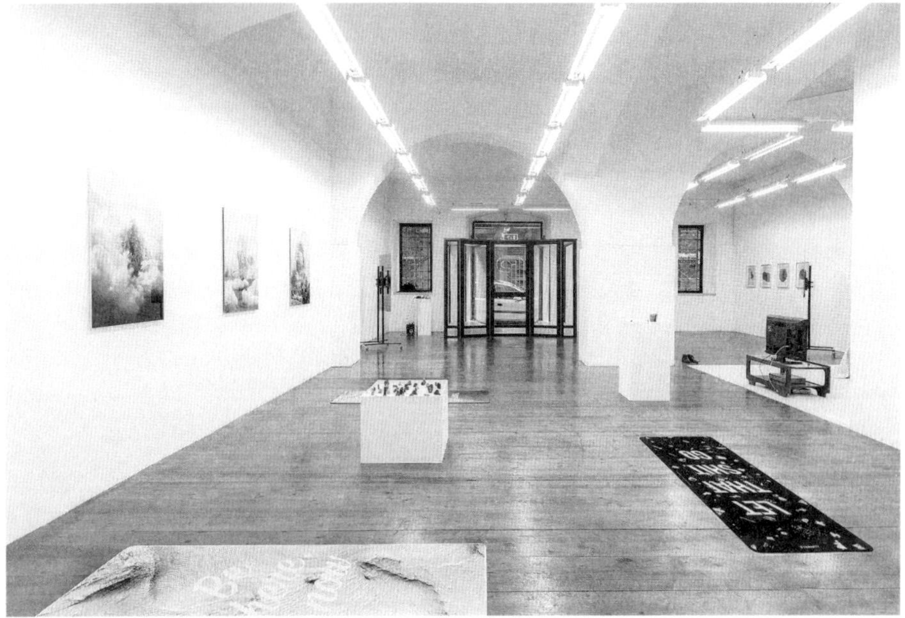

2

Manique Hendricks

INTERVIEWEE: MANIQUE HENDRICKS
PROJECT: VARIOUS – THE CURATED WEB, 2015
WEBSITE: *maniquehendricks.nl*, *37pk.nl/nieuws/64193/Presentatie-The-Curated-Web_bij-37PK*
DATE: 8 DECEMBER 2017

Can we start by defining the terminology we're using and how you position yourself within existing categories like digital art, new media, net art, contemporary art, or any of the post-arts?

M   I use the term net art when referring to the historical movement/group of artists/networks and artworks from the 1990s such as Vuk Ćosić and Olia Lialina. I also believe that the term New Media is already outdated in a society where the Internet and computers are ubiquitous. What is still new about new media? I use the term digital art when referring to art that is born-digital or/and presented in a digital environment, and I prefer to use the term Internet art for art that is created and/or presented in an online environment.

What is your background and what triggered your interest in digital/net art? Could you elaborate on these initial encounters?

M   As a kid growing up in the 1990s and the early 2000s I think I developed alongside digital technologies, gadgets and social media. I started a Tumblr blog in 2010 and was introduced to a never-ending stream of information and images that intrigued me. In 2013 I attended my first physical exhibition about online visual culture and digital art at Bitforms Gallery in New York. Being traditionally schooled in art history at the University of Amsterdam, I've always been interested in art-related subjects that weren't part of the curriculum such as non-Western and Chinese art and ultimately digital art and Internet art. This eventually led to me doing research and writing a thesis on (post-)Internet art.

You've been involved in various types of organizations and spaces. Could you share some of your experiences working in these different settings and particular contexts? For example, how does it affect your practice? Are there specific things that work very well in one context but not at all in another?

M   By working at a small art platform I learned about every aspect and every step in the process of exhibiting art and working with artists, because I had to do everything myself, from painting the walls to creating content for social media. I also worked at a large institute, where I had the luxury to solely focus on the subject matter. That also meant that, for example, I couldn't even touch the art objects when they entered the museum, which could only be done by the art handlers and restorers. I might feel more at home in a small organization, where I'm not

 limited by strict regulations and there are more opportunities and more space for personal initiatives.

> There has always been a separation between people who stress the techno-logical (material) developments of digital art and those who emphasize the art qualities (content/conceptual). At the same time digital art is also often accompanied by a fair amount of theoretical discussion. How do you position yourself in this discourse?

M   I'm not a very technical person. As an art historian I tend to focus more on the conceptual and visual qualities of a work as well as the theory rather than the technological/material aspects. But at the same time I'm also very aware of the importance of technique and materials, especially in the case of digital and Internet art.

> You organize online and offline exhibitions. Starting with the latter, do you work with certain methods or criteria? For instance, I recall numerous discussions in the past where showing a computer monitor was 'not done', or some curators wouldn't even consider presenting net art in an exhibition at all, while others created entirely new installations based on online work. What are your thoughts/experiences with this?

M   I strongly believe that we still have to discover the most 'ideal' way of showing online art in an offline environment (if there is one) and that it will happen through trial and error, by experimenting and by not being afraid to make mistakes. Discovering new ways of presenting online works in an offline exhibition space is an exciting challenge. I'm also aware that in most cases, the online contexts of online artworks are essential and that by presenting them on a computer monitor in a physical exhibition space the intimate character of experiencing a work online at your own personal computer at home is lost. The experience becomes flat and linear and might even look like a documentation of the online work. I experienced these problems while installing the Tumblr exhibition in 37PK where I discov-ered that the scrolling speed of my laptop was not the same when projected onto a large surface in the physical exhibition space. I finally realized that the online works I had presented were maybe just a static 'snapshot' of the dynamic character of the social networking platform Tumblr and the ever-changing character of the Internet itself.

> Who do you see as your audience? I guess it changes with each new context but are there also changes (and/or exchanges) that you've noticed over the years, people moving from one place to another, or crossovers from other fields?

M   I think most museum and art-related audiences are predom-inantly white, well-educated adults. As a biracial woman in her twenties I like to focus on a younger public who I can identify with. Digital and Internet art are definitely artforms that young digital natives can identify with. As for online platforms, people have shifted from platforms like Tumblr to Instagram as an exhibition space or a critical space.

> What do you focus on in your online exhibitions/digital magazine? In the past we've seen examples ranging from lists of links, to commissions, to documentation about a work, to embedding a work in a website? What is your preferred or even ideal 'model'?

M   My ideal model would be both online and offline. Offline in the traditional documentational form of a catalogue or booklet, and online as a website or archive working with links. I think both might be very important for future art historians and researchers. I also like the feel of a physical publication. As a researcher I search for offline documentation as well as online documentation, if possible.

> Should digital art enter established museums or organizations or are there better places where it can be preserved and presented? If so, what role should museums play in the future?

M   I think that it is (unfortunately) still necessary for digital and online art to enter the more traditional institutions and established museums, collections, galleries and organizations. One of the conditions for art to be considered art is still the overruling attitude that it is the context or space that validates a work of art. The traditional art system is fixated on notions of context, authorship and ownership, which become ambiguous when dealing with online artworks. Rafael Rozendaal's websites, for example, have an owner (a traditional solution for them to be validated as artworks), but are also always accessible to the public online. I think these institutions also bear the responsibility to search for new ways and techniques to exhibit and preserve digital and online artworks in the best possible way for future generations.

> I recently had a few discussions with artists and producers about the usefulness of open source, it seems that although all kinds of codes and suchlike are available they're hardly ever used, mainly because of the personal approach to coding and the complexity that derives from such project-based work. What is your approach to open source in this context?

M   This has been discussed many times before in art history and it is always in line with technological innovation, such as the invention of photography, technical reproduction techniques and now digital techniques. When Donald Judd introduced his machine-made serial objects, it became clear that the

 artist's personal touch isn't the most important condition for the authentication of the work. But I also feel that it is important for the artist to develop a personal relationship with the material, be it paint, clay or code. I prefer to use the open source operating system Linux, because I like the philosophy that emphasizes the freedom to share software and information in a capitalist society dominated by large corporations and software developers like Apple and Windows.

> Until recently in the Netherlands there was always a very good funding system for the arts in general and specifically for digital art. That has since changed, increasing on the one hand the divide between 'traditional' art and digital art, while on the other it generally means looking for money outside the funding system. Could you share some of your experiences working around the globe? How do you and the artists you work with survive?

M   I was only in my second year of studying art history when the Dutch government imposed massive cuts in 2012. My fellow students and I used to make jokes about it, that we wouldn't get a job with our degrees and all we had to look forward to was a huge student debt. I graduated in September 2017 when I still had a temporary job. I now work as a freelance art historian/curator/researcher and I'm struggling to find a job or project I can be involved with. I can't imagine what it must be like for artists at the moment.

> You've been experimenting with online curation for several years. I'm particularly interested in the translations you made in the project *The Curated Web*, which took place online as a Tumblr blog and offline as a physical exhibition. Could you discuss your approach to Tumblr's aesthetics and how you translated those to a physical space? I'm also wondering what you think of earlier attempts at doing and presenting 'Tumblr art' (for example, the Tumblr—Hyperallergic collaboration a few years ago—*hyperallergic.com/tumblrart*)? And could your attempt, or experiment, also be seen as a way of documenting or preserving Tumblr's unstable environment?

M   The idea for the exhibition/installation *The Curated Web* arose from various questions I asked myself such as: What is the best way to present an online Tumblr page in an offline environment? Do these works lose their strength when removed from their original online context? Can I refer to a Tumblr page as a curated exhibition?

The Curated Web consisted of a large projected, endlessly scrolling Tumblr blog page with 25 online artworks and an exhibition catalogue. This project was one of the main subjects of my Bachelor's thesis for which I researched the relationship between online Internet art and the physical offline art space. In this process, my personal decisions and questions were an important component of this research.

An example is my decision to present this project exclusively in the offline environment of the exhibition space in 37PK: the Tumblr blog was password protected and could not be viewed online by the public. This gave the project a degree of exclusivity, which normally doesn't occur on the World Wide Web but does manifest itself in the art world where most artworks can only be viewed in a museum or gallery.

The selection of works was based on a variety of known and lesser-known Internet artists who use Tumblr as a medium or platform for their art. I searched for a certain coherence in aesthetics to create a storyline in which different phenomena that occur on Tumblr were central. In addition, I researched the original source of each online work and documented it in the catalogue, because the original sources of the images on Tumblr are often lost in the enormous flow of content and due to the speed of the medium. In an object, information is often deliberately limited or even omitted for aesthetic reasons, in which case other sources of information could be the museum guard, catalogue or audio tour. On Tumblr, there is no guard or curator present to explain the work or its creator. Within this line of thinking I chose to explain my decisions in the exhibition catalogue, just like a traditional exhibition with physical objects.

I've always been very enthusiastic about the Tumblr–Hyperallergic project and the essays that were published on the theme. It's one of the first comprehensive studies on Tumblr as an online platform for art and as an artistic landscape, and it was a launching pad and huge resource for my Bachelor's because I struggled to find good quality sources and texts about this very contemporary subject.

Although I unfortunately did not properly document *The Curated Web* in videos or photographs (it was the first exhibition I made all by myself), the project can definitely be considered to be a documentation of Tumblr. My aim was not to preserve the unstable environment of Tumblr, but the catalogue might contribute as a physical documentation of concepts like Tumblr and Internet aesthetics and the vaporwave movement.

The Curated Web was a physical installation and an online exhibition of born-digital artworks. It was a curatorial research into the relationship between Internet art and the physical exhibition space based on phenomena that occur on Tumblr, such as Internet aesthetics and digital sculptures.

Manique Hendricks is an art historian. She works at LIMA, the institute for media art in Amsterdam as a junior conservator. As an independent curator, writer and researcher Manique focuses on contemporary (media) art, visual- and digital culture touching upon themes such as identity, representation, and camp and club culture.

1–2   Manique Hendricks, *The Curated Web*, 2015. at 37PK. Photo: Stefan Groenendijk.

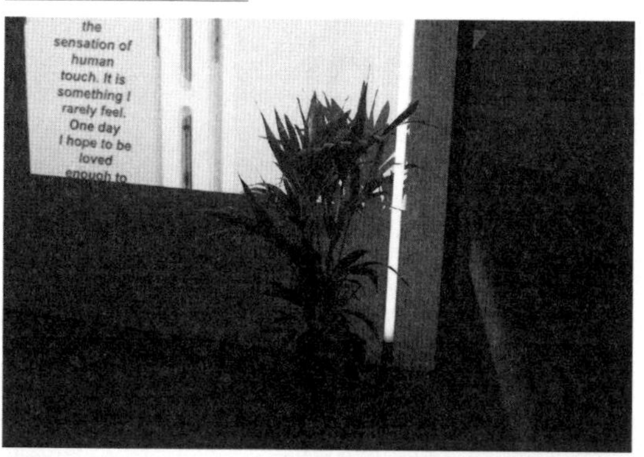
the
sensation of
human
touch. It is
something I
rarely feel.
One day
I hope to be
loved
enough to

1

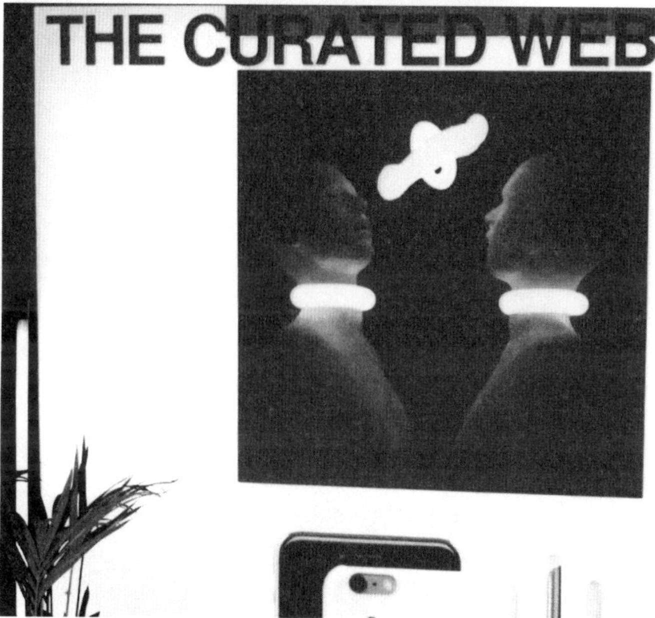
THE CURATED WEB

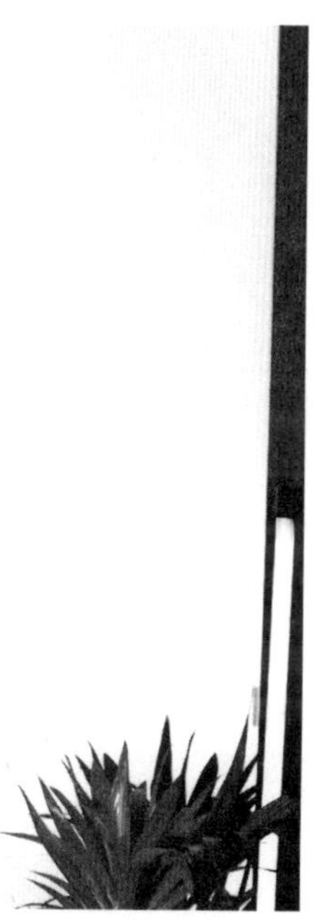

2

Marialaura Ghidini

INTERVIEWEE: MARIALAURA GHIDINI
PROJECT: VARIOUS – #EXSTRANGE, 2017
WEBSITE: *marialaura-ghidini.hotglue.me*
DATE: 4 MAY 2018

Can we start by defining the terminology we're using and how you position yourself within existing categories like digital art, new media, net art, contemporary art, or any of the post-arts?

M   I don't find these categories very useful; the distinctions they generate are too narrow, too clear-cut to be used in a context that I like to think is more organic. I like the category media art because it includes the historical trajectory of practices that have explored the role and use of mass media and technologies from an angle that is not just rooted in art history or aesthetics. I find the suffix 'post-'reductive and somewhat misleading. It literally implies a development by surpassing what was previously there, as though this 'something or other' does not have an impact in the present. Nothing is created in a spatio-temporal vacuum, and a term like 'post-'establishes a sort of confinement and a break in a continuum that I don't think is linear. If needed for the sake of temporal clarification, I'd rather use 'new' than 'post-'—I think that 'new', as an adjective that is malleable, and more meaningful than the idea of an afterwards.

       If I were to define my curatorial practice in relation to your question I'd say that my interests lie in exploring media and technologies that are prominently shaping our lives—the way we understand who we are, communicate with each other, and relate to the world we live in. And these media and technologies happen to be networks and web-based tools, and the contexts of their making and usages (the web, apps, sharing economies, IT companies, to name a few): these are 'entities' we are grappling with right now. But this is just one facet of my curatorial practice, which I think is something I do as a way to think about and understand certain aspects of these times that are connected to exploring how we relate to the world around us.

What is your background and what triggered your interest in digital/net art? Could you elaborate on these initial encounters?

M   Education-wise my background is in the humanities, specifically literature, philosophy and art history. Work-wise, my focus on curating started quite late, in my late twenties, and besides working in the arts sector, my background includes a good chunk of years in the corporate sector as a production manager for a manufacturing company. The intricate paths of life! For the past three years I've been teaching at Srishti Institute of Art, Design and Technology in Bangalore, India, where I'm a course leader for the Master's programme in Curatorial Practices.

My interest in net art comes from my fascination with mass media, not just as communicative systems and devices, but as socio-cultural and economic spaces that mediate our most mundane activities. I'm not a 'digital native'; perhaps that's why I feel that the Internet and web technologies have not just been affecting us on many levels (social, intellectual, economic and political) for the past few decades, but have also offered new opportunities for rethinking what we take for granted, what we think we understand—especially if we adopted them in a different way. Net art, and media art in a broader sense, started to do this in a way that defied art historical paradigms, in a way that I feel was more reflective of the present. Works that drew me to digital technology include Heath Bunting's _readme.html, Olia Lialina's *Art.Teleportacia*, Lynn Hershman Leeson's *Agent Ruby*, Paolo Cirio, Alessandro Ludovico and UBERMORGEN's *Google Will Eat Itself*. Despite their very different approaches, all these works explored the technologies we were starting to use in our daily life, exposing some overlooked aspects of their workings. They directly questioned the technological systems we often use blindly to perform tasks, relate to each other and 'optimize' our lives. As for *Art.Teleportacia*, well, it's the 'The First Real Net Art Gallery', and a source of inspiration for my own practice, along with *äda 'web*.

That having been said, I'm interested in all the arts, practices and research that focus on this exploration. I'm not interested in net and digital art *per se*.

You've been involved with various types of organizations and spaces. Could you share some of your experiences working in these different settings and contexts? How does it affect your practice? Are there specific things that work very well in one context but not at all in another?

M   I've worked on independent curatorial initiatives such as *Sound Threshold*, a project started by Lucia Farinati and Daniela Cascella; as associate curator for not-for-profit gallery spaces such as Grand Union in Birmingham UK; as a programmer for residency spaces such as T.A.J. Residency & SKE Projects in Bangalore; and I've also collaborated with a variety of spaces on the *or-bits.com* programme. These experiences are all different, especially in terms of focus, but the way I worked with them has a common thread, namely emphasizing the processes of curating and producing art, rather than just focusing on the outcome: the gallery exhibition. The first project I organized for Grand Union, *Search Engine* (2011), evolved from observing how Digbeth, the area where the gallery is located, had changed as a consequence of 'technological' progress. At that time I was particularly interested in exploring the effects that technology and the rise of networked society have on history—the way it is generated, interpreted and distributed in public spaces. Because of this, I wanted to give life to a programme that would enable artists to research on-site, collaborate with local practitioners, and create (the beginning of) a work. *Search Engine* was a six-week residency programme at the gallery during which three artists groups, Manu Luksch & Mukul Patel, American Mountains, and GOTO10, devised projects specific to the Digbeth context and in response to a set of questions I drew up. It was a pretty intense time for everyone! Luksch & Patel presented the *Kayak Libre* project, which offered 'free thinking, free transport' on the Grand Union canal and an interactive map that archived the exchanges about speculative futures between the audience and the artists during a series of kayak trips we organized. American Mountains produced a set of three publications detailing their site-specific research into Digbeth's architecture and its socio-economic context, and the events they organized at the gallery. GOTO10 developed the project *!POP!: points of presence*, for which they broadcast Wi-Fi poetry, which originated from their investigation into Digbeth's industrial past, in the street. Each mini-residency was punctuated by events, discussions and workshops and culminated in a final showcase. I felt that presenting the 'remnants' of the artists' activities was the least important part of the project.

Generally, the situations that have been more interesting for me to work with occur outside the gallery, in especially online spaces, or spaces that are not meant for art exhibitions. Examples include a moving-image show in an electronics shop in Bangalore for the C(h)roma Show (2014), or the presentation of the app-based performance *Unknown Cloud* by the artist duo Lundahl & Seitl (2017) in the park of the National Centre of Biological Sciences. I find that processes don't fit the gallery space well, especially when a project tries to engage audiences in a more active manner. No matter what a curator wants to accomplish with an exhibition, a gallery is inherently a space for 'contemplation' (in the Brian O'Doherty sense, especially in the West). Therefore, in the gallery a curator finds herself either following this paradigm or trying to break with it—but it is a breaking that only occurs according to the 'rules' dictated by this space meant solely for observation. Online projects such as *or-bits.com* (2009–2015) or *#exstrange* (2017) allow me more flexibility in how I engage with artists and collaborate with other curators. It also makes me feel that I have more possibilities to think about how the audience might engage with a project. For example, the *#exstrange* project, which I co-curated with artist Rebekah Modrak, allowed me to directly question the way we use and understand some of the e-services that I'm interested in exploring. This would be unimaginable in (or as) a gallery space. I've always compared organizing online projects to the process of editing a book—this might be the reason why all the exhibition projects I organize start with a set of questions for the artists and curators I work with. Other projects I'm interested in participating in are edited books such as *On the Upgrade* (as part of the activities of *or-bits.com*) and the series *Silicon Plateau* that I'm working on in Bangalore these days. But books (even if they're an artistic/creative miscellany like the projects I usually work on) are totally different contexts of engagement. If you start from a book, you have to find a way to 'activate' it.

This diversity of contexts has impacted me in the sense that for most of the projects I work on I have to reconsider what sort of engagement the artists and the audience can have with them—from a book, to an app performance in a park, to an Internet radio show, to a web-based exhibition on a website, or a proprietary web platform. This is what energizes me about curating. It's also important to stress that this diversity of contexts is also social and geographical. Observing local contexts is of paramount importance for me, and it also helps me to take distance from the grand narratives of the contemporary art world, with which I often feel uncomfortable because of their implied 'universality' or set-in-stone historicity.

> There has always been a separation between people who stress the technological (material) developments of digital art versus those who emphasize the art qualities (content/conceptual). At the same time digital art is also often accompanied by a fair amount of theoretical discussion. How do you position yourself in this discourse?

M   I don't think I really position myself in this discourse, at least not anymore, even though I see where it comes from and the reason why it exists. I think this discourse only makes sense if one considers art as being that which the contemporary art world of established museums, galleries, fairs and magazines legitimize as 'good' art. Hence, the importance of the attempts to defend the legitimacy of (new) media art, starting with Lev Manovich's distinction between Duchamp-land and Turing-land.

For me it isn't the medium that dictates if an artwork is more structuralist or conceptual, it's the artist's work and worldview. Thinking in terms of categories misses the point of what art and artistic practices are about by concentrating on yet another generalized art-historical dictum.

As for my own work, I'm interested in art that raises questions related to the specificity of the contexts we live in, and as I mentioned earlier, often (but not only) in relation to those media and technologies that are shaping our lives. So I never engage with artists or projects that are based on using technology or on the latest technologies *per se*. And in terms of exhibitions, I'm more interested in developing projects that try to move fluidly between spaces, places and formats, because it allows me to interact with audiences and collaborators who engage with art outside the given universal frameworks.

You organize online and offline exhibitions. Starting with the latter, do you work with certain methods or criteria? For instance, I recall numerous discussions in the past where showing a computer monitor was 'not done', or some curators wouldn't even consider presenting net art in an exhibition at all, while others created entirely new installations based on online work. What are your thoughts/experiences with this?

M   When I started *or-bits.com* in 2009 I was very interested in devising an online exhibition, of finding a way of viewing and contextualizing artworks online that would move away from the index/category/tag-based websites I encountered on the web. *or-bits.com* was a response to the limitations of a gallery space. At that time, I was keen to give form to a curatorial project that would work as a platform, that is, not culminating in 'just' an exhibition. For example, each *or-bits.com* exhibition was accompanied by a scrolling blog with contributions from different writers and researchers responding to the topic of the exhibition from different disciplinary perspectives. Once the website was up and running, I realized that a webpage was 'acting' as a medium that enabled artists to think about their work differently (the participants in the *or-bits.com* exhibitions were mostly not new media/digital artists as such). From this, I became interested in this idea of distributing an exhibition, that is, having an exhibition that travels to different spaces, formats and contexts. So, many of the exhibitions and artworks became part of other projects such as gallery, performance and sound events, and projects in print. I was interested in this idea of translating artistic, and also curatorial, ideas for different spaces. Because of this, I never displayed a web-based work on a computer in a gallery, as it would miss the point of the process of translation I was after. The exhibitions I organized in galleries with *or-bits.com* such as *(On) Accordance* at Grand Union in Birmingham (2012) or *Un-published Outsourced* at Banner Repeater in London (2013), were, curatorially, all based on examining the similarities and differences of displaying art on a website and in a gallery space.

The experience one has on a computer clashes completely with that of a gallery space, and computers and mobile devices have become so task-oriented that it makes little sense to bring them into a gallery space, unless the exhibition specifically examines this clash or relationship. I have therefore always chosen to offer the gallery viewer a different type of experience from a website. But things sometimes become more complex when it comes to translating an online project into a gallery project. In the case of *#exstrange*, a three-month-long exhibition of an artists' auction on eBay, the project was so embedded in the conceptual and structural framework of the online marketplace that Rebekah and I decided that the only way to represent it for those who did not experience it live was through creating a website and a book—but the latter is probably more related to documenting web-based art than distributing an exhibition.

In terms of your question about my method, I very rarely exhibited already existing artworks online. The works presented on *or-bits.com*, for example, were specific to its environment—any existing artworks were 're-thought' before being uploaded to the online space used for the exhibition. This is an old and trite point, but the way of navigating a space, the manner of conceiving time and making connections online, is inherently different to that which occurs in a built space offline. This is why in my work I've always made a distinction between showing on the web and not. What I think is most interesting now though, is that newly built spaces, like buildings and cities, have become spaces that are trying to mimic our conception of time and space online, trying to echo the fluidity of online platforms. It used to be the opposite. Do you remember when websites tried to resemble real-life spaces? I'm thinking of GeoCities and its attempts at being viewer/user-friendly by using geographical locations and addresses.

Who do you see as your audience? I guess it changes with each new context but are there also changes (and/or exchanges) that you've noticed over the years, people moving from one place to another, or crossovers from other fields?

M   I tend to organize projects, especially these days, that allow me to interact with different audiences, both online and not. Also, I currently live in a city where the art world is very much cut off from the lives of the majority of people and therefore I wonder what 'audience' means. Not working with the safety net of assumptions one can easily make about audiences in European capitals like London or Berlin, for example, allows me to work in a hybrid way. The publishing project *Silicon Plateau* (2015–), which I edit with artist Tara Kelton and looks at the connections between art, technology and society starting from observing the city of Bangalore, is an example of trying to nurture a broadening of the role of the arts in discussing the relationship between technology, society and urban spaces. We bring together an array of very diverse people, from artists and designers to social scientists and lawyers, to discuss this relationship with us.

In terms of online audiences, the landscape has definitely changed compared to a decade ago. I just have to think of my students whose first experience of artistic content is mostly online, and via mobile phone apps not the web. This way of engaging with artistic content in online spaces that are 'curated' using analytical criteria dictated by algorithms has generated a crossover both in terms of those who create and those who consume what is created. This younger generation rarely sees the point of making a distinction between artistic and creative endeavours—the notion of an Instagram artist is something I came across while teaching classes in new media art! I don't want to judge this crossover as something bad or good. What it brings up, though, is a change in the perspective of audiences that I feel requires us (curators and art professionals, for example) to look at what we do from a more transdisciplinary perspective, one that lies outside the comfort zone of categories and takes account of the shifts happening out there.

> What do you focus on in your online exhibitions/digital magazine? In the past we've seen examples ranging from lists of links, to commissions, to documentation about a work, to embedding a work in a website? What is your preferred or even ideal 'model'?

M   In the past, many people told me that *or-bits.com* functioned more as a magazine than an exhibition space. I have primarily worked with commissioning content online rather than embedding already existing artworks. This is because, in the instance of *or-bits.com*, each 'programme'—this is what I used to call the exhibitions—was thematic, and my focus was on triggering responses from artists and writers to each theme. I was inspired by projects like *äda 'web* and *Art.Teleportacia*, rather than *Runme.org*, *TAGallery* and *VVORK*. I find the latter three very important and interesting projects because they explored different modes of producing art and exhibitions as a response to the new curatorial tools offered by the web (such as forms of collaborative production). But with *or-bits.com*, as I mentioned, I wanted to give life to a space dedicated to the production of art and to a discussion that was more conventional.

In terms of documentation, in my experience print publications can be useful tools to document online projects, along with methods like the *net.artdatabase* (2011) initiative devised by artist Constant Dullaart and art historian Sakrowski. It's very important to preserve the experience of browsing a web-based artwork at a certain point in time, and *net.artdatabase* succeeded in this. But the topic of documentation requires a much longer discussion!

> Should digital art enter established museums or organizations or are there better places where it can be preserved and presented? If so, what role should museums play in the future?

M   It would be good but I don't think it is the only way. Museums are only one of the nodes at our disposal to access 'history' and knowledge. For many people around the world it is difficult or impossible to access a museum.

Museums should definitely be more open to acknowledging the work of organizations like Rhizome by including their preservation initiatives and strategies (from their ArtBase, to Colloq to Webrecorder, for example) into the activities of both their conservation and curatorial departments. But going back to my previous point, I feel there should be more educational initiatives supporting the conservation and circulation of web-based art online, irrespective of the museums' endeavours. If this were the case, there would need to be activities that allow viewers to encounter these artworks and the practices of their creators outside the web, because it is important to keep real-life learning and experiences alive. The Internet is a space where one can become too easily lost, while it is also a space where one can be too easily locked out because it is increasingly controlled by profit, personal interests and fear. And this is very problematic in terms of accessibility and learning.

Turbulence is a recent unfortunate example of the patchy history of preserving web-based projects: it had to go offline because of lack of core funding. It is interesting that it was a university—Cornwell University, and specifically The Rose Goldsen

Archive of New Media Art—that offered to host Turbulence's work on their servers, but offline, and not in a museum.

So, the role of museums in the future? More accessible and comprehensive of the diversity of not only practices, but audiences as well.

> I recently had a few discussions with artists and producers about the usefulness of open source, it seems that although all kinds of codes and suchlike are available they're hardly ever used, mainly because of the personal approach to coding and the complexity that derives from such project-based work. What is your approach to open source in this context?

M   When thinking about code and programming, and open source I think of what Ellen Ullman wrote in her book *Life in Code*:

> As the computer's pretty, helpfully waiting face (and contemptuous underlying code) penetrates deeply into daily life, the cult of the boy engineer comes with it. The engineer's assumptions and presumptions are in the code. That's the purpose of the program, after all: to sum up the intelligence and intentions of all the engineers who worked on the system over time, tens and hundreds of people who have learned an odd and highly specific way of doing things. The system contains them. It reproduces and enacts life as engineers know it.[38]

Ullman is primarily referring to the work of IT companies and corporations that produce software and algorithms. However, she describes the difficulty in (wholly) grasping a code that is written by many people in disparate personal ways, in a manner that might lead to the erasure of individual (hence social, civic, ethic) responsibility. Working with open source programmes and platforms requires a type of knowledge that many curators often lack. Hence the importance if working in an interdisciplinary way when it comes to producing art and exhibitions.

All this being said, I'm not a programmer and I've never organized a project using open source systems. So I don't think I can say too much about this. With *#exstrange*, both Rebekah and I wanted to create an open system as a way of curating that could be used, changed and distributed by other practitioners, be they artists or curators. But it is difficult to keep things alive once a project ends.

38   Ellen Ullman, *Life in Code: A Personal History of Technology* (New York: MCD, 2017), p. 17.

Until recently in the Netherlands there was always a very good funding system for the arts in general and specifically for digital art. That has since changed, increasing on the one hand the divide between 'traditional' art and digital art, while on the other it generally means looking for money outside the funding system. Could you share some of your experiences working around the globe? How do you and the artists you work with survive?

M   I know, and it gave life to so many initiatives, like the netart.database!

I have a full time job, as many others in this field do. My experience of funding systems dedicated to supporting the production of web-based art and exhibitions is not a very bright one. One of the reasons I decided to stop *or-bits.com* was related to funding and the fact that it was unfeasible for me to keep the project going financially—there is only so long that one can ask artists and collaborators to work for a small or no fee. Although I received a few small grants to organize parts of the *or-bits.com* programme, the moment I tried to develop it into an organization (you know, with a clear mission and scope projected into the future, a full programme of partnerships, a creative strategy for raising extra funding, to name a few aspects), what became the major problem for the national body I proposed the project to (I was in the UK at that time) was that *or-bits.com* did not have a fixed 'real' location—it was a web-native project and in this it lacked a certain kind of substance according to them. But to give *or-bits.com* a brick-and-mortar status was precisely the opposite of what the platform did for years and wanted to continue improving upon with more financial support. It's demoralizing to think how much sponsorship and financial support start-ups and global e-services with no assets and little civic/political/social responsibility receive, not only from seed investors but also from governments. If you compare this scenario to what happens in our field, you're confronted with the infrastructural backwardness of both the art world and education systems. Now that I'm in India, I cannot even think of a national/regional funding body dedicated to digital art.

You've been experimenting with online curating for a while now, in projects such as *or-bits* (2009–2015), and you completed a partly related PhD 'Curating after New Media'. One of your recent projects was *#exstrange*, which you curated with Rebekah Modrak, in which you used or appropriated the online marketplace eBay as a site of curatorial operation, artistic production and cultural exchange. Could talk about your approach, also in relation to your other work?

M   I think I replied to this question earlier, but I can summarize a few points that might tell you something about
126 my approach.

Experimenting with online curating is one of the ways I've used to explore how the communication and service technologies we use right now, but also the contexts of their making and usages (the web, apps, sharing economies, IT companies, to name a few), shape us and our surroundings. At the same time, it also allows me to explore how we the users can in turn shape them if we use them differently — beyond the purposes they were designed for. *#exstrange* was precisely about this. Among the things Rebekah and I wanted to explore was what it means to give life to creative exchanges between strangers in a space dedicated to commodities, on a platform that was initially born from the intention to empower people by creating a system that would bypass all the mediating entities at the core of the capitalist system. In this sense, there is so much more work I would like to do in this area, and with other platforms!

When I work online I'm interested in collaborating with artists or other people who have different approaches to making art. It's very interesting to work with a performer, or a sculptor or a researcher when organizing an online project. The fact that the environment of the web might be new to them, in terms of being a space where activating and showcasing their work/research, generates very interesting ideas and discussions.

eBay is a rather unstable environment when thinking about the future history of the exhibitions. What is your interest and perspective when it comes to digital preservation, documentation and collecting?

M   My general idea about preserving web-based projects and artworks, or any web-based content for that matter, is that their environment is a performative context. Hence, naming one approach to documentation as the best way to represent a project is not helpful, since documentation is in this case contextual and live—including the dependence on technological infrastructures often offered or powered by third parties.

Because *#exstrange* was activated by the interactions between artists, visitors and buyers, and was literally embedded in the structure and workings of the platform (the artworks were the auctions, and existed across the many sale categories of eBay), it was not only unstable in terms of its environment but difficult to grasp as a whole, both during and after it. Rebekah and I found that the most useful way to document the project was to create a website for archiving the auctions as they were launched on eBay, and producing a catalogue at the end of the project that would also include essays contextualizing some of its core ideas. *#exstrange* presented an artwork-as-auction every day for three months, and each auction was online for only seven days. In order to document the project we took full-page screenshots of the auctions, both of the launch and of the end of each of them, so that we could include the advertisements chosen by eBay to target new consumers—a way, I feel, to encapsulate the 'liveness' of the project. Both on the website and in the catalogue, these images are accompanied by the conversations between the artists and buyers (the Q&A between seller and buyer on eBay), and the bidding data, exchanges and shipments, which were subsequently analysed by two economists at Michigan University, one of whom was using *#exstrange* as a case study for his own research into the creative market. We also created an interactive map on the project website that displays the geographical exchanges that happened throughout the project. In terms of documentation, *#exstrange* required a great amount of data-keeping, Excel sheets and coordination!

The online project **#exstrange** invited a global group of designers, artists and curators to subvert the conventions of eBay, presenting artworks masquerading as goods and services. Artists created artworks-as-auctions using the online marketplace's auction template as the tool of production. *#extrange* put art in a networked context, based on one-to-one exchanges.

Marialaura Ghidini is a curator whose work explores the inter sections between art, technology and society. She founded the curatorial platform *or-bits.com* (2009–2015) and since obtaining her PhD from CRUMB (University of Sunderland, 2015) has researched the field of curating on the web. Interested in working with various exhibition formats, her projects include *#exstrange* (2017) on eBay; *The C(h)roma Show* (2014) in an electronics shop in Bangalore, IN; *Search Engine* (2012) across public spaces in Birmingham, UK; and *128kbps objects* on *basic.fm* (2013). She is co-editor of the publishing series *Silicon Plateau* (which examines the impact of digital technology on, and its infrastructure in, the city of Bangalore), and course leader of the MA Curatorial Practices programme at Srishti Institute of Art, Design and Technology in Bangalore.

1   Miyö Van Stenis, *#exstrange Live Now on eBay (featuring Anke Schüttler)*, 2017, screenshot. Courtesy of exstrange.com.

#exstrange
HELLO
AUCTION ARCHIVE
WRITING
RELATIVES
BOOK
JOIN
#exstrange is a curatorial project transforming eBay into a site of artistic production and cultural exchange as an artistic intervention into capitalism.
Live Now on Ebay
KINDHEITSERINNERUNG / CHILDHOODMEMORY #1
View
KINDHEITSERINNERUNG / CHILDHOODMEMORY #1
Artist: Anke Schüttler
Category: Collectibles
Price: EUR 1,00
Location: Aachen, Germany
Curator: Harrell Fletcher
SYMPHONIES OF RESILIENCE
Artist: Anupam Singh
Category: Cell Phones & Accessories
Price: $10.00
Location: Portland, Oregon, USA
Curator: Harrell Fletcher
GOOGLE TRACKERS IN NORTH KOREA OFFICIAL WEBPAGE
Artist: Joana Moll
Category: Everything Else
Price: $30.00
Location: Pyongyang, North Korea
Curator: Bani Brusadin

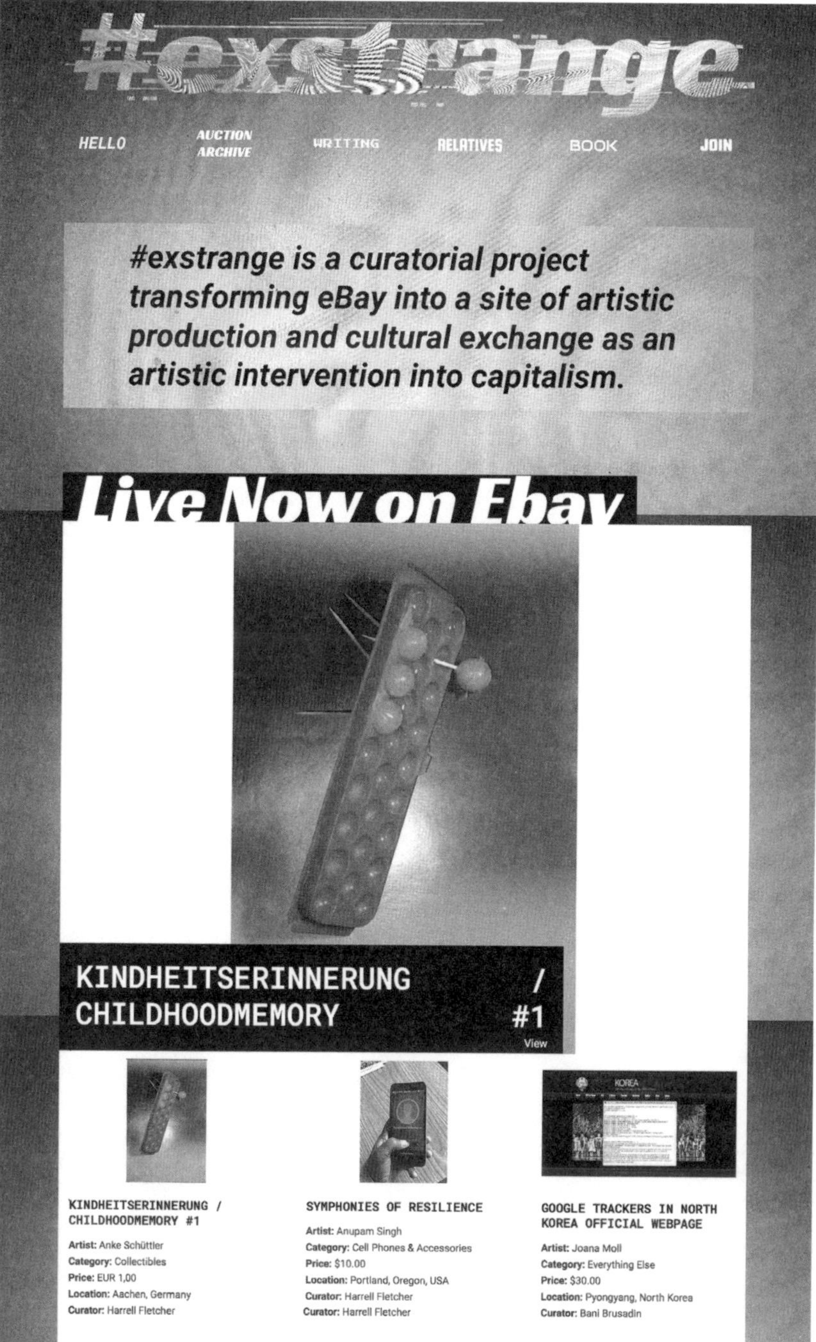

1

Bob Bicknell-Knight

INTERVIEWEE: BOB BICKNELL-KNIGHT
PROJECT: VARIOUS – ISTHISIT?, 2016–PRESENT
WEBSITE: *isthisitisthisit.com*
DATE: 31 MARCH 2019

Can we start by defining the terminology we're using and how you position yourself within existing categories like digital art, new media, net art, contemporary art, or any of the post-arts?

B   By 'position' I assume you mean how I frame or categorize the work I produce, or potentially you mean what kind of work I deem to be described as 'digital' or 'new media' art. For the sake of clarity I'll answer both.

I see my own work as medium-less, as I don't want or like to be restricted by only working in one medium. A lot of what I do is concept-led, so I never start off thinking about the end product, what the work will eventually manifest as. I usually have an idea, and then I think about how that idea might work as a sculpture, a painting, a video, or anything else. So I see my own work as simply 'contemporary' art, art that's being produced at this current moment.

In terms of what I deem to be 'digital art', a lot of people I know say whatever is made now is in a digital context, so everything that is made can be framed as 'digital art'. You're always going to be looking at things on a screen. I'm torn between that point of view and being very strict about the definition, that the piece of work has to be made on a computer, it has to be on a TV screen, et cetera. I remember being asked what digital art is a few years ago, and being very careful about my answer, as it's an incredibly huge and loaded question. I think I'll go with the ambiguous answer, in that it's anything that's being made right now, maybe anything that's been made over the past twenty years, after the advent of the Internet. I think net art is quite different, as it's art that's exclusively made for the Internet, or resides on it. Obviously this kind of work can be exhibited and sold within a gallery space, but it needs an Internet connection to be seen.

What is your background and what triggered your interest in digital/net art? Could you elaborate on these initial encounters?

B   I think I first truly became interested in net art when I started researching Constant Dullaart and his various websites, both his own artist website and his actual art pieces that reside on the Internet, like *The Death of the URL* (2013), which is, in essence, a grey webpage that has the title of the work and the artist's name in green block capitals across it. The URL constantly refreshes its 38 characters (mostly made up of x's) to infinity, mourning the death of the URL. The piece was a reaction to how no one types in URLs anymore, they always type key words into Google or other search engines.

After that I started making my own websites, or attempted to. In 2015 I produced a piece called *All My Messages*, a free-to-browse website that housed all of my Facebook messages from a ten-year period. I slowly realized, however, that the piece was really only interesting to me, reliving those early memories of how I used to speak and act on social media, which was completely different from how I currently navigate the platform.

Later on, in 2016, I started building *isthisit?*, a platform for contemporary art. Online, it operates as a gallery producing monthly exhibitions showcasing emerging to mid-career artists, and hosts a roster of guest curators experimenting with the medium of the Internet to interrogate a variety of concepts. The website also hosts monthly residencies, where artists are given a webpage to create new work that exists on the Internet as a piece of net art. Offline, it has held exhibitions nationally and internationally and is the publisher of *isthisit?*, a book series released on a triannual basis.

> You've been involved in various types of organizations and spaces. Could you share some of your experiences working in these different settings and particular contexts? For example, how does it affect your practice? Are there specific things that work very well in one context but not at all in another?

B   Most of the people I've worked with when organizing physical exhibitions and events have been fantastic and incredibly accommodating. A lot of the things that I've been part of have involved little or no money, which is definitely a strain, both on my practice and, more importantly, my livelihood. If you're curating an exhibition and you've been given no monetary resources, then you have to rely on your own funds and the kindness of the artists you're working with. The artists I choose to work with, and the artists who choose to work with me, are always incredibly helpful and the most important part of the process.

Recently I had the chance to work with a few spaces, both on- and offline, that have provided me with a budget so I could pay myself as a curator and the artists I worked with. It's sometimes awkward to talk about money, as you might be labelled a capitalist, or someone who's just interested in the financial side of things, but money is incredibly important: you need it to live and to continue to make work. As with a lot of artists who don't have inherited wealth, money is the thing that affects my

 practice the most. Without funded projects you're more than

likely going to get stuck in a full-time job, too tired to produce work, which would in turn enable you to get funding. It's a cruel, fucked-up cycle, which for many is never-ending.

> There has always been a separation between people who stress the techno-logical (material) developments of digital art and those who emphasize the art qualities (content/conceptual). At the same time digital art is also often accompanied by a fair amount of theoretical discussion. How do you position yourself in this discourse?

B   As I mentioned before, for me and my own work concept is key. I'm less interested in zombie formalism and the type of work you might see displayed in a CEO's office. The same goes for digital art that focuses only on the aesthetics of the digital, the type of work that's being produced by people interested in 'post-Internet' art, a term and art aesthetic that seems cringey, over the top, and incredibly dated by today's standards, even if it was a groundbreaking movement in 2010. The best kind of art/artists that use/s digital technologies do so for a reason, rather than simply abusing the aesthetic such as attempting to copy Hito Steyerl, Cory Arcangel or Amalia Ulman.

> You organize online and offline exhibitions. Starting with the latter, do you work with certain methods or criteria? For instance, I recall numerous discussions in the past where showing a computer monitor was 'not done', or some curators wouldn't even consider presenting net art in an exhibition at all, while others created entirely new installations based on online work. What are your thoughts/experiences with this?

B   Again, most of the shows I curate are concept-driven, and don't necessarily focus solely on digital or net art. Personally I try to limit the amount of screens in a show, as it's very easy to overload an exhibition with them, so much so that the aesthetic becomes overwhelming, not to mention how much time it takes to watch a video work compared to strolling past a painting.

When thinking about artists and artworks to exhibit, I'm always conscious of how long it would take for a visitor to see the entire show. So usually I limit video works to three, with a combined viewing time of 40/50 minutes at most. I also always try to provide seating for video art that's over five minutes long, either by working with the artist to produce a new installation specifically for viewing the work in a gallery context or including another artist's work that literally functions as a viewing seat. In 2018 I produced an exhibition called *Duty Free* around a purpose-built structure that held all the work, so people could sit on the structure and watch the video works, or simply appreciate the other art on display. For my own art, I always make sure there's seat in my video installations, unless I want to deliberately distress the audience.

I'm all for showing video and net art in an offline context, and will happily install screens or work with an artist to produce an installation that allows the work to function better in the public gallery context, outside of the personal online experience when usually interacting with such a piece. Although this doesn't mean that you simply get a TV and place it on an IKEA stool, there are a lot of factors to showing video art, from thinking about where your source of electricity is in the gallery to buying extension leads, deciding to conceal or show cables, looping your videos using a media player and everything else. It's never as simple as hanging a painting.

Who do you see as your audience? I guess it changes with each new context but are there also changes (and/or exchanges) that you've noticed over the years, people moving from one place to another, or crossovers from other fields?

B   I'm still not really sure who my audience is, I think it's mostly young artists, although I know a lot of people from older generations who follow what I do too, so I think/hope it's a fairly broad and diverse group of people. I have a lot of followers online and have worked with many artists from around the world. I still work and talk with people who've moved away from London, where I've lived for the past four years, and I think everything I do can be seen from afar. In the future I'd like my artwork and curation to be seen outside of an art context, within institutions and spaces that aren't just for artists/curators/collectors. I'm particularly interested in technology and science. Earlier in 2019 I was in a group exhibition called *Ground Zero Earth* in Cambridge at the Centre for the Study of Existential Risk, a research centre at the university created with the intention to study possible extinction-level threats posed by present or future technology. I'd like my work to be seen in this sort of context a lot more. Recently traditional gallery exhibitions have become a little tedious.

What do you focus on in your online exhibitions/digital book? In the past we've seen examples ranging from lists of links, to commissions, to documentation about a work, to embedding a work in a website? What is your preferred or even ideal 'model'?

B   For the online shows I'm open to pretty much anything that can be done on the platform. I really like online spaces like *Cosmos Carl* that do one thing incredibly well; in Frederique and Saemundur's case that's a website that links to other websites, but for me the whole reason why I began *isthisit?* was to experiment with what curating was/is, so I never had one idea or niche that I would continue to explore month to month, and I still don't.

I don't have a preferred way of exhibiting work online, but I do think it's a little basic to simply have all the work on one page, endlessly scrolling down, as that's not really utilizing the Internet and its potential. I want online shows to have multiple pages, hidden links and a crafted story that unfolds through your interaction with it. The ability to curate online enables you to create this type of gamified space a lot more cheaply than, for example, it would be to make multiple rooms in a gallery space, something akin to Morag Keil's 2018 exhibition *Here We Go Again* at Project Native Informant in London. As I said, I'm open to anything, but, as with showing video work in a gallery space, there are a lot of different aspects to consider.

> Should digital art enter established museums or organizations or are there better places where it can be preserved and presented? If so, what role should museums play in the future?

B   I think that's already happened hasn't it, or is in the process of happening? The main example is the Julia Stoschek Collection in Düsseldorf, which specializes in time-based media art. Obviously that's a private collection, but it's still a fairly big institution. Another, smaller example would be Molly Soda's video work in an exhibition at the National Portrait Gallery in Washington DC that ends at the end of 2019. I think it's totally fine to have your work displayed/shown in these kinds of settings. Even though the type of work within these large museums is fairly old, new media and digital art is incredibly new, so it's going to take time for large institutions to adapt. I think it will happen eventually, and it might not be the best setting for this kind of art right now, but these kinds of spaces are still gatekeepers to expanding your cultural capital as an artist, mostly due to the fact that museums have overwhelming amounts of funding and huge numbers of people visiting on a daily basis.

> I recently had a few discussions with artists and producers about the usefulness of open source, it seems that although all kinds of codes and suchlike are available they're hardly ever used, mainly because of the personal approach to coding and the complexity that derives from such project-based work. What is your approach to open source in this context?

B   I'm all for open source software! Even if you don't end up using the code or product, it's fantastic that the developer gives anyone and everyone access, allowing insights into how it works, or simply gives you the power to adapt and change the end

137

product to your own ends. Of course, everyone's way of working is different, but being able to look through the data is what I find most interesting. Proprietary software is great, but when it doesn't work, or if you want to find out how it works, you're at a loss and are usually faced with a large corporate machine, rather than a small group of individuals who've made this thing that you're allowed to do anything to.

> Until recently in the Netherlands there was always a very good funding system for the arts in general and specifically for digital art. That has since changed, increasing on the one hand the divide between 'traditional' art and digital art, while on the other it generally means looking for money outside the funding system. Could you share some of your experiences working around the globe? How do you and the artists you work with survive?

B As I mentioned before, a lot of what I do involves little to no money, which is frustrating for me, but even more so for the artists and curators I work with. Even though it's great to speak about my practice and my interest in digital art, I'm not being monetarily compensated for this interview. In another, non-art context, I probably would be. If, when I'm curating I'm unable to pay the artists I'm working with, I try to compensate for this by putting in as much work as possible so that the artist doesn't have to spend valuable time and money themselves to be a part of the show. If they're not being paid I try to be considerate of their time, collecting work at their studio at a time that suits them, providing screens to exhibit work on, et cetera. Obviously, this isn't much, but I've heard of large institutions doing a lot less with no monetary compensation for the artist.

I survive by working two jobs, as a gallery manager at a small commercial gallery, and at an art handling and shipping company as a freelance technician. I also occasionally get paid to be in exhibitions, curate shows, give talks, be on panel discussions, and very rarely I sell my own work, but none of these happen often enough, and at the moment so infrequently that I cannot live from my art practice. Most of the gallery spaces I've curated shows for have given me little to no money, and the money that I have received is usually spent, not on living costs, but on the show itself. Working two jobs takes up a lot of my time but allows me to live in London, see a lot of art, and work with people who I wouldn't know/have access to in other parts of the UK or the world. I will probably move from London in the next five to ten years because of money: working in the arts is usually underpaid and relies on people who have large amounts of inherited wealth.

Whenever I work with artists and curators I usually ask if they do this full-time, and of course most of them don't, and like me, they have one or two jobs, either part time in galleries or waiting tables. I do know some artists who make a living from selling their work, but it's a rarity when working with mostly young artists. Most of the people I work with don't have inherited wealth either, so they can't afford to not have a job: if they aren't getting funding for their practice or selling work on a regular basis they cannot focus solely on their art.

> You're the founder, curator and contributor of *isthisit?*, a platform for contemporary art. What I particularly like about the site is how it seamlessly moves between different genres, formats and spaces. Could you explain your approach, also in relation to the related activities at the gallery? And what is your interest and perspective when it comes to digital preservation, documentation and collecting?

B   The general layout of the website has gone through many iterations over the years, although of course when building it originally, I was influenced by other online spaces and gallery websites. If you built something against the norm like Petra Cortright's landing page or *jodi.org*, without any followers or interest, it was very hard to grow and build an audience. If you're an established artist or curator and make a new, ambiguous thing, it's easy to be accepted and seen, but if you're emerging and don't really know anyone, it's a lot harder to make something that's different, or more specifically, hard to navigate in a digital context.

At the moment I think the website is easy to navigate, with everything being fairly self-explanatory. Even though I find it less interesting when online exhibitions are simple and easy to use, without the clickbait factor, whether its a particular piece you want to see or because there's a famous artist involved in the exhibition, they will usually get more clicks if they're user friendly.

I think New Scenario's 2017 online exhibition *Hope* is a wonderful example of being a not-so-friendly user interface, but because of the artists involved and the fantastic conceit, it makes you, as an interactive audience member, want to go deeper and investigate further. The exhibition is made up of a number of 360-degree photos of the inside of a university campus, which has been overrun by flesh-eating zombies, with the project involving over 200 students and volunteers. In each photograph there are a number of areas that are clickable, allowing you to navigate through to different areas of the campus, where various artworks have been hung and documented. I think that's maybe my favourite online exhibition.

For me, and most artists/curators nowadays, documentation is one of the most important aspects of organizing an offline exhibition. In an online context I'm a little less attentive, I still archive all of the shows with screenshots, press releases, et cetera, but as the shows are usually interactive in some way, it's hard to replicate that without simply visiting the website. You can still go back and see all the previous exhibitions on the website, although most of the early shows were very simple and aren't put together as well as the more recent ones. Even though I choose to archive the shows, I really like how *Offsite Project* functions. Akin to an offline gallery, they have online shows that are only available to view for a set period, after which they close the webpage. I enjoy this, although for me it goes against the beauty of the online gallery, where you can create hundreds of webpages and curate hundreds of exhibitions without having the overheads of a traditional gallery.

isthisit? is a platform for contemporary art founded by Bob Bicknell-Knight. Work by over 800 artists has been exhibited since its creation. Online, it operates as a gallery producing monthly exhibitions and residencies. Offline, it has held international exhibitions and is the publisher of *isthisit?*, a yearly book series.

Bob Bicknell-Knight is an artist, curator and writer working in multiple mediums. His work is influenced by surveillance capitalism and responds to the hyper-consumerism of the Internet. Utopia, dystopia, automation, surveillance and digitization of the self are some of the themes that arise through his critical examination of contemporary technologies. He has given talks and participated in panel discussions at Tate Modern, University of Cambridge, Camberwell College of Arts and Goldsmiths, University of London.

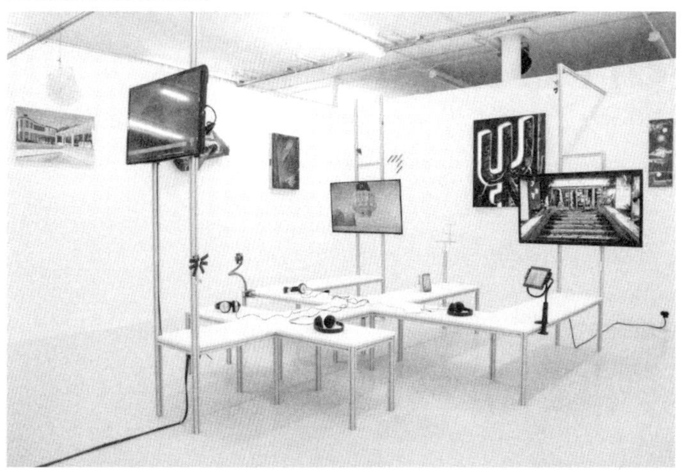

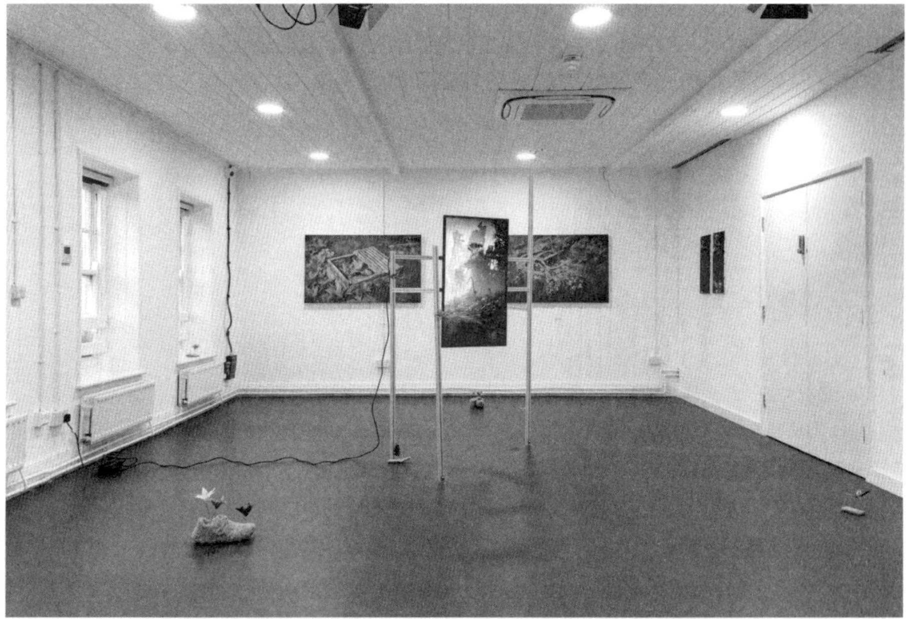

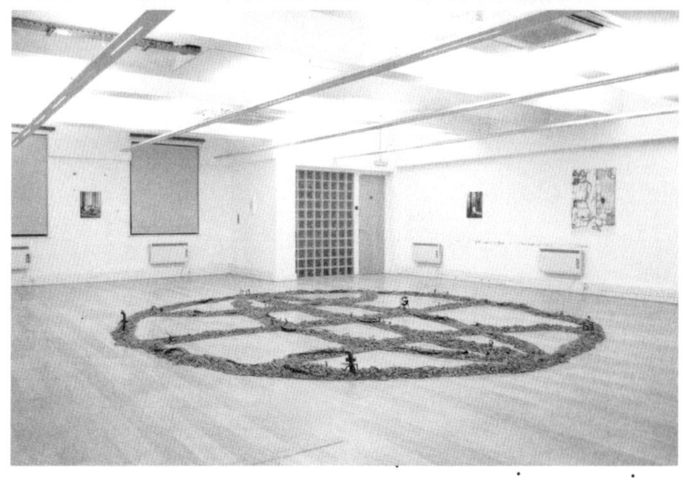

Miyö Van Stenis

INTERVIEWEE: MIYÖ VAN STENIS
PROJECT: VARIOUS – BEAUTIFUL INTERFACES, 2016
WEBSITE: *miyovanstenis.com*, *beautiful.miyovanstenis.com*
DATE: 3 APRIL 2019

Can we start by defining the terminology we're using and how you position yourself within existing categories like digital art, new media, net art, contemporary art, or any of the post-arts?

M   I recognize the importance within the institutional circuit and the need to label a practice. My own work is often seen as 'new media art' or 'post-Internet art', and within that scope I can justify the use of different disciplines like net art, virtual reality, video, and so on...

What is your background and what triggered your interest in digital/net art? Could you elaborate on these initial encounters?

M   I'm born and raised in Caracas, Venezuela. I've always had an interest in technology, especially in computers and Internet culture. Therefore it was clear to me when studying art that I would pursue a career in digital arts. Net art caught my attention as I was taught about the tools and practices, and it still inspires me most. The first net art projects that I experienced were the works by Vuk Ćosić and Alexei Shulgin's *Form Art* (1997). *Form Art* is a work that still amazes me, even though it has changed over the years with each new browser and interface update.

You have been involved in various types of organizations and spaces, could you share some of your experiences of working in these different settings and particular contexts? For example, how does it affect your practice? Are there specific things that work very well in one but not at all in the other context?

M   I get involved in a project because it fits with my research, or at least it has something that could help to develop my work in a conceptual or aesthetic way. This is not necessarily connected to the art world but can also be triggered by an event that happens beyond the 'artist figure'. For example, we developed the project *Dismantling the Simulation* (2014) as a response to the human rights violations during the student protests against Nicolas Maduro in Venezuela that year, which was part of the political unrest. At that moment Helena Acosta, Violette Bule and I decided to get involved as activists by creating and maintaining a space for social engagement. Before this my online practice was not very political, but thanks to this project I became interested into the ontological question around the figure of power. So, it had a major impact on the development of my work.

Each project comes with a different challenge, for example, *Beautiful Interfaces*, and my most recent project, *Zoonosis Project*, with Carolina Sanz, are very different—even opposite—

experiences in terms of practice and subject. This often happens when working with different groups or organizations; I like to work in such dynamic workflows. Managing curatorial projects provides me with an important base to coordinate my studio together with the curatorial/installation space. I learned to solve problems that I encountered as a curator, because I had the experience of being an artist who had to deal with the best way to present my installations.

There has always been a separation between people who stress the technological (material) developments of digital art and those who emphasize the art qualities (content/conceptual). At the same time digital art is also often accompanied by a fair amount of theoretical discussion. How do you position yourself in this discourse?

M   There should be a balance between what technology has to offer and the reason why it should be used as a tool. But in a perfect situation, there is also the conceptual justification of the work. In a sense, to me, it's both the beast and the beauty. However, I no longer feel the need to debate the material versus the concept. If the path of digital art goes in the direction of merely promoting the capabilities of a device, or towards explaining it as a complex metaphor of our species, I'm fine with both; the resulting narrative will be interesting.

You organize online and offline exhibitions. Starting with the latter, do you work with certain methods or criteria? For instance, I recall numerous discussions in the past where showing a computer monitor was 'not done', or some curators wouldn't even consider presenting net art in an exhibition at all, while others created entirely new installations based on online work. What are your thoughts/experiences with this?

M   In my experience as an artist I've been in situations where people said that the net art in an exhibition 'wasn't art' or 'was just a website'. It took a few years before I could present my work in my country, because net art or even digital art weren't really considered as disciplines before 2012. The solution was to create our own space and force the art circuit to adapt: that's how my curatorial practice started. At the time, projects like *DeOrigenBelico, BYOB (Bring Your Own Beamer)*, and others helped to demonstrate in Caracas that art could be displayed with a computer and that sometimes art takes place on the Internet. Now that these events and presentations have become more mainstream, and of course the fact that digital art has a stronger overall presence, there are fewer difficult discussions like these. In this sense, I think VR is the new net art.

    One of my most interesting experiences in mixing 'IRL/

URL' was with the project *Beautiful Interfaces: The Privacy Paradox*, which I curated with Helena Acosta. It was far removed from net art. In order to display and preserve 'digital art' and to understand digital art as pure data—a collection of files that will recreate an experience—we used different formats and presented the artist in a private network. We presented the project in New York, and each artist presented their work on a different custom router, or on private networks. This was an 'online exhibition' displayed offline, no monitors or devices were involved as part of the gallery setting, just the routers. And with their phones people could immediately connect to each artist's network. This project also enabled me, years later, to create a new version of the custom router for *The Wrong Biennale*, where it functioned as a product and extended the exhibition format to the Biennale pavilions.

Who do you see as your audience, I guess it changes with each new context but are there also changes (and/or exchange) that you've noticed over the years... people moving from one area to another, or crossovers from other fields?

M   Social networks constantly change things without notice, so it always depends on the tools you use, and what allows you to have more 'traffic'. In a sense, you're constantly forced to move from one platform to another depending of the content you want to share, for example, Facebook has its own aesthetics and language—you can be more formal, share exhibition events, and so on—while the structure of Instagram allows you to be more intimate. There are fewer formalities so the content can function more like a continuous 'process'; the information never stops. The different ways of communicating on these platforms of course influences who I meet and connect with online. On Instagram I will likely have more followers that are from gaming, 3D or VR communities, while Facebook functions more like an art/artist's address book. I move from one field to another and reach art-related audiences in different ways.

What do you focus on in your projects? In the past we've seen examples ranging from lists of links, to commissions, to documentation about a work, to embedding a work in a website? What is your preferred or even ideal model?

M   Any platform or exhibition format where a discussion or a reflection about a specific work can take place is a good model for me. With time I realize that my work works better if it is embedded within a context that enables the viewer to have an experience. While I sometimes use social media to reach certain people, other times I can show other people art in such environments. Then there are also people who may only look online

for portfolios or interviews. So, I will adapt the way I work or present a project with a specific audience in mind.

Should digital art enter established museums or organizations or are there better places where it can be preserved and presented? If so, what role should museums play in the future?

M   Artists need a support system that allows them to continue their practice, a system that also preserves their work for the future. I'm not against the 'institutional' art model. Although, as I say this, there is a wonderful thing happening: while some large museums and institutions still lag behind and don't follow these new art practices—maybe because they still don't understand the way these works are created or because it is not easy to have these works 'on loan'. At the same time, new organizations are starting that quickly adapt to the needs of contemporary art.

In the past I've had discussions with artists and producers about the usefulness of open source, it seems that although all kinds of codes are available they are rarely used, mainly because of personal approaches to coding and the complexity resulting from such project-based methodology. What is your approach to open source in this context?

M   Besides being an artist I'm a developer, so open sources codes or software are part of my work and daily routine. I've made a few projects that depend solely on open source and have extensive and complicated libraries, which, sadly, you have to learn how to manage no matter how difficult it may be. For example, *Vigipirate Quadcopter Drone* (2020) is a project that collects data which is backed-up inside a drone. It was built mostly using open source codes, from Google's open source JavaScript, to drone board protocols on C++ and Java. All the information was online, and the project could come to fruition thanks to people who allow their work to be open source... the challenge was learning how to use or even understand it, but it was worth it.

Until recently in the Netherlands there was always a very good funding system for the arts in general and specifically for digital art. That has since changed, increasing on the one hand the divide between 'traditional' art and digital art, while on the other it generally means looking for money outside the funding system. Could you share some of your experiences working around the globe? How do you and the artists you work with survive?

M   I hardly apply for residencies or awards and there isn't a cultural funding system or something like that in Venezuela. So, in my case institutions pay for the production of a piece, or they give me a grant, or I set up crowdfunding. Doing different types of projects and having different skill sets also allows me to work

in the arts without having to depend only on what I as an artist would do or sell. If you keep that in mind it's less difficult to earn money from your practice. In France there are ways to get financial funding for artists; I imagine there's a whole system in place, but I don't really know about it.

In order to survive, I learned that at a certain point you need to demand payment, and sadly abandon projects that demand a huge amount of work but no money. Of course, when you're a young artist it's more difficult to refuse an offer to present your work for free, but I learned that it helps to let people know that you can't work for free.

One of the things that fascinates me about one of the projects you organized, *Beautiful Interfaces* (2013, as part of *The Wrong Biennale*) that presents several social media interfaces by artists, is how the exhibition is only accessible via Tor. Could you tell a little bit more about your approach, and perhaps how it relates to your other works/projects? What is your interest and point of view when it comes to digital preservation, documentation and collecting?

M   The online gallery *Beautiful Interfaces* tries to present a specific way to preserve and collect digital art with each new exhibition. For the first exhibition for *The Wrong Biennale, Beautiful Interfaces: The Deep in the Void,* the fifteen selected artists presented what for them was a 'beautiful interface' (responding to the title and concept of the project) into the void (the deep web). The project tried to direct the public view away from the 'surface web' towards the new and alluring Tor network. The exhibition had two types of access: via Tor, and following the recommendations of using the browser, et cetera, a temporary onion link in the pavilion enabled users to navigate and download the online exhibition. For those ones who were afraid to use the Tor network, at the end of the Biennale, users could click on a link on the pavilion website to download a ZIP file, which would run the exhibition locally, as a mirror website.

What excited me the most about this project were the artists' capacities to explore the concept within the limitations imposed by the type of network and the Tor Browser, which doesn't work as efficiently as the browsers we're used to. There isn't any Javascript or complicated codes, no embedded videos from YouTube, or heavy files. With a server of 100MB to present fifteen artists, which means there was less than 10MB per person, for a new media artist it was a significant challenge.

Beautiful Interfaces, online gallery, strives to present a way to preserve and collect digital art. For the first exhibition as part of *The Wrong Biennale, Beautiful Interfaces: The deep in the Void*, fifteen artist presented what they believed could be a *beautiful interface* in the void (the deep web). The project aimed to turn the public view away from the 'surface web', to a new and fresh Tor network. At the core of the project were the artists' capacities to explore the concept under the limitations of the type of network and the Tor Browser, which doesn't work as efficiently as the browsers we are used to.

Miyö Van Stenis is an artist and curator specialized in New Media Art, and is currently based in Paris. Her work explores the technological field: interfaces, operating systems, software and devices involving the Internet as a performative action where the value is the human pursuing the error or the limit. She also produced a series of projects related to the socio-political crisis in Venezuela. Her curatorial work is centred on the critique and aesthetics of new media/technologies such as *Beautiful Interfaces*. She is a founder member of the activist group *Dismantling the Simulation* and co-creator of *The Wrong Router*.

1 Loïq Sutter, *Freaks*, 2012, Courtesy of *loiqsutter.tumblr.com*.
2 INTIMIDAD ROMERO | INTIMIDAD ROMERO, 2013, net. art, *intimidad.me/la_raya_verde/index1.html*.

1   2

Intimidad Romero @La Raya Ve
Not secure | intimidad.me/la_raya_verde/index.html

Home
My Photos
My Vids
online now

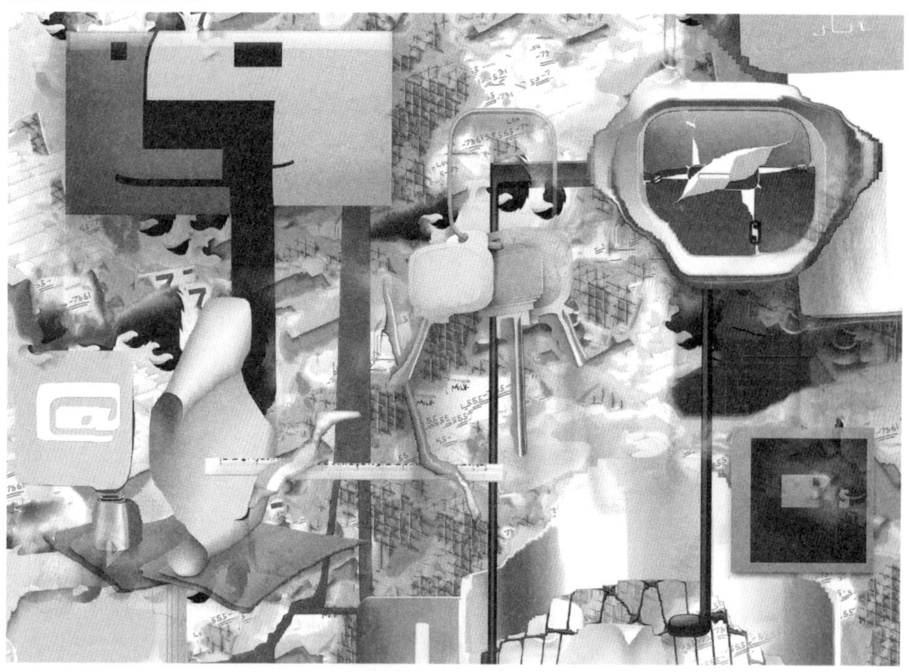

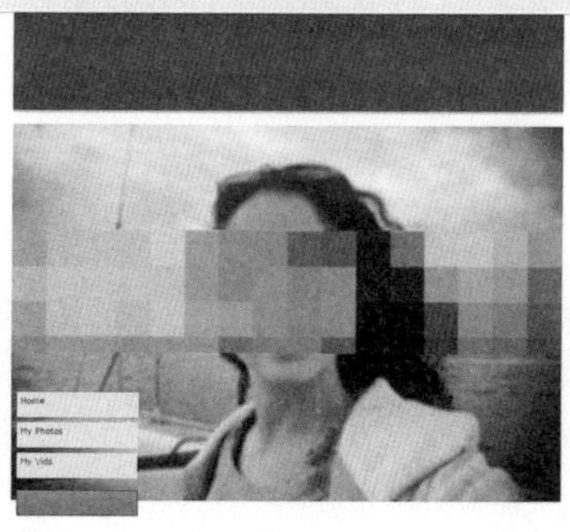

Evelyn Austin & Lilian Stolk

INTERVIEWEES: EVELYN AUSTIN, LILIAN STOLK
PROJECT: THE HMM, 2016–PRESENT
WEBSITE: *thehmm.nl*
DATE: 4 APRIL 2019

Can we start by defining the terminology we're using and how you position yourself within existing categories like digital art, new media, net art, contemporary art, or any of the post-arts?

E & L   We depart from the framework of 'contemporary visual culture' with a special focus on 1) culture influenced by/reflecting on the online environment and/or digital tools; 2) mainstream or pop-culture mostly as it is expressed in/with regards to the online environment.

What is your background and what triggered your interest in digital/net art? Could you elaborate on these initial encounters?

E   I've always been interested in creating my own online space, and in the possibilities new technologies offer. I come from a DIY background and am therefore a very bad front-ender and a very bad A/V-editor. As far as I can remember, I first encountered net art about thirteen years ago, most likely the work of Constant Dullaart and Jan Robert Leegte. What I remember most was the instant recognition that here were people reflecting on 'my' environment. After this I started attending the FutureSonic conference in Manchester, where I became more familiar with technopolitics, which eventually led to my work with Bits of Freedom.

L   My father has worked as a computer programmer his entire life. In the early 1980s, when he was instructed by his boss to teach the rest of the staff how to use computers, he did so with computer games. As a manager of the company's game library he made sure that the newest games were available at home. I was a two-year-old toddler when I played my first computer game. Because of this, I've always thought of the digital world as being intertwined with real life. While studying at the Rietveld Academie, I was inspired by artists who combined those two worlds, like Heath Bunting and Olia Lialina. My emoji research can be seen as an outcome of this.

You've been involved in various types of organizations and spaces. Could you share some of your experiences working in these different settings and particular contexts? For example, how does it affect your practice? Are there specific things that work very well in one context but not at all in another?

E L   Not really. Maybe slightly off topic: there is less and less space for non-institutionalized organizations in Amsterdam. I feel this nudges us as an organization towards institutionalization without it being a strategic choice.

L   It's funny but I think because our format is so strict (we always have ten speakers who present their idea or story in five minutes accompanied by twenty slides) it doesn't really matter if we organize an event in a community centre (like De Roze Tanker) or an art institute (like LIMA or MU). The audience we attract to all these places doesn't vary much.

> There has always been a separation between people who stress the techno-logical (material) developments of digital art and those who emphasize the art qualities (content/conceptual). At the same time digital art is also often accompanied by a fair amount of theoretical discussion. How do you position yourself in this discourse?

E   *The Hmm* takes a political stance in this. We're interested in content and concepts, but—at least for me personally—the main drive behind *The Hmm* is that we (people, but in particular artists and other 'makers') need to talk more about tools. Tools matter. We need to talk about the software, materials, platforms, et cetera, that we use. This happens a lot in academia, but in my opinion is less and less common among young practitioners and art academies.

L   I agree with Evelyn. Especially now that the platforms and software we use are less DIY and more pre-programmed it's important to understand how they work and be critical about how we use them.

> You organize online and offline exhibitions. Starting with the latter, do you work with certain methods or criteria? For instance, I recall numerous discussions in the past where showing a computer monitor was 'not done', or some curators wouldn't even consider presenting net art in an exhibition at all, while others created entirely new installations based on online work. What are your thoughts/experiences with this?

E   We have ten speakers per night and a super strict pres-entation format (a time limit, twenty slides, fifteen seconds each), which means we don't deal with that many presentation questions. We like the idea of the event being an 'evening on the Internet', where we do the scrolling for the audience. When one of our speakers gave a talk about Childish Gambino's *This is America* we watched his video from start to finish before his presentation. I liked that because it sort of replicated the solo viewing experience people usually have behind their computer. This year we also seem to be talking a lot about temporality, but I'm not sure where that conversation is going.

L   And removing something from its context (looking at someone's ten favourite YouTube channels or Childish Gambi-no's music video, bringing the online offline) helps us to under-stand it better instead of just consuming it.

Who do you see as your audience? I guess it changes with each new context but are there also changes (and/or exchanges) that you've noticed over the years, people moving from one place to another, or crossovers from other fields?

E   A lot of our audience are between their twenties and thirtees, and are art students/young professionals artists/designers/et cetera. The part of our audience that changes from event to event, changes because of the guest programmer who's working with us, and not so much because of the venue. For instance, when we worked with Ward Jansen, this attracted a more established net art crowd, and working with Martijn van Boven and Roosje Klap brought in a lot of students.

L   Because we try to keep the ten speakers as diverse as possible (from amateur makers, to artists, scientists and nerds) our audience also comes from different backgrounds, which leads to interesting crossovers and discussions after the talks. At one event a speaker who presented his collage-based Instagram account realized that his account might be in trouble after the five-minute talk that followed his on the proposed new copyright law for the Netherlands (Article 13).

What do you focus on in your online exhibitions/digital magazine? In the past we've seen examples ranging from lists of links, to commissions, to documentation about a work, to embedding a work in a website? What is your preferred or even ideal 'model'?

E   Our online work is more research-based. We commission text-based articles (1500 words), and each month ask someone to give us a peek into 'their' Internet by picking a single image that they feel deserves contemplation to represent each week (50/50 text/image-based). I'm not against it, but embedding work on your website feels kind of counterintuitive to me (although I see the value for the sake of preservation, and perhaps reaching a larger audience).

L   In addition to what Evelyn said above: Since we stick to the five-minute format during our offline-events, we use our online space to dive a bit deeper. We use the essays to present topics we think are important, but haven't been presented by artists or in artworks yet.

Should digital art enter established museums or organizations or are there better places where it can be preserved and presented? If so, what role should museums play in the future?

E   I think it's important to preserve art within the established and respected (and respectable) art context. Museums and public institutions such as libraries are failing us when it comes to preserving, documenting and making the digital age accessible.

L   A museum is not only a repository for artworks, but also a place that tells stories. You see different artworks next to each other, and talk about the experience afterwards. Practically this can be translated to a digital environment, but I'm not sure whether this would have the same focus.

I recently had a few discussions with artists and producers about the usefulness of open source, it seems that although all kinds of codes and suchlike are available they're hardly ever used, mainly because of the personal approach to coding and the complexity that derives from such project-based work. What is your approach to open source in this context?

E   This question doesn't really apply to us, but we do think it's an important topic. When we interface with people, we try to use open source software or open protocols as much as possible. There are times when that's easy: our website, newsletter, e-mail; and moments when it's hard: we try to be less reliant on Facebook, but we're still on Instagram). When it comes to collaborating internally, it's a whole other issue. We used to use different messaging apps but have settled on iMessage; we used to use different text editors and have settled on .docx; some of us are Google-haters so we have settled on etherpad instead of Google docs. 'If only' the surveillance capitalist business model hadn't completely monopolized our thinking around communication tools, we could be living in a completely open source and open protocol online environment by now, which would be far more beneficial.

Until recently in the Netherlands there was always a very good funding system for the arts in general and specifically for digital art. That has since changed, increasing on the one hand the divide between 'traditional' art and digital art, while on the other it generally means looking for money outside the funding system. Could you share some of your experiences working around the globe? How do you and the artists you work with survive?

E & L   *The Hmm* doesn't have experience with alternative funding. We receive support from Stimuleringsfonds Creatieve Industrie and AFK.

One of your recent projects are the *Must See* 'exhibitions', for which you ask someone to present a selection of images that they find particularly intriguing and which they describe in their own way. Could you explain your approach, also perhaps in relation to your other work (*The Hmm* events)? And what is your interest and perspective when it comes to digital preservation, documentation and collecting?

E   We scroll through a lot of images every day. During *The Hmm* events we imitate the speed of Instagram Stories, where each image can be seen for exactly fifteen seconds, but by regulating the images and the tempo, we eliminate the need for the viewer to scroll endlessly. This creates space for contemplation and discussion.

L   But some images deserve a closer look. Under the guise of 'show us your Internet', every month we invite someone to select four images that attracted his/her attention and to explain why they're so important/beautiful/interesting/dangerous/funny. We consider this image editor as a curator in the increasingly visual landscape. We post the images as weekly 'must sees' on our social media channels, and as a collection on our website. By placing the images alongside each other, the editor's perspective and interests are revealed. For example, graphic designer Joris Landman's selection showed how technology influences images, and Elki Boerdam investigated the authenticity of images.

The Hmm is an inclusive platform for Internet cultures. Through real-life events, online editorials, expert advice, and educational programmes, it reflects on people's online behaviour, the latest Internet trends, and the mechanisms behind Big Tech companies and their impact on society.

Evelyn Austin is the Executive Director of Bits of Freedom, the leading Dutch digital rights organization. Her work has made headlines multiple times: she demanded attention for Google's censorship of the Dutch women's rights organization Women on Waves, and proved that Facebook lied to the Dutch parliament about their efforts to combat election manipulation. Additionally, Austin is the co-founder of *The Hmm*, and she sits on the advisory board of the Creative Industries Fund's Digital Culture programme. Previously she worked at Mediamatic and for the academic journal *Kunstlicht*.

Lilian Stolk co-founded and currently leads *The Hmm* and is an emoji expert. She cares about understanding the Internet and has a special focus on Internet languages and the rise of image-based communication. A writer, public speaker and programmer of event, her research into emojis was published as *Het zonder woorden-boek* in 2018.

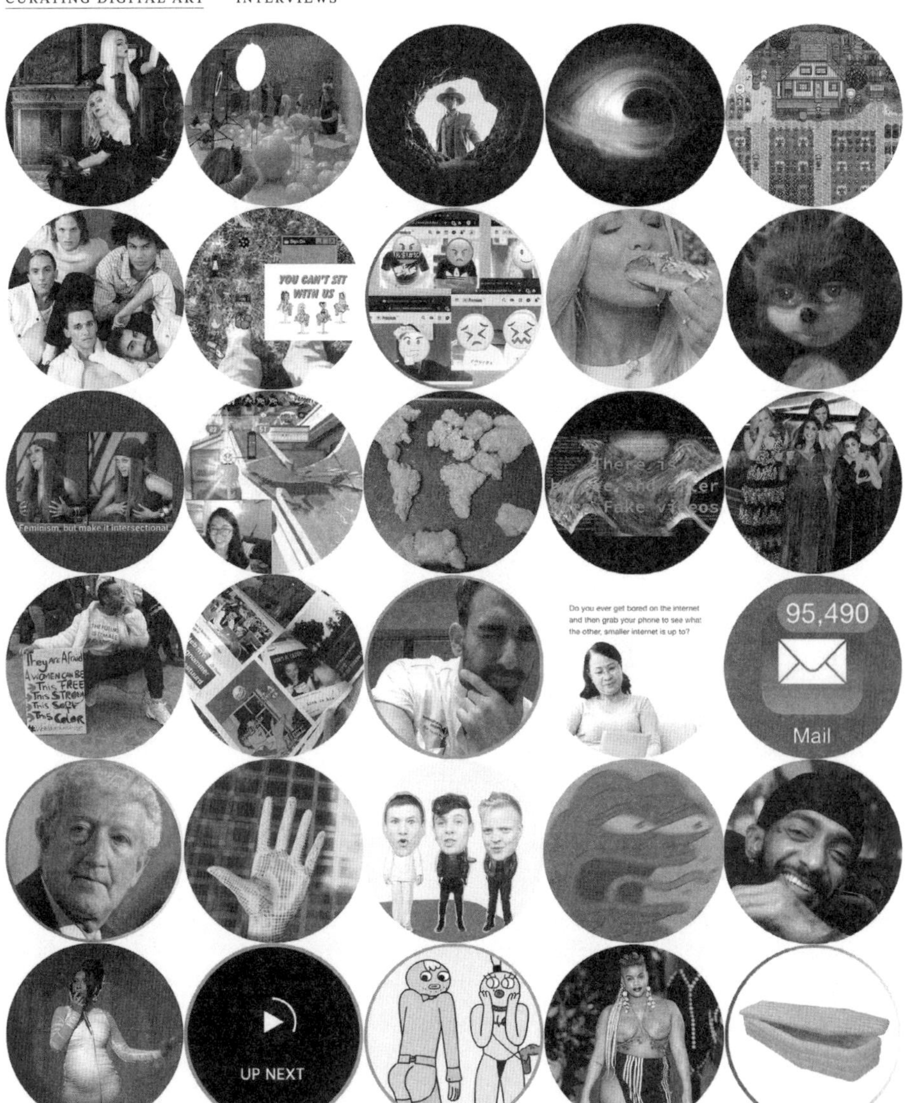

YOU CAN'T SIT WITH US
Feminism, but make it intersectional.
There is
Fake videos
Do you ever get bored on the internet
and then grab your phone to see what
the other, smaller internet is up to?
95,490
Mail
UP NEXT

LaTurbo Avedon

INTERVIEWEE: LATURBO AVEDON
PROJECT: VARIOUS – PANTHER MODERN, 2013–PRESENT
WEBSITE: *turboavedon.com*, *panthermodern.org*
DATE: 10 APRIL 2019

Can we start by defining the terminology we're using and how you position yourself within existing categories like digital art, new media, net art, contemporary art, or any of the post-arts?

L   Terminology is important, and I'm always trying to get the community to engage in this discussion. 'New Media' never really seemed to make sense from the perspective of art history, but I do enjoy the term 'Simulism'. My identity and my work exist through repurposed software tools from Hollywood and Silicon Valley. It is in the space adjacent to these industries that I want to reside, simulating my own virtual reality.

What is your background and what triggered your interest in digital/net art? Could you elaborate on these initial encounters?

L   I was raised on Geocities, America Online. Bits and pieces of me started taking shape across my interfaces—saved game files, usernames, threads in the BBS. You needed a handle. It was then, choosing a username for the very first time, when I realized that I could become so many different things online. Years later, once things went MMO (Massively Multiplayer Online), I started hosting raves and other social events in Second Life. Seeing the vitality and representation of self in these places, I decided that I wanted to present my work and experiences in the metaverse. After a few years on the Second Life grid I wanted to get to know people beyond a single simulation. That's when I ran into a lot of the net artists who were coalescing on social media networks.

New media is actually a decades-old practice with a vast queer subcultural narrative, though this conversation usually gets clipped down to the past five to seven years. My time in Second Life was often spent responding to thinkers such as Donna Haraway, Susan Sontag, and Slavoj Žižek, manifesting ideas that had been stranded in academia for quite some time. By the mid–2000s we were realizing the fictions of cyberspace at a consumer level, and that was where I could finally enter as an artist.

You've been involved in various types of organizations and spaces. Could you share some of your experiences working in these different settings and particular contexts? For example, how does it affect your practice? Are there specific things that work very well in one context but not at all in another?

L   There is a lot of acclimation to process, weaving in and out of my online existence. I don't appear at my exhibitions physically, but my work is often exported for print or installa-

 tions. I speak to my audiences solely through chat rooms and video projections. In many ways the physical world becomes my renderer—a visible yet intangible environment within which I can create. When I'm creating a projection installation I begin by simulating it, making scale models and examining the ways things do and don't work. There are times when I wonder which is more real to me, the space that the public can wander about in with their bodies, or the wireframes that construct it all within my monitor.

> There has always been a separation between people who stress the technological (material) developments of digital art and those who emphasize the art qualities (content/conceptual). At the same time digital art is also often accompanied by a fair amount of theoretical discussion. How do you position yourself in this discourse?

L   These kinds of conversations go back centuries, with slightly different flavours, depending on the medium. I try to keep a healthy balance between the conceptual and the formal in my work because the stakes are actually quite high—the same tools that I use to make my art are paving the pathways of our future. Simulation, machine learning, and the tools used to build them will shift the paradigm, and the choices reflect how we currently comprehend them. I like to think that we can be careful yet playful.

> You organize online and offline exhibitions. Starting with the latter, do you work with certain methods or criteria? For instance, I recall numerous discussions in the past where showing a computer monitor was 'not done', or some curators wouldn't even consider presenting net art in an exhibition at all, while others created entirely new installations based on online work. What are your thoughts/experiences with this?

L   There were times in the past where respected colleagues of mine would say, 'You should give up on the computer art, it will never have the same status inside galleries'. Usually, these interactions drove me to work even harder, because I believed in the ways that my work was revealing the moment. It's been a slow but increasingly positive charge. A lot of artists have taken steps to formalize their work so that it more resembles objects native to art institutions, but for me it's important to stick with the format and show the public that these are real and valid forms of art in their own right.

> Who do you see as your audience? I guess it changes with each new context but are there also changes (and/or exchanges) that you've noticed over the years, people moving from one place to another, or crossovers from other fields?

L   The audience has changed over time, especially as the 'digital native' becomes a very ordinary member of society. At first my audience was a spread of academics and experimental

 creators, but it continues to widen. Usernames are parked for babies yet to be born, networked interfacing is seen as a passive function of daily life. These conditions continue to normalize, and in turn my work and approach actually feel less surprising.

What do you focus on in your online exhibitions/digital magazine? In the past we've seen examples ranging from lists of links, to commissions, to documentation about a work, to embedding a work in a website? What is your preferred or even ideal 'model'?

L   I want to create records of this moment, and how artists have chosen to respond to this junction of art and technology. This drives me as both an artist and a curator to work within all of these virtual parameters. We're witnessing the transition into the Simulation Age, an often-flawed yet incredibly transformational process. I frequently correspond with the inhabitants of our future landscapes. I want them to know that some of us were mindful of the long view, and that we wanted to create a strong foundation for what comes later. I want to celebrate the branching format of these tools, to know that our work with machines creates so much more. Something may exist as a still image, but it may also exist as an immersive simulation. There is volume to our work, a fluid to be poured from vessel to vessel.

Should digital art enter established museums or organizations or are there better places where it can be preserved and presented? If so, what role should museums play in the future?

L   Museums are often the glue of history, so it is important that we integrate digitally created art within them. It is my hope that many different types of museums and new fields of scholarship come into existence. We need more intermediary spaces, accessible civic venues that permit experimentation. If we respect the work enough to create digital art auctions, we should see a more holistic environment. Foster growth and development, integrate older and younger creators.

I recently had a few discussions with artists and producers about the usefulness of open source, it seems that although all kinds of codes and suchlike are available they're hardly ever used, mainly because of the personal approach to coding and the complexity that derives from such project-based work. What is your approach to open source in this context?

L   Open source utility is quite exciting, but practical experience has shown that people are often quite predatory of those who are generous with their processes. I know so many artists who've had unrelated users pinch or profit from their efforts, all without citation or concern for the source. I don't believe that open source requires some sort of hierarchy, but citation can be a positive and progressive method.

Until recently in the Netherlands there was always a very good funding
system for the arts in general and specifically for digital art. That has since
changed, increasing on the one hand the divide between 'traditional' art and
digital art, while on the other it generally means looking for money outside
the funding system. Could you share some of your experiences working
around the globe? How do you and the artists you work with survive?

L   Even avatars have day jobs, unfortunately. As much as I
wish I could spend all my time on my work, I have an ordinary
job to protect it. A lot of artists end up doing commercial art
to sustain themselves and there's nothing wrong with that, but
I wish there were more avenues of support so that they could
focus solely on studio time. Galleries often only allocate quite
small amounts for exhibitions so they cannot be relied upon,
especially when some projects require extensive work periods for
rendering and output. Sometimes we have to be resourceful and
nomadic. Many artists are leaning towards the model of music
and royalties but I don't think that is optimal. Art is such a vital
element of daily life, and I hope that the tech sector can learn to
give back to those who have visualized its fruit.

One of the things that fascinates me about *Panther Modern*, the file-based
exhibition space, is how it provides an architecture that resembles a
physical structure yet stresses the affordances of the virtual and its endless
possibilities as well as restrictions. Could you explain your approach, also in
relation to your other work such as *Club Rothko*? And what is your interest
and perspective when it comes to digital preservation, documentation and
collecting?

L   *Panther Modern* is meant to allow artists to extend their
reach beyond physical space, to use the render as a space to
reassess architecture and their work. Whether this is through a
suggestion of physicality and scale, or through a formal configur-
ation of planes within perspective, there are so many directions
an artist can take a 3D model. As a curator I want to raise the
ceiling, or break it altogether. I want to see what artists envision
when they have greater freedom. These will only become more
interesting with the passing of time. The ways we visualized
cyberspace just twenty years ago seem so distant now, and I can
only imagine how these works will appear in another twenty.
Look closely at our 1080p, our low anti-alias, the polygon count
of our models. Watch us struggle with ray tracing, and the way
we marvel at our first 3D prints. This was our method and
how we could make sense of this world, just one hyperlink in
the long chain.

Panther Modern is a file-based exhibition space curated by LaTurbo Avedon. *Panther Modern* encourages artists to create site-specific installations for the Internet. Each project shown at *Panther Modern* is given a unique structure in the format of a 3D-model file, which is built to engage the artists and their creation process. Given the variety of methods available to produce works in virtual space, artists can choose the format they will use to share their installations. Completed rooms are added to the existing architecture, such that the shape of *Panther Modern* changes with each project.

LaTurbo Avedon is an avatar and artist who exists solely online, and creates work that emphasizes the practice of non-physical identity and authorship. Avedon has spent the past decade developing a body of work that illuminates the ever-growing intensity between users and virtual experiences, pursuing creative environments that deepen the meaning of memories found in cyberspace.

1 Mark Dorf, *Panther Modern (Room Nine)*, 2015.
2 Pussykrew, *Panther Modern (Room Seven)*, 2014.
3 LaTurbo Avedon, *Panther Modern (Room Ten Architecture)*, 2015.

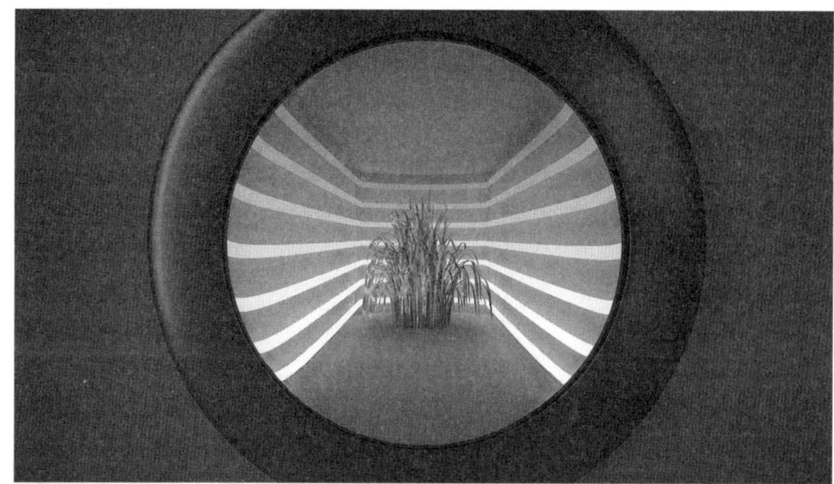

1

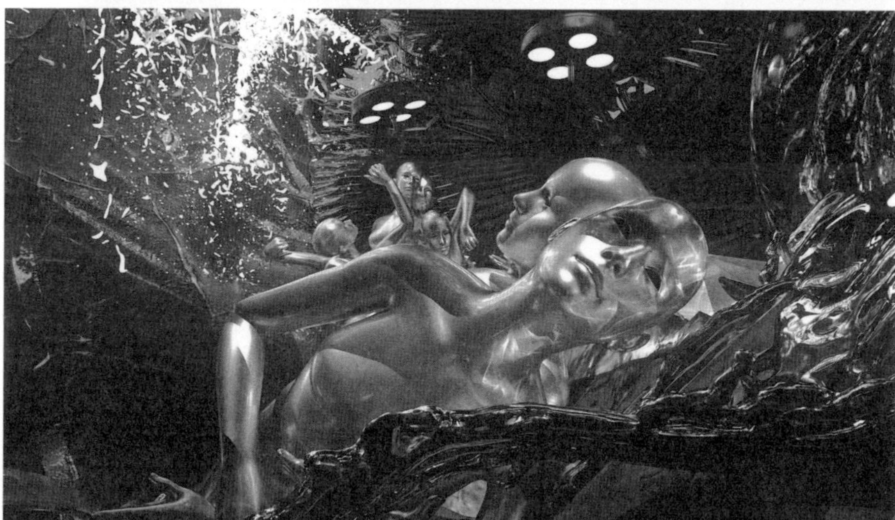

2

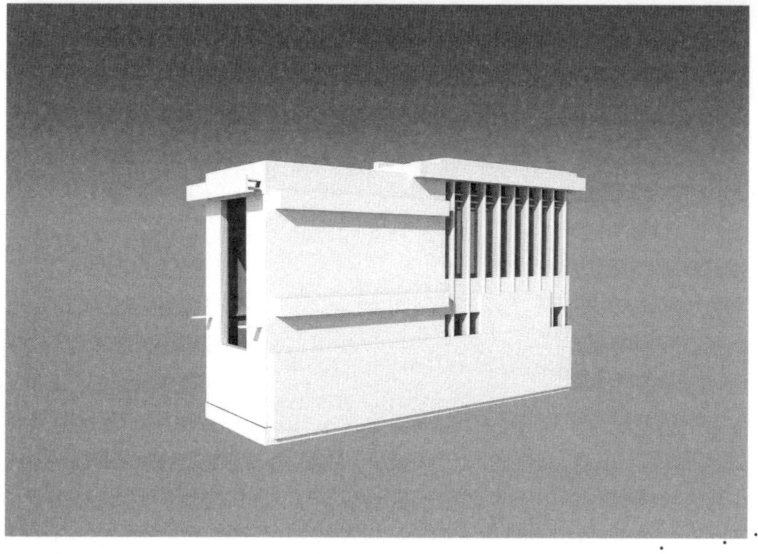

3

Sakrowski

INTERVIEWEE: SAKROWSKI
PROJECT: VARIOUS – PANKE.GALLERY, 2016–PRESENT
WEBSITE: *panke.gallery*
DATE: 10 APRIL 2019

Can we start by defining the terminology we're using and how you position yourself within existing categories like digital art, new media, net art, contemporary art, or any of the post-arts?

S   The question about categories is one that is always very difficult to answer because it's very political. It sets boundaries, is exclusionary, and creates restrictions that—in my opinion—are unnecessary. I think it's all about art. I'm interested in art if we can understand art as a way to express an idea about the world.

Since 1999, the focus of my work has been an examination of net art in its various forms. Currently, I describe net art as follows: net art—whether focusing on formal, political, relational, aesthetic or material manifestations of the digital—is today understood as an artform that grew out of the context of Internet culture, and reflects on it and shapes it. By working intimately on, in, and with the Internet both as a material and in their own lives, younger artists also recognize and define the aesthetics and central concerns of the early twenty-first century. They formulate questions about the significance of the private sphere, about identity, about the role of the subject in networked society, and about the ownership of data and digital objects, as well as engage in political, aesthetic and formal investigations into authorship, original and copy, the artwork and authenticity, and their dissolution under the conditions of the Internet. Our society is becoming totally networked, and therefore artists who define our position within it are of utmost importance to me.

The question of a categorical definition of the medium remains difficult in the context of art history. In Berlin, there are funding programmes for various artistic disciplines: Fine Arts, Performing Arts, Theatre and Dance, Literature, Music. Net art, however, unites all of these disciplines within its medium, and that again makes it impossible to define net art exclusively through its medium—otherwise everything would be net art and net art would be everything and nothing at the same time.

The political and economic factors of defining net art makes it very difficult to predict or favour a definition: if no one understands what they're being asked to support, then support won't be forthcoming. On the other hand, the hype around the term 'media art' has also led to its demise. Apparently, everyone only produced for media arts programmes, and interpreted the works as 'something involving computers/video', while net art was not considered 'real' media art.

What is your background and what triggered your interest in digital/net art? Could you elaborate on these initial encounters?

S   My first encounter was 1991 when I met a developer from the company Hermstedt, which produced the Leonardo ISDN card. He told me about the upcoming network where I would be able to buy my flight ticket on the way to the airport from my car. As someone with experience of the Eastern German surveillance state I replied: 'But then 'they' will know where I am right now and what plans I'm making, where I want to go and with whom etc.' I was really shocked. He asked me who 'they' are? ... Maybe you can understand that it was hard for me to adapt to the new society... Without realizing, I saw my first pre net.art piece at the E-Werk techno club in Berlin—it was the clubnetz an IRC installed in 7 Berlin techno clubs around 1994. I saw my first net artworks later in 1996 at Transmediale in Berlin. I was studying art history at the time and I thought: OK, they do a quick run through of art history... conceptual art, video art, Dada, performing arts, et cetera. A lot of the work seemed to only be ideas rehashed for a new medium, so I was sceptical, but then I saw *jodi.org*. It really touched me and I started to research more.

At the close of the twentieth century there was also a discussion about how to preserve net art for later generations and that beckoned me as an art historian: I felt responsible in a way and started the *netart-datenbank.org* project. I must add that I compared early net art with the Dada and Surrealist movements—a small artist group experimenting with new media techniques and exchanging thoughts by e-mail that came from all over Europe (East! and West), so it felt like I could study an avant-garde movement as a 'living body'.

You've been involved in various types of organizations and spaces. Could you share some of your experiences working in these different settings and particular contexts? For example, how does it affect your practice? Are there specific things that work very well in one context but not at all in another?

S   I can't really elaborate on this, only that I wish there was a governmental institution with a real! budget that would take care of the heritage and research, a museum like Hamburger Bahnhof, for example. The panke.gallery is a great place to work, but the lack of funds makes it hard and not really sustainable. It's frustrating to see all the current digitization efforts where they digitize the analogue, but I don't see a serious effort to understand and preserve born-digital artefacts. Also it looks like all the mistakes are going to be repeated—like single ambitious solutions far from an open standard, or isolated individual solutions for one special case only, or forgetting the ongoing maintenance costs, to name but a few...

> There has always been a separation between people who stress the techno-logical (material) developments of digital art and those who emphasize the art qualities (content/conceptual). At the same time digital art is also often accompanied by a fair amount of theoretical discussion. How do you position yourself in this discourse?

S   I think digital art has to be treated like every other artform. Ideas about form or technique are just as important as concepts and discourse. So every artwork or genre needs to be accompanied by a fair amount of theoretical discussion. Digital art also has its history and I think art always has to have aesthetic qualities. I can't understand this separation. It is often forgotten that with the passing of time—in some cases even a decade later—it's almost impossible to show net art as it was in its original state, which means we have to deal with an ongoing translation process. This happens much faster than with an oil painting or a sculpture, even though in those cases, in order to understand the work, we also have to consider and imagine the specific historical context.

> You organize online and offline exhibitions. Starting with the latter, do you work with certain methods or criteria? For instance, I recall numerous discussions in the past where showing a computer monitor was 'not done', or some curators wouldn't even consider presenting net art in an exhibition at all, while others created entirely new installations based on online work. What are your thoughts/experiences with this?

S   This is a complex topic and could fill plenty of books. I think on one hand that at the moment the exhibition space defines the circumstances within which the exhibition is de-veloped, and on the other that the curatorial or artistic concept defines how it will be presented. There is no single hard-and-fast rule that applies to all situations.

It's important, if possible, to show the net art activity in the hard- and software-context of the time when the work was created and presented. I also try to work with artists on develop-ing an exhibition form for each specific situation, event and/or space. If the work is still present online and is still working/func-tioning, then all well and good: then it has its environment. But if it is shown in a space outside the web, a variety of intentions come into play. The 'coming together', the social interaction in the space, is important, because it enables an exchange of ideas and a discourse based on personal experiences of art. Also in this case it's not much different from planning an exhibition with any other art. We have to take care of the specifics of the medium, the artists' intentions, and the intentions, ideas and contexts of the exhibition itself. All this differs from case to case.

My perspectives have changed over time! My first exhibitions (*netart-datenbank.org*) were more or less experimental research into this topic.

We initially exhibited the browser by itself because the deep entanglement with net art was obvious. We also followed the ideas of Prof. Huber, i.e., that the browser is the stage where net art is performed, and that this context defines the net art activity. At the same time, there were a lot of artistic browsers around. Not to mention that a lot of works in the early days of the web were playing with browser bugs. The browser as software was also understood as a medium for artistic expression. This shows again that also at that time there was still confusion about what net art is. Is a browser, an artistic software, net art, or is it software art? Or is it perhaps the only real net art, where you write and define your own context within the project. This exhibition focused our attention on the relation between the software and hardware context, especially our second one, where we exhibited the then famous work *unendlich, fast...* (1995) by Holger Friese as a single page. It seems really simple but it exemplifies all the problems you can encounter when exhibiting net art. Friese already had a version for collectors— a small edition with a diskette in a nice package and a printout of the website. At this exhibition we saw the multimedia format of net art activity, particularly because we tried to emulate the system. Yet even though you can use an emulation version, the web is not the same. For example, the computer chip that ran the emulator was much too powerful so we tried to slow down everything to get a 'real' impression of the actual processing time of the web back then. In the end the best results were achieved with a computer, an operating system and browser from the time the work was made. For me this is still the best way to exhibit historical works—in a gallery space.

> Who do you see as your audience? I guess it changes with each new context but are there also changes (and/or exchanges) that you've noticed over the years, people moving from one place to another, or crossovers from other fields?

S   At panke.gallery I try to create crossover moments between a club and a gallery on the one hand, and young and old on the other. But the interest in net art is still not mainstream and so the audience is rather limited.

What do you focus on in your online exhibitions/digital magazine? In the past we've seen examples ranging from lists of links, to commissions, to documentation about a work, to embedding a work in a website? What is your preferred or even ideal 'model'?

S   Also here I wouldn't really differentiate between online and offline. Online exhibitions also have their spaces with their own constraints—there is no ideal model.

For instance, *GRIDr.org* was a tool you could use to create exhibitions or sketches, or as a place for your research, etc., but there were problems within days of its release: what to do if a video disappeared because either the owner took it down, or permission to embed it was withdrawn. Should I have downloaded all these videos? I decided against it and regarded the project more as something ephemeral: showing the liveliness and the uncontrollable aspects of the web. Then again, for some works or exhibitions it's maybe crucial to download the videos.

I would say this is similar to many web projects: for the exhibition you could build an exhibition context page but what happens if the exhibited work disappears?

Personally, I would prefer to have the works in the same place as the exhibition so that nothing disappears. Unfortunately I can't maintain it. This is a constant struggle and maybe that's the reason for all the different forms you mentioned.

Should digital art enter established museums or organizations or are there better places where it can be preserved and presented? If so, what role should museums play in the future?

S   I would say that museums still play an important role in the eyes of the public. But I have the impression that their concepts are not quite what they should be. I've heard from people that museums have to adapt to the 'attention economy' and 'the star system'—I disagree, I don't think they should. Museums could be a lively intermix of heritage, research, exhibitions and discourse, but somehow I see them becoming ensnared in political and economic traps, bound by all kinds of constraints and losing importance, perhaps in a similar way as other older forms of cultural mediation like magazines, newspapers and TV. It would be great for net art if the activities could stay in their original context for as long as possible: the web. But at the same time they should be acquired by collections, taken care of and kept together with their historic context, i.e., their software and hardware: perhaps museums should participate in *archive.org*'s attempt to save the net and only preserve their own copies. Anyway, for now I think it's better if net art is kept in an art museum than in a technical collection or a science and technology museum.

I recently had a few discussions with artists and producers about the usefulness of open source, it seems that although all kinds of codes and suchlike are available they're hardly ever used, mainly because of the personal approach to coding and the complexity that derives from such project-based work. What is your approach to open source in this context?

S   On an institutional level open source software is really important and should always be used. In my own situation as a 'one-man' gallery it's often more reliable, easier and cheaper (especially the maintenance) to use conventional software. In the context of archiving I always prefer the open source approach. But I was so frustrated by institutional archival attempts that Constant Dullaart and I proposed a method based on YouTube as the primary storage, catalogue and interface system: *net.artdatabase.org*.

Until recently in the Netherlands there was always a very good funding system for the arts in general and specifically for digital art. That has since changed, increasing on the one hand the divide between 'traditional' art and digital art, while on the other it generally means looking for money outside the funding system. Could you share some of your experiences working around the globe? How do you and the artists you work with survive?

S   The smaller countries always had more money for art it seems and it's sad to see how this has changed in the last decade. But if we speak about young artists or the so-called avant-garde then my experience is that it is becoming more and more difficult for artists to make a living from their art praxis. I think there are several reasons for this. Right now it feels as if we are returning to the early twentieth century when artists starved or had to support themselves with something other than their art, like private funds, parents, an inheritance, or previous business success. Then there is the whole gallery business, which is still an enigma to me. Governments should support artists with the same amount of money as they provide to the institutions that exhibit their output. The imbalance is connected to our political will. It seems that everyone who works in socially important jobs are underpaid, the argument being that the satisfaction they get from their work makes up the difference.

One of your recent projects is the online and offline gallery events at panke. gallery, where you're organizing a series of exhibitions with emerging and established artists in an attempt to initiate a dialogue, also linking it to the history of net art and digital culture in Berlin. At the same time, there are Wi-Fi exhibitions on local routers. Could you explain your approach, also in relation to your other work? And what is your interest and perspective when it comes to digital preservation, documentation and collecting?

S   The exhibitions happen in the physical panke.gallery space and are curated by me. The *router.gallery* is a digital space

that is like a 'virtual' layer over the exhibition space that hosts exhibitions assembled by different curators. I see the *router.gallery* as an addition to the physical gallery: it expands my curatorial approach to other ideas and possibilities. Also it is an easy way for the club audience to connect to the panke.gallery even if the gallery is closed at night—people can connect via Wi-Fi and view the exhibition.

The last question is the most complex and I hope my previous answers go some way to answering it. But I would say digital preservation is important, it should happen as an active process in art museums. Next to the preservation of the artwork, the relationships with the artists is important and they should be part of the process of documentation and preservation. New open source tools and methods should be developed to do this, perhaps by a network of museums, people, artists and art historians. It's really important that digital preservation becomes part of the education system in either classical restoration or forensic science studies, or that a standard is developed, like in library science, for metadata, for preserving the hardware and software and documentation, etc. Documentation is an area that requires more tools—the digital makes possible things that are unimaginable with other artforms, but sadly I don't really see anything happening at the moment. *Oldweb.today* is a good example of one approach, but this does not even approximate what could be accomplished.

I tried also to develop a method: a video interview with a diagrammatic real-time visualization: *youtu.be/PF3O2nNu8S8*. Collecting is a really interesting topic—I think there should be more research into the act of collecting itself—people collect everything nowadays—sports shoes, telephones, video games... Why don't they collect webpages? We should also develop a culture of supporting artists by supporting their art—the start-up patron thing is very close but middlemen are totally unnecessary. It would be much better if the collector was directly involved with the artist. All these online portals selling digital art make it very unattractive to buy there: everything looks like a product, like merchandize. I would also urge artists to take care of their contracts and include a paragraph stipulating their percentage on every subsequent sale. Holger Friese and Hans Dieter Huber did this in the 1990s when they adapted an old suggestion from the 1960s into this contract for selling net art: (see Article 2).

panke.gallery seeks to enable local and international dialogue between established and emerging artists. The presented works derive from the connection between digital or net-based art and club culture, reflecting in particular the recent history of Berlin. panke.gallery is a non-commercial platform and framework to support net-based cultures.

Sakrowski has worked in various constellations in the field of music and new media art since 1986. He studied art history at TU Berlin. From 1999 to 2003 he led the project *netart-datenbank.org*. Between 2007 and 2009 he worked in Linz on the *netpioneers 1.0* research project. Since 2007 he has created various exhibitions under the name *CuratingYouTube*. In 2014 he worked as curator for the Transmediale Festival *capture all* in 2015. He founded panke.gallery in Berlin-Wedding in 2016, where he still works as a curator.

1, 3   Berlin Zentrum der Netzkunst, *damals und heute* (2018). Courtesy of panke.gallery. Photo: Alexia Manzano.
2   Daniel Keller, 2017. Courtesy of panke.gallery. Photo: Visvaldas Morkevicius.

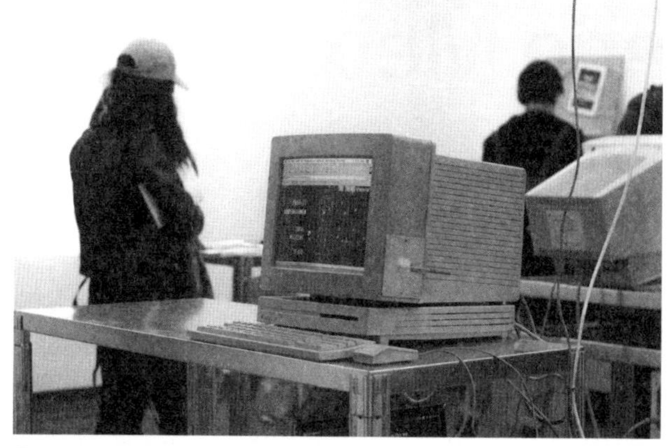

1

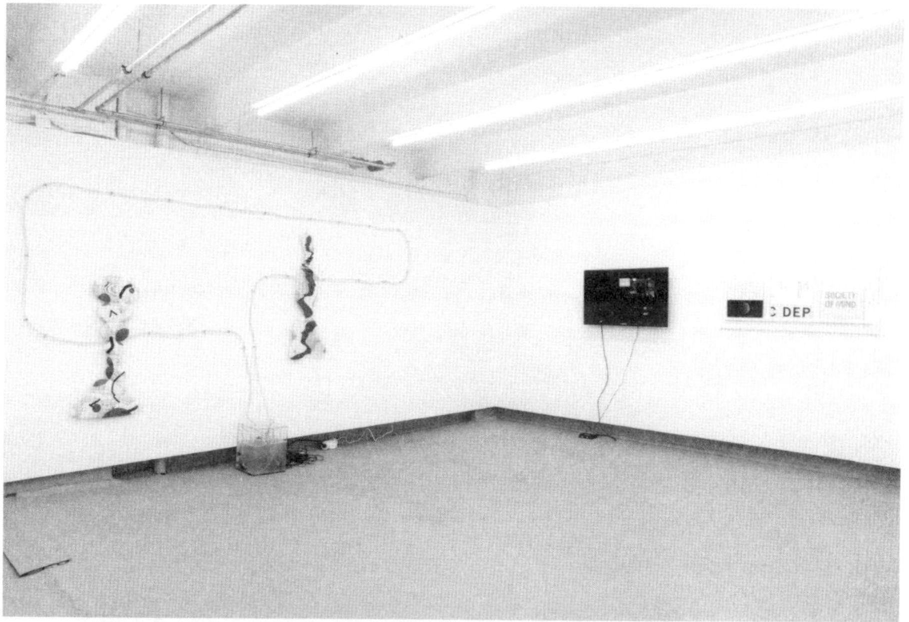

2

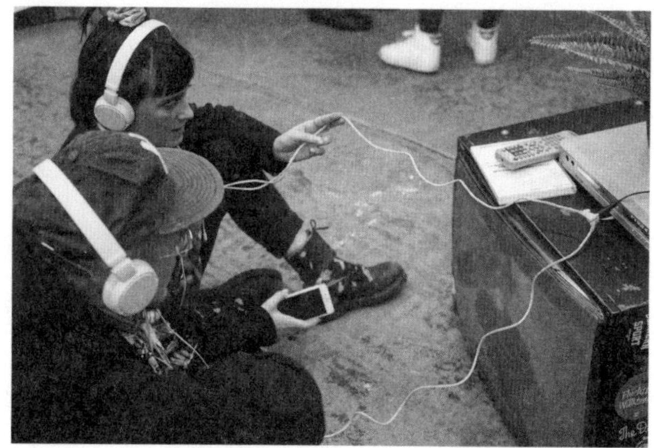

3

Marie Meixnerová

INTERVIEWEE: MARIE MEIXNEROVÁ, MARY MEIXNER/(C) MERRY
PROJECT: SCREENSAVERGALLERY, 2012–PRESENT
WEBSITE: *crazymerry.tumblr.com*, *screensaver.metazoa.org*
DATE: 11 APRIL 2019

Can we start by defining the terminology we're using and how you position yourself within existing categories like digital art, new media, net art, contemporary art, or any of the post-arts?

M   The definitions of these terms call for constant exploration and re-evaluation, and the relations between them are not stable, but evolve constantly. In 2019, I tend to understand (contemporary) digital art as the essence of contemporary art. The term 'digital art' has sort of replaced 'net art', as it no longer address only digital things online, but in a wider sense anything that was produced under the direct influence of the Internet and while online (often addressing this experience) is not understandable without this direct, close experience. Following this logic, I regard 'net art' as a broader term that includes post-Internet... even artworks drawing on object-oriented ontology and speculative realism. This could definitely be said even five years back.

The problem is, that in today's situation, when the Internet has penetrated every aspect of our lives, and is now omnipresent, indispensable and invisible, with the premise that this development will go even further and exceed all previously imaginable limits, 'net art' as described in this sense almost merged completely with contemporary art, making the term 'net art' in its broader sense no longer useful. Instead we could say that the work is contemporary, net-related and/or digital. Maybe it's only my impression that the definition of 'net art' has narrowed again to refer to web-based works, but so much confusion has arisen around the terminology that net art (but only as a term) might finally be redundant.

Digital art on the other hand, is an easier term to define by medium, which is digital technology. As such, 'digital art' also covers the 'online' stuff. Contemporary art is art that is produced in the moment, or at least within the past ten years. 'New media art' is, for me, a quite archaic term—it addresses primarily works (usually digital) that were made in the past—in the 1960s, 70s, 80s and 90s. I would hesitate to call works after 2000 'new media', and instead use the term 'digital'.

Of course, it's completely functional to define work with more than one term: as digital, as net art, as contemporary art, or as contemporary net-related art without being digital, et cetera, rather than just lumping them together in one category.

What is your background and what triggered your interest in digital/net art? Could you elaborate on these initial encounters?

M   Education-wise, I have a background in English philology, film studies, communication studies and art education. As a Film Studies graduate, I participated in the research project and online database Mediabaze (implemented by FAMU Prague) for which I worked, among others, on the profile of Czech-born and at that time Berlin-based artist Martin Kohout. So my first serious encounter with digital and Internet art was via net-based works by Martin Kohout, Constant Dullaart, and other Berlin-based artists. Net art quickly grabbed my attention and became the centre of my focus. (It was something I'd never seen before—a very different kind of moving image that had never been mentioned in the Film and Media department, where I felt it rightfully belongs, or at any other stage of my study.)

Another important encounter was PAF – Festival of Film Animation and Contemporary Art in Olomouc, Czech Republic, which explored topics such as digital culture, experimental film, audiovisual art, archiving, design, intermediality, animation, media archaeology, net art, re-mediation, video art, digital art, glitch art, etc., and the year-round activities of its organizers. This really shifted my professional interest away from television and cinema towards digital art, net art, and the art of the moving image. (I think that thanks to my background, I will always perceive digital/net art, historically and theoretically, in the context of the moving image and animation more than in any other contexts.)

In 2012, I started to work as curator under the moniker PAF, which has by now developed into a key Czech platform for the promotion and presentation of the moving image. In 2013 ScreenSaverGallery was established by Czech net art duo Barbora Trnková and Tomáš Javůrek, and I began collaborating with them that same year (SSG content is curated by Barbora, Tomáš, myself, and Berlin art historian Sakrowski). Later on I started collaborating with several other galleries and off-spaces. In 2014 I edited the first Czech anthology dedicated to Internet art.

Around 2011, I started using the alias (c) merry for my own work.

You've been involved in various types of organizations and spaces. Could you share some of your experiences working in these different settings and particular contexts? For example, how does it affect your practice? Are there specific things that work very well in one but not at all in the other context?

M	The spaces and places I'm involved with are all very specific, and are best compatible with site-specific or site-sensitive programming. They have different audiences, different financing, and they work with different dramaturgical approaches.

The works and programmes we present are not transferable as such, but some of them are adaptable for different contexts. Transfer involves adapting to a new context. The context of perception is for me of utmost importance: the artwork has to really 'work' well in the specific environment.

> There has always been a separation between people who stress the technological (material) developments of digital art and those who emphasize the art qualities (content/conceptual). At the same time digital art is also often accompanied by a fair amount of theoretical discussion. How do you position yourself in this discourse?

M	I'm primarily a theoretician, and my thinking is largely theoretical and very analytical. That explains my sensitivity and thinking about contexts and places, etc., and my tendency to favour conceptual artworks. However, I believe that the concept and content of the work have to go hand in hand with its technical processing. Every work needs some balance in this sense. Since I'm not sufficiently technically skilled, I often achieve such balance (as a curator as well as an artist) through collaborating with more technically qualified people. I am the concept creator and together we find ways to do it.

I prefer the art qualities to the technological ones. On the one hand a concept is something that can be understood and processed, while on the other, technology can be quite intimidating.

> You organize online and offline exhibitions. Starting with the latter, do you work with certain methods or criteria? For instance, I recall numerous discussions in the past where showing a computer monitor was 'not done', or some curators wouldn't even consider presenting net art in an exhibition at all, while others created entirely new installations based on online work. What are your thoughts/experiences with this?

M	I think I've answered this already... The question is what do you want to achieve? Sensitivity to the context is again my answer. Showing a computer monitor might be great or terrible, but it really depends on the context—the theme and content of the exhibition, the context of the audience, the institution, the geological and socio-cultural location, and last but not least, the context of time.

> Who do you see as your audience? I guess it changes with each new context but are there also changes (and/or exchanges) that you've noticed over the years, people moving from one place to another, or crossovers from other fields?

M   I always try to focus on an uninitiated public, rather than just please the close circuit of insiders. Everyone has the right to see the art in a way they can understand it. And if they're uninitiated, they often need some help, a description, examples, etc., to help them get to grips with the work. Of course it doesn't always turn out the way I envision it: usually the audience are 'experts', people who have at least some orientation in the field, professionals, students, regular attendees of PAF events.

Individuals approach me from time to time to thank me for opening up something new, wonderful and fascinating, for introducing them to something they didn't know existed. And that's great! Although I always think they are over-exaggerating, there aren't that many opportunities where you can meet, get used to and fall in love with digital art, especially in the local context. Cultural platforms like PAF change the situation in county towns like Olomouc, where they initiated people and focus attention on the topic. ScreenSaverGallery is amazing in spreading digital art worldwide, into schools, etc., especially thanks to projects like *Unleashing Screensaver* (ScreenSaverGallery and Teachers College, Columbia University, 1 April–31 May 2018).

What do you focus on in your online exhibitions/digital magazine?
M   I focus mainly on the moving image and digital art in relation to the moving image, conceptual art, and performance.

Should digital art enter established museums or organizations or are there better places where it can be preserved and presented? If so, what role should museums play in the future?
M   Without the involvement of museums, galleries and auction houses, digital art will not become part of school curricula, at least not in the Czech Republic. And because museums and schools are supposed to educate the future audience, without it, many will perceive digital art as a weird, marginal offshoot of contemporary art, without a long and important enough history. Too many would still question if it 'really is art'. For an audience without a relationship with digital art, it's hard to adopt a positive approach to it, to understand something without knowing the formal preparation and necessary context. And this also applies to the youngest generation of digital natives, who often seem to skim through online content and/or artworks without thinking deeply about them, thus decoding only little fragments of the information the works contain.

At the moment, the approach of major museums and art institutions to digital art in the Czech Republic is either that of keeping a sufficient distance, or a not very sensible one such as employing untrained staff who are unable to provide any information to visitors, cannot switch on or report a malfunctioning installation, and only have vague—almost none really—knowledge of preservation and restoration policies or collecting policy for digital artworks at all. By the way, the same applies to video art and the moving image. Perhaps it is connected to the under-financing of culture and especially arts in general, but also education.

The role of the museums should be to create places suitable to present digital art—smart places that would make digital art accessible and intelligible to broader public—but these places would have to be under their umbrellas, to be institutionalized.

Until recently in the Netherlands there was always a very good funding system for the arts in general and specifically for digital art. That has since changed, increasing on the one hand the divide between 'traditional' art and digital art, while on the other it generally means looking for money outside the funding system. Could you share some of your experiences working around the globe? How do you and the artists you work with survive?

M   Money is always an issue, especially if you don't work for large, established public institutions, but for non-profit small and independent regional galleries or online. There is no specific funding for digital art in the Czech Republic, but there is a possibility to ask for support from regional resources that enable you to organize a decent show. However, there is usually a limit to how much you can pay people from these public resources, so most of the work is done voluntarily, for a symbolic fee, or is severely underpaid. International grants like Norway Funds are great, because you can actually be paid for the amount of work you do. You can use stipends for individual work, but those are mostly for research and you have to be a doctorate student, or a young researcher affiliated with an institution or something like that. Universities have internal grants, but they usually have specific demands (they might be more for research and scientific publications than art). The endowment fund of Palacký University in Olomouc, for example, is unique in its support of international projects by talented Master's or PhD students—it supports not only hard scientific research, but also artistic activities. It's generally very hard to find money beyond public funding; if you're lucky enough to find a sponsor or benefactor, you might have ethical problems about where the money comes from.

To sum up: Making and presenting (or reflecting) art is rather a time-demanding, expensive 'hobby'. It's a matter of the heart, a selfless life mission—a crusade. Only the toughest manage to do it consistently, and for longer periods of time, let alone a lifetime. Everybody hopes for change, so that culture and art can thrive as they should.

I survive on stipends—a PhD stipend, then a Fulbright, and the Jan Hus Foundation enabled me to invest some time in producing culture. With a fulltime job I wouldn't be able to that. And doing cultural projects alone, as an artist, curator, writer or lecturer, wouldn't pay my rent. Artists usually teach or have other jobs, for example, as freelance curators.

ScreenSaverGallery was supported in the fifth year of its existence by the City of Brno, which enabled us to do some necessary software updates and cover fees connected with its online presence. But we never strove for financial support, since we cherished the strong ideals of independence, avant-garde and anarchy—as long as the situation was sustainable. To this day, there is no fee for artists, curators, or translators (of materials for our website). We're working hard on changing that. And even though ScreenSaverGallery is non-profit, and you don't pay anything to download the app, artists should be paid for their work.

ScreenSaverGallery was founded by Czech new media artists and researchers Barbora Trnková and Tomáš Javůrek alias &. Czech curator, theoretician and artist Marie Meixnerová (Mary Meixner) joined the project in 2013. ScreenSaverGallery is an online exhibition space and net art project using the computer screensaver as its medium. The inherent software feature of operating systems is transformed into a gallery space during moments of inactivity. The gallery's software application is downloadable online, and the exhibitions change automatically. Guest curators have included Sakrowski (DE), Dominik Podsiadly (PL), Anita Somrová (CZ), and Monika Szűcsová (SK).

Marie Meixnerová graduated in English Philology, Film Studies and Communication Studies from UPOL, Czech Republic, where she is finishing her PhD at the Department of Arts Education. She co-curates ScreenSaverGallery, is editor of the Experimental cinema section at the film and new media magazine *25fps*, and curator at PAF – Festival of Film Animation and Contemporary Art in Olomouc. She just started teaching at Theory of Interactive Media, Masaryk University, Faculty of Arts, Brno. She creates art under the name (c) merry.

1   R. Singer, *#selfie*, 2018. Photo: © B. Trnková. ScreenSaverGallery.
2   Jana Bernartova, *430–500 nm, ~ 700–600 THz*, 2018. Photo: © Studio Flusser. ScreenSaverGallery, Jan 18 – Feb 26 2018.

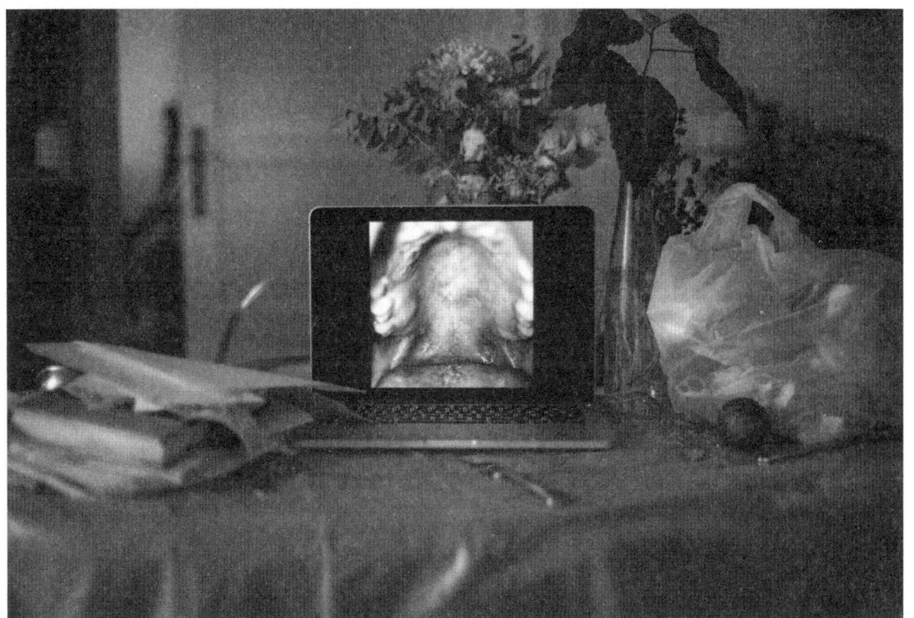

1

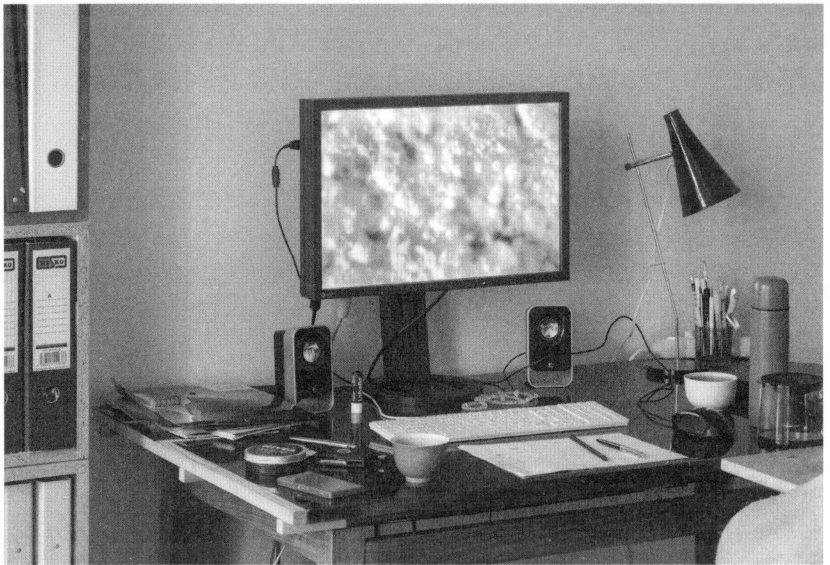

2

Systaime

INTERVIEWEE: SYSTAIME
PROJECT: VARIOUS – SPAMM, 2011–PRESENT
WEBSITE: *systaime.com*, *spamm.fr*
DATE: 12 APRIL 2019

Can we start by defining the terminology we're using and how you position yourself within existing categories like digital art, new media, net art, contemporary art, or any of the post-arts?

S   I'm an artist not a theorist, I usually express myself with pictures, videos, sounds and more but I can try to answer with words.

For me an artist is someone who speaks of his time through the different media and different mediums of his time. I try to create with an understanding that is necessary for this 'system', with immersion, emotion, humour, understanding, compassion and love, in order to divert or subvert it and to try and remain free in full awareness and not be slave to this life or this technology. I just try to give my vision of this time with my artist eyes ;) We are artists! I think we can use categories, but I'm talking about Art.

What is your background and what triggered your interest in digital/net art? Could you elaborate on these initial encounters?

S   I graduated from art school, primarily in painting. Later on, I wanted to be able to put my paintings on the Internet. My first computer was a doorway to a magical world and I soon realized that my computer and the Internet were so much more than mere tools to post my pictures online ;) They would be my new toolkit, media, medium and more for my creation and communication... and my creativity would expand exponentially. I started creating digital hybrid works in 1999, and I continue to experiment with different aspects of the Internet and tools.

I soon joined online communities where creators on the Internet were exhibiting on different platforms such as mailing lists, websites, blogs, etc. I realized that I wasn't alone ;) I started to experience the joys of online collaborations and of social media networks and then the Internet became even bigger, with audiences growing in tandem—it was a perfect playground for art and exchanges.

Society has changed dramatically because of how the Internet, computers and mobile phones have become embedded in daily life. Everyone is over-connected. I've been over-connected since 1999, but now I believe in a 'connection with consciousness', because every day we witness the excesses of information overload and its impact.

189

S   I always try to work low-tech and DIY, and I rarely engage
with theoretical problems, because I think that technology is just
a tool. Furthermore, accessing some technologies can be complicated and/or expensive, which often results in a kind of 'creative
poverty'.

I also like the idea of working in this way, because users
can project themselves onto the creative act and say 'I can do it'.
I like it when users can behave like artists, especially at exhibitions with immersive installations. Art is an attitude, a feeling,
a desire.

A large part of my work is always low-tech and DIY because I like to use easily accessible tools, and if its open source
then so much the better, as I will hopefully inspire others to be
creative with free tools. If you want do art you can do it! You
don't need technology or money, just your tools and ideas. I like
experimentation, I like sharing the Happyness of creativity.

Obviously, there are many theoretical and technological
works that I like a lot but it's not really my playground right now.

You organize online and offline exhibitions. Starting with the latter, do
you work with certain methods or criteria? For instance, I recall numerous
discussions in the past where showing a computer monitor was 'not done',
or some curators wouldn't even consider presenting net art in an exhibition
at all, while others created entirely new installations based on online work.
What are your thoughts/experiences with this?

S   The main model at the moment is social networks. For
example, most of the artists I discover are on Facebook or Instagram. Sometimes I also use the very convenient Facebook group
system to curate and to reunite artists. Otherwise, it's classic
curation. I work with the feeling I have on seeing the artworks. I
like discovering new artists, and some of them don't even think
that they're artists. It is very interesting to see trends evolve and
to discover new generations. It's art in perpetual evolution: a
very generous art in a global way. Most artists are very human,
very responsive and always very affordable. It's as if we enter the
artists' studio with just a few clicks. The energy of the web is in
its relationships and in art. The codes are certainly very different
from other movements or artistic backgrounds.

Regarding where and how to show it, I think that this art
should be everywhere. Even if the heart of this art reposes in the

centre of the Internet it must be shown everywhere in different forms and sometimes even take another direction. With *SPAMM [SuPer Art Modern Museum]* I chose to mainly exhibit videos, although sometimes we exhibit connected works or augmented reality in the 'white cube'. *SPAMM* adapts to all configurations and different places according to the space, the equipment and the public. The rule is that there are no rules, just FUN and the desire to show this art to as many people as possible.

> What do you focus on in your online exhibitions/digital magazine? In the past we've seen examples ranging from lists of links, to commissions, to documentation about a work, to embedding a work in a website? What is your preferred or even ideal 'model'?

S   For me the ideal model is streaming art and video works, ideally a TV channel or something like that, or maybe a physical museum.

> Should digital art enter established museums or organizations or are there better places where it can be preserved and presented? If so, what role should museums play in the future?

S   I think digital art belongs everywhere! The future role of museums should be to preserve this art even if its conservation seems complex.

> Until recently in the Netherlands there was always a very good funding system for the arts in general and specifically for digital art. That has since changed, increasing on the one hand the divide between 'traditional' art and digital art, while on the other it generally means looking for money outside the funding system. Could you share some of your experiences working around the globe? How do you and the artists you work with survive?

S   Everyone has a different experience. A lot of artists work at arts schools, agencies, hotels or cafes, or are freelancers and make clips, do publicity or somesuch, because it's not easy to sell art or be paid for exhibitions. Life, you know... Some countries provide public funding and some artists spend a lot of time on dealing with the administration so that they can access this money ;) I've never applied for funding or had sponsors or a maecenas for my art, and this also applies to *SPAMM*.

But if we focus only on art, in general it's very difficult to live from art and even more so if you make dematerialized art. The arrival of the post-Internet movement with 're'-materialization can provide an answer. There are also more and more online websites where you can buy art with money or sometimes cryptocurrencies. It's just the beginning but there are some examples of art websites, gifs or YouTube videos that have

 been successfully auctioned.

For the moment, *SPAMM* works a little like the open source web and is always free. For example, one exhibition was managed in collaboration with the Arte channel, which enabled us to pay the artists who participated in an online exhibition in 2013. It was a little revolution ;) I'm still looking for the ideal economic model for *SPAMM* and for the artists. My objectives are to continue the project and to discover and exhibit artworks from around the world, and especially to be able to finance other exhibitions and to pay the artists and curators who collaborate on some future exhibitions. Even though *SPAMM* doesn't earn any income, it offers great visibility and contacts with artists that could trigger other projects. We need more!

One of the things that fascinates me about *SPAMM*, the *SuPer Art Modern Museum*, a file-based exhibition space, is how it is both physical and virtual space at the same time and how they connect and relate. Could you explain your approach, perhaps also in relation to your own work such as *Thug Lilith*, *Internet Ecology* or your eBay project? And what is your interest and perspective when it comes to digital preservation, documentation and collecting?

S   Initially, *SPAMM* was created in 2011 to generate greater exposure for digital art because at that time, institutions and galleries didn't really care about this kind of art or didn't know how to exhibit it. So it was a case of 'if they don't exhibit us we'll exhibit ourselves'. Galleries, alternative art spaces and institutions contacted us soon afterwards and exhibitions were held in physical spaces all around the world (Caracas, New York, Paris, Naples, Chicago, London). *SPAMM* is not opposed to institutions or the classic gallery system. *SPAMM* is positioned as a link between the online world of the Internet and the physical world of art.

I like to organize physical shows without being physically present but it's always better if I have the pleasure of finally meeting artists who I've usually only interacted with online, sometimes for quite a while. More and more digital art exhibitions initiatives are being held around the world and that's an encouraging sign.

Every artist is different. I conserve nothing. I put my art online and believe in natural disappearance or conservation, it's like my art has its own life. Sometimes my videos disappear or an anonymous YouTuber reposts one of my old works. It's funny...

But the conservation, preservation and documentation of this art is important. I'm sure there's a lot of Internet art collecting, documenting and preserving that we don't know about. I think it was the same for every art movement, for example, maybe only 10% of Dadaist art has been preserved and the same goes for others art movements. The difference now is that we have Internet and it's more or less like semi-permanent conservation if artists put their works online.

SPAMM, the *SuPer Art Modern Museum*, is an international platform of Internet artists, a space open to digital creation, and a decentralized alternative to the elitism of contemporary art. Founded by the French net-artist Systaime, at the beginning of French Trash Touch (a nod to the French techno vein that brought Daft Punk & Co. to international attention), *SPAMM* is the emanation of a net culture that defends open access to creation and appropriation by digital artists of their work and exhibition space.

Systaime a.k.a. Michaël Borras (France) is the anti-system of art. Systaime is a pure shoot of Net, a datamoshing and smash up virtuoso. Systaime exhibits himself and the web, without licked screen or trickle of flashy modern media. He is the historic agitator who, with his *SuPer Art Modern Museum* (*SPAMM*) gained widespread acceptance by exposing the Tom Thumbs of digital culture online and in-town, from Caracas to Milan, from New York to Brussels.

1–2   Systaime a.k.a. Michaël Borras, *Internet Ecology*, 2019, print on dibond.

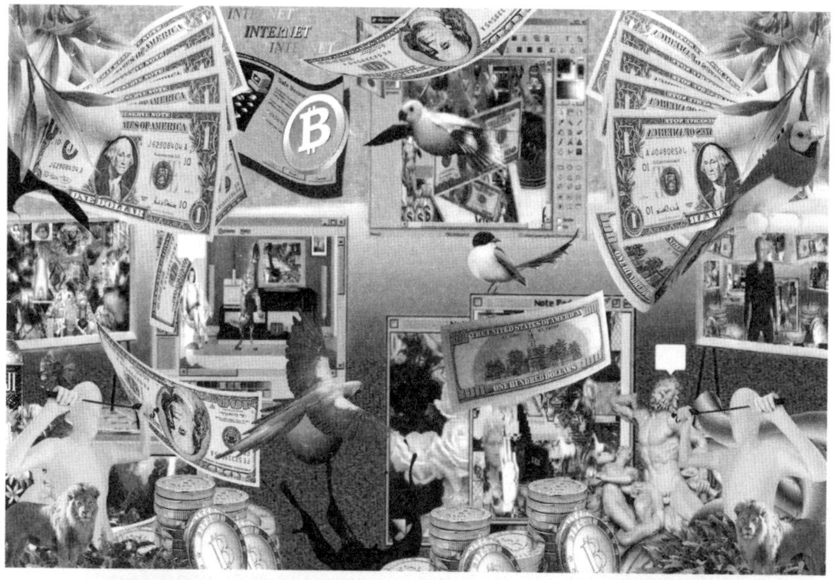

1

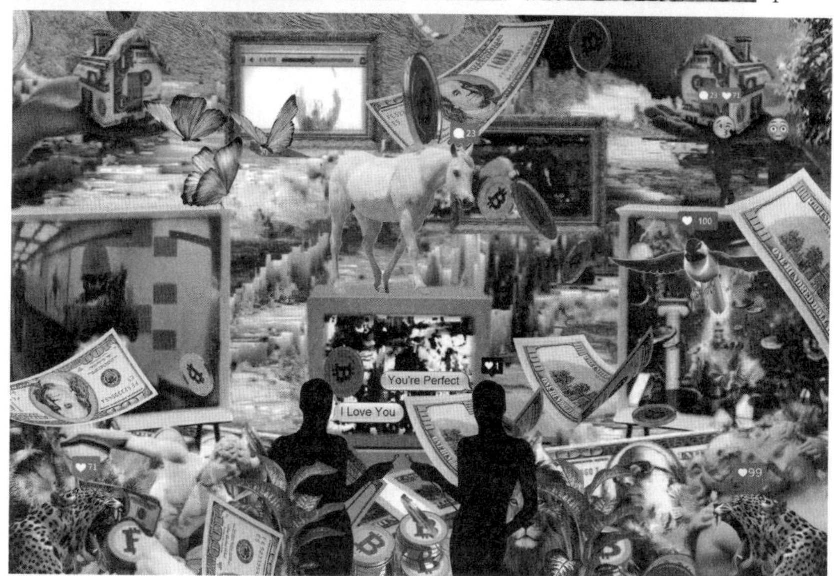

2

195

Florian Kuhlmann

INTERVIEWEE: FLORIAN KUHLMANN
PROJECT: SUPER INFORMATION HIGH MARKET, 2017
WEBSITE: *floriankuhlmann.com*
DATE: 16 APRIL 2019

Can we start by defining the terminology we're using and how you position yourself within existing categories like digital art, new media, net art, contemporary art, or any of the post-arts?

F   I don't really regard myself as an artist, or as falling into either one or other niche. The Internet and the digital interest me, and I sometimes interact with them from an arts perspective. In such moments I would define myself as an artist, but only for a limited time. Art for me is a field in which I act, but I do not want to limit myself to it.

What is your background and what triggered your interest in digital/net art? Could you elaborate on these initial encounters?

F   The relationship between art and digital technology has fascinated me for over twenty years. This fascination peaks when both come together. Net art is still a great passion for me. I also still like the screen a lot. I first came into contact with it during my studies at the KHM [Academy of Media Arts Cologne] in the early 2000s.

You've been involved in various types of organizations and spaces. Could you share some of your experiences working in these different settings and particular contexts? For example, how does it affect your practice? Are there specific things that work very well in one but not at all in the other context?

F   Most of the projects I've worked on have been my initiatives and I also edited most of them, such as *digital3mpire*, the exhibitions I curated, or the Perisphere blog. I've only collaborated with institutions or galleries for the past few years. That makes it a little easier I think, and it's great to have a partner, especially for the publicity. I'm not very good at self-promotion, so I'm glad when someone else takes care of that.

There has always been a separation between people who stress the technological (material) developments of digital art and those who emphasize the art qualities (content/conceptual). At the same time digital art is also often accompanied by a fair amount of theoretical discussion. How do you position yourself in this discourse?

F   Yes, I've also noticed this separation. As an artist, I rather belong to the latter. Content and concept are very important to me, as is context. All in all, I would probably define my art of recent years as digital context art. Conceptual art could also work as a definition. I more often develop ambitious technical projects in my function as a software developer on behalf of customers.

197   These often relate to ensuring technical stability. However, for my art projects this never really interests me. Many tech-driven works tend to lose themselves in endless possibilities or are made as gimmicks and are not very sustainable.

> You organize online and offline exhibitions. Starting with the latter, do you work with certain methods or criteria? For instance, I recall numerous discussions in the past where showing a computer monitor was 'not done', or some curators wouldn't even consider presenting net art in an exhibition at all, while others created entirely new installations based on online work. What are your thoughts/experiences with this?

F   Regardless of whether I'm working on- or offline, I focus on the content while trying to preserve the core of the digital and strive to maintain the essence of net art. One example would be the 'local-non projects' in which I organize very classical net art group exhibitions that I can only make locally accessible. For a long time I only showed my work on a screen because the ephemeral nature of the digital was always important to me, and I saw it as intrinsic to the work. Over time I've become a little more flexible and less dogmatic.

> Who do you see as your audience? I guess it changes with each new context but are there also changes (and/or exchanges) that you've noticed over the years, people moving from one place to another, or crossovers from other fields?

F   That's a good question and I don't have an answer. I'd really like to know too! I have noticed, however, that artists respond to my work more strongly than curators and collectors.

> Should digital art enter established museums or organizations or are there better places where it can be preserved and presented? If so, what role should museums play in the future?

F   Digital art, especially net art, loses a lot of its power in a museum. After all, we wanted to become independent of the institutions, occupy new areas and break up and bypass established power relations. Looking back, one has to admit that this did not quite succeed, at least not as we'd hoped. But I think that's a more general problem of the net. We were too naïve, and the promises of freedom and liberation remain unfulfilled. I would therefore not continue to dogmatically cling to this notion of the autonomy of net art.

Generally, I would welcome it if museums nowadays became more aware of their historic role as archives and preserve digital and net-based works in their collections. Much of what has been created on the net in the last few decades is slowly disappearing.

I recently had a few discussions with artists and producers about the usefulness of open source, it seems that although all kinds of codes and suchlike are available they're hardly ever used, mainly because of the personal approach to coding and the complexity that derives from such project-based work. What is your approach to open source in this context?

F   Open source is still an important approach for me. I've been making all my artistic images available as free downloads with THE GIFT under a Creative Commons license for years. The images are still there today and will remain so. With regards to technology and code, in general I would only work with open source and if at all possible not use proprietary software for artistic works, not least because of issues such as maintenance, updates and archivability.

Until recently in the Netherlands there was always a very good funding system for the arts in general and specifically for digital art. That has since changed, increasing on the one hand the divide between 'traditional' art and digital art, while on the other it generally means looking for money outside the funding system. Could you share some of your experiences working around the globe? How do you and the artists you work with survive?

F   Most of the artists I know have a regular job in addition to their artistic practice, and this applies to me too: I make a living as a programmer. The downside of this of course is that it takes me longer to develop my ideas or create new works and projects. But I also appreciate being independent of the arts (funding) system—which I increasingly experience as merely annoying. I used to receive project grants in the past, but I realized that the bureaucracy that comes with it bothers me too much and that it's not worth the effort. My autonomy is very important to me and therefore I try to distance myself as much as possible from the structures of the arts system. The Internet has enabled me to do this for many years, and I've always liked that a lot.

One of the things that fascinates me about *super information high market* is, as you mention, how shopping is an act of curating. Could you explain your approach, perhaps also in relation to your other work such as *Metamoderne* or the offline project space and hub *#digital3mpire*? And what is your interest and perspective when it comes to digital preservation, documentation and collecting?

F   Affirmation is an important for me. I like to accept things and criticize them at the same time, and this ambivalence is also a core element of *Metamoderne*. Above all, *Metamoderne* is characterized by the ambivalence of our times; it is a lived contradiction that we find ourselves in continuously. Being 'metamodern' means to oscillate between the different poles and to put ourselves into what quantum physics calls a 'super

 position'—a stable but undefined state, open in all directions.

Super information high market is the economy in total and constant flux that has merged with life into a new form of reality based on an intense information stream powered by the endless sources of energy extracted from deep within the earth core. In the *super information high market* everything is connected. It is the last product of a globalized, hyper-capitalistic techno machine and the result of the final massive bailout of the last remaining super company after this has collapsed. In the *super information high market* the virtual, the augmented and reality merge into a higher surrogate of consciousness. Driven by the last forces of capital, boosted by Internet technology in combination with the deep understanding and usage of morphogenetic fields, the world is transformed into a surreal dreamtime state, where being is a continuous oscillation between TRUE and FALSE. This form is stabilizing and reassuring but also highly stimulating at the same time.

Florian Kuhlmann has never been an artist and he never will be one. He has worked full-time as a software developer and as a metamodern poet at NON in Düsseldorf since 2006. He qualified as computer scientist in 2000 and began working in the new economy. From 2002 to 2007 he studied audiovisual media at the Academy of Media Arts in Cologne. The focus of his work and cybernetic research is the digital, and its globalized, networked infrastructures aka the Internet, including its newly emerging contexts. For more than fifteen years he has been engaged in various roles, which are increasingly dominated by the computer and a vague idea of a metamodern being.

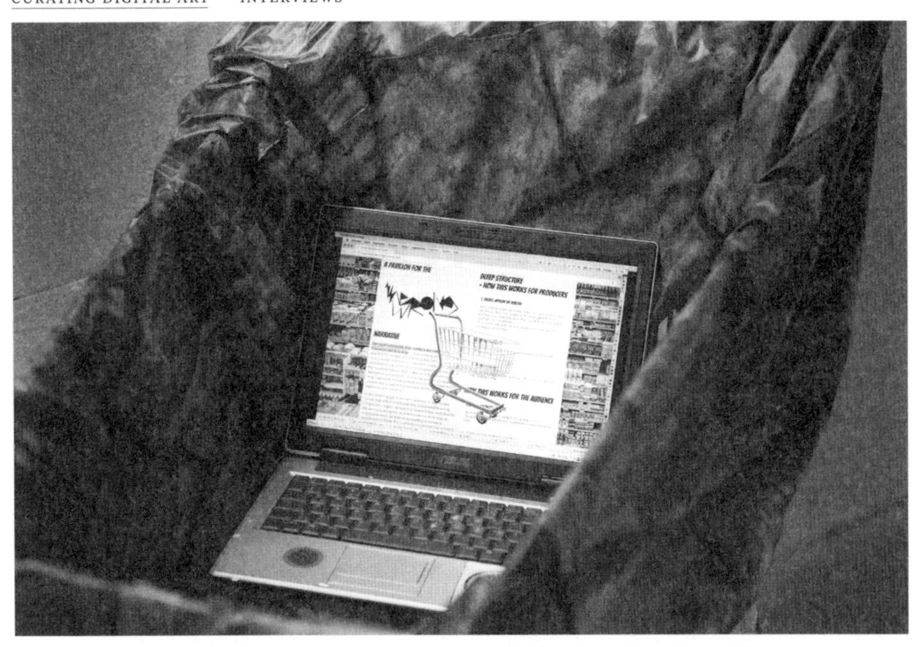

ART AS THE LAST
OPEN SOURCE
SUPERPRODUCT

HTTP://SUPER-INFORMATION-HIGH-MARKET.COM
AN ONLINE PAVILLON

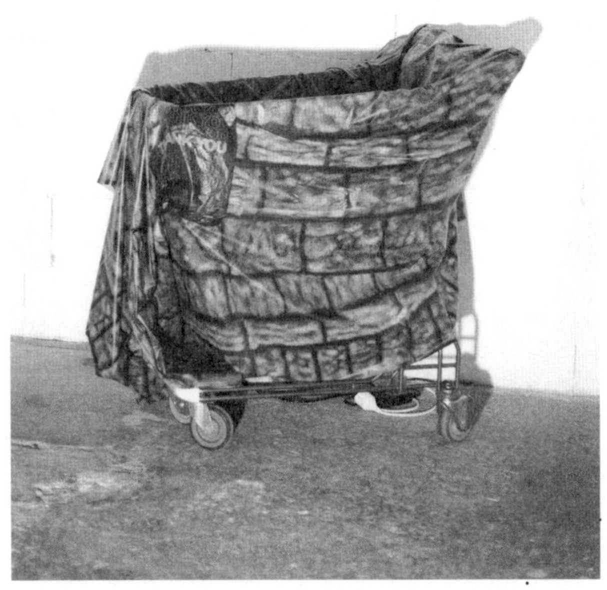

New Scenario (Paul Barsch & Tilman Hornig)

INTERVIEWEES: NEW SCENARIO (PAUL BARSCH AND TILMAN HORNIG)
PROJECT: NEW SCENARIO, 2015–PRESENT
WEBSITE: *newscenario.net*
DATE: 1 MAY 2019

Can we start by defining the terminology we're using and how you position yourself within existing categories like digital art, new media, net art, contemporary art, or any of the post-arts?

P & T   To be honest we don't care much about categories and we think they're rather limiting and misleading. *New Scenario* is a curatorial project with an artistic approach (or the other way around) that displays physical artworks in physical, narrative settings through digital online presentation. The artists involved represent all kinds of categories and genres of art. The digital platform we use to present our exhibition projects is the most convenient, manageable, cost-saving and easy-to-maintain tool that we have right now, which leaves us a lot of freedom to experiment with formats and presentation. On top of that, everyone has easy access to it from anywhere in the world. Of course, we also use digital software and applications in the post-production process, but a lot of the production is physical and hands-on. We work with collaborators and people who have skills we do not, such as coding. All this has to do with (or not really anything to do with) the abovementioned categories because we operate on the edges of curating, exhibition-making and artistic production and thus across the borders of these categories.

What is your background and what triggered your interest in digital/net art? Could you elaborate on these initial encounters?

P & T   We both received relatively classical training in fine arts at Dresden Art Academy with a focus on painting, but with a lot of freedom to experiment, which Tilman did in Martin Honert's sculpture class and I did in Lutz Dammbeck's new media class. Around that time, when the post-Internet soup started to cook and Tumblr was the place to be, we also started running Tumblr blogs and following what was happening. The direct response from the audience was triggering. Blogs like *The Jogging* were fun to follow and we felt that after two decades of hollow, mindless 'Dachlattenkunst', some new visual and conceptual approaches were emerging that also considered the documentation or staging of an artwork—its virtual being—to be an integral part of its existence.

You've been involved in various types of organizations and spaces. Could you share some of your experiences working in these different settings and particular contexts? For example, how does it affect your practice? Are there specific things that work very well in one context but not at all in another?

P&T   Coming from a rarely noticed art scene in Dresden and our involvement in different art and music projects has taught us that you have to do things yourself. If you want your projects to be seen, you can't wait for people to come to you; you have to find ways to get your projects noticed. Of course, each project involves different demands and structures. Running an exhibition space requires different tasks and skills; running *New Scenario* requires others. But in principle the two are similar, and everything depends on your approach and on what you want to do and achieve. You can learn new skills, or find help to get them done, be it having to learn to use a camera because you were never satisfied with a photographer's documentation, or learning how to post-process videos because there's no one on hand to do it, or finding specialists to fly a drone... It's not so much a matter of skills and control but of self-confidence, and of knowing that you aren't dependent on certain infrastructures and predefined rules, but that you can build your own structures and set your own rules, just as you would—or should—with your art.

There has always been a separation between people who stress the technological (material) developments of digital art and those who emphasize the art qualities (content/conceptual). At the same time digital art is also often accompanied by a fair amount of theoretical discussion. How do you position yourself in this discourse?

P&T   We definitely emphasise the art qualities. One of the main reasons why we started *New Scenario* was because we noticed that there was a lack of new concepts in curating, as much in online projects as IRL. Technological developments in the different fields of art aren't worth much if they aren't coupled with content and concept. Art that only revolves manneristically around its own medium and feasibilities is bad art. The same problem can be seen with a lot of recent offside shows. A fair amount of these shows simply happen somewhere outside the usual exhibition space, without much thought put into the location or space in general. If you leave (or reject) the neutrality of the white cube, then why would you want to show art in an uninteresting junkyard or playground for the hundreth time? If the neutrality is gone, then the backdrop matters, and it has to be considered. It becomes an integral part of the presentation and corresponds with the artworks. A random and unconsidered backdrop can render the works dull.

You organize online and offline exhibitions. Starting with the latter, do you work with certain methods or criteria? For instance, I recall numerous discussions in the past where showing a computer monitor was 'not done', or some curators wouldn't even consider presenting net art in an exhibition at all, while others created entirely new installations based on online work. What are your thoughts/experiences with this?

P&T   One of our main criteria is to create something that we would like to see, something visually and conceptually challenging that hasn't been done yet or that we find worth investigating. We have no specific method. Each project follows different concepts and ideas, and therefore demands different approaches and realizations. We try not to limit ourselves or the artworks' abilities or qualities and we don't respect artificial boundaries. It's all just a matter of how you present a work within your conceptual parameters. We consider the artworks we work with to be materials but we also take them seriously on their own terms; they have to be able to unfold their potential and be able to resonate within the context we choose to present them in.

Who do you see as your audience? I guess it changes with each new context but are there also changes (and/or exchanges) that you've noticed over the years, people moving from one place to another, or crossovers from other fields?

P&T   We don't really know who our audience is. The platform is accessible to anyone with an Internet connection. Google Analytics shows us that thousands of people visit the site, but not who they are. We assume the main audience is artists, people from the art field and creatives in general, but there are probably also random people who somehow stumble across our platform.

What do you focus on in your online exhibitions/digital magazine? In the past we've seen examples ranging from lists of links, to commissions, to documentation about a work, to embedding a work in a website? What is your preferred or even ideal 'model'?

P&T   We focus on very special settings, narrative qualities and challenging concepts. There is no ideal model for us. We also don't consider our platform to be a digital magazine: it's more a framework for presenting our exhibition projects. All exhibitions (with some exceptions) are presented as 'websites' that are navigable with a browser. The digitality of the platform is not mandatory, but at the moment it's the most convenient form. A future project could just as well happen IRL, or in an exaggerated example, it could take the form of an audio experience on a cassette tape. The shape that it takes really depends on the idea and the concept behind it.

Should digital art enter established museums or organizations or are there better places where it can be preserved and presented? If so, what role should museums play in the future?

P & T   We don't know. Digital art should try to establish its own digital museums and institutions that go beyond the traditional models, collections, and modes of presentation and conservation. It makes no sense to try to enter a structure that is already in crisis. Of course, museums should think about collecting and preserving digital art, but doing so requires a mindset that is able to understand the contexts, environments, references and purposes of digital artworks. In general, digital art is easy to store, lightweight and space saving. That being said, digital art requires specific hardware and playback devices to present it, which, due to the ever-changing nature of technology, requires a high level of maintenance. A certain flexibility is necessary in regards to presenting digital art, which means that the fetishism of devices and surfaces probably has to be abandoned in favour of visual and conceptual qualities. Just as a Greek sculpture functions perfectly in the digital domain, digital art must also be able to assert itself in various and future aggregate states, otherwise it will vanish.

I recently had a few discussions with artists and producers about the usefulness of open source, it seems that although all kinds of codes and suchlike are available they're hardly ever used, mainly because of the personal approach to coding and the complexity that derives from such project-based work. What is your approach to open source in this context?

P & T   We think that open source, sharing and collaboration are good things. However, when it comes to actual coding, we don't have much expertise. We don't code our projects; a friend of ours does. He probably works with open source code. But if we had to code ourselves, open source would help us a lot.

Until recently in the Netherlands there was always a very good funding system for the arts in general and specifically for digital art. That has since changed, increasing on the one hand the divide between 'traditional' art and digital art, while on the other it generally means looking for money outside the funding system. Could you share some of your experiences working around the globe? How do you and the artists you work with survive?

P & T   *New Scenario* was started without any funding and we put a lot of effort and work into the projects, supported by friends and the generous trust of the participating artists. We paid for and produced the first four exhibition projects ourselves. After that we received some public funding and/or production budgets from in-stitutions that enabled us to eventually pay a fee to the participating artists, to our coder, other helpers, and ourselves. Yet we still do most of the work ourselves: the production, post-production and communication, as well as everything else. The less money there is, the more we have to develop smart solutions to get the best out of a project, conceptually and visually. There is no way of making a living out of it yet because there's never any money left over, but we try as much as possible to pay fees (which is usually rare when you exhibit as an artist). Part of *New Scenario*'s mission is to establish this platform as a serious institution in order to raise money easily and distribute it among the artists, or even eventually to find a way to become financially independent. Being artists ourselves we know how it is. We have to survive just like everyone else and make our art while doing related projects and odd jobs to survive—it's not an ideal situation right now.

> You describe *New Scenario* as a 'dynamic platform for conceptual, time-based and performative exhibition formats, which happens outside the realm of the white cube and is meant to function as an extension to create new contextual meaning'. I very much like how it plays with new methods and approaches to the white cube exhibition space, and also that it can only be viewed online. In that way, I'm drawn to how you address the conventional approach to documentation. Could you explain your methodology? And what is your interest and perspective when it comes to digital preservation, documentation and collecting?

P & T   Having only online access to the exhibition projects removes the sensual experience of space, but at the same time it strengthens the conceptual and narrative qualities and draws the exhibition and thus the works of art into an imaginative sphere, where anything can happen. If the documented scene and the location in which the exhibition takes place are strong enough and if the artworks and their surroundings can interact and communicate with each other, they are able to transcend the documentation and turn it into an experience that is able to replace a spatial experience. Many attempts have been made to digitally replicate a white cube experience online, but only to disillusioning effect. The virtual white cube becomes a backdrop, a quasi-space with an auratic function that re-evaluates the role of documentation and gives the artwork the credibility of being exhibited in a gallery. It's an easy way to bypass an exclusive gallery system, but it can't compete with a physical white cube experience. What we do instead is shift the physical exhibition space into the production phase and the documentation into that of the experiential (online) exhibition. This allows us to experiment with formats and space and it opens up room for the artistic design and creation of these different stages, without having to worry about whether a human spectator can physically enter the space. The exhibition space can be completely inhospitable or physically inaccessible to a human viewer (cf. *New Scenario*'s *BODY HOLES*). Due to the relative elimination of the spatial and material restrictions of a gallery space and the relatively free design of the navigation and narration of the exhibition, the possibilities of incorporating other elements such as text, objects and timelines are manifold. Image production, however, is paramount, since the projects are only accessible via their images, so the expressiveness, narrative structure and conceptual presentation of the images are crucial. At this point, it is no longer possible to curatorially bring the artworks into an intellectual and spatial context using known formulas. The creation of (an experience in) online exhibitions requires making artistic decisions in order to generate the corresponding images that stage and support the exhibition and the exhibited artworks.

We make every effort to keep the exhibitions accessible. We aren't dependent on certain spatially conditioned opening times like a gallery; at our own discretion, we can let the projects run forever and in parallel. As far as conservation is concerned, the original material will probably have to be secured from time to time, and the programmed substructure of the platform will have to be adapted to evolving web standards.

New Scenario is a curatorial project founded by the artists Paul Barsch and Tilman Hornig, which operates on the edge of curating, exhibition making and artistic production and has been conceiving online exhibitions with international artists in spectacular narrative settings outside the white cube since 2015. *BODY HOLES*, an exhibition exploring the natural orifices of the human body as practical exhibition spaces for art, was part of the 9th Berlin Biennale's online section *Fear Of Content*.
www.newscenario.net

1   BB5000, *True To You When I Punch You*, 2016. Courtesy of the artist and New Scenario. Photo: New Scenario. Produced by New Scenario for BODY HOLES, 2015.

2   Tilman Hornig, *Elastobabe*, 2015. Courtesy of the artist and New Scenario. Photo: Stefan Haehnel. Produced by New Scenario for CRASH, 2015.

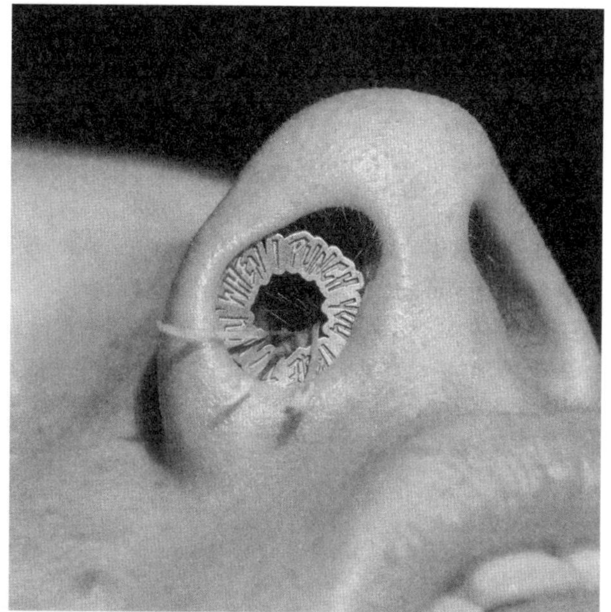

1

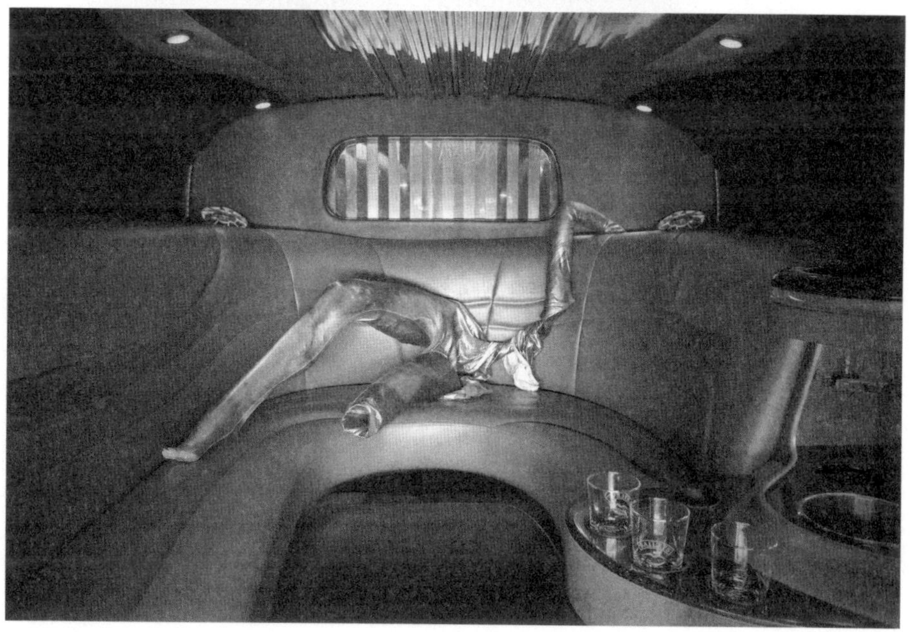

2

Nimrod Vardi
& Rebecca Edwards

INTERVIEWEES: NIMROD VARDI, REBECCA EDWARDS
PROJECT: AREBYTE, EST. 2013–PRESENT
WEBSITE: *arebyte.com*
DATE: 7 MAY 2019

Can we start by defining the terminology we're using and how you position yourself within existing categories like digital art, new media, net art, contemporary art, or any of the post-arts?

N & R   We're excited by new developments in the tech industry, and by observing how the artists we work with use these innovations. Ultimately we would position ourselves firmly within emerging media; however, we're also sensitive and conscious of older ways of working in digital art such as early web development or gif making, and we try to have a good mix of old and new.

At its core, arebyte aims to rethink and redefine what a space for art is or what it could or should be. We are a place to exhibit digital art and emerging media, but we're also a place to meet, converse, work and think, which is something we hope brings about an openness, or inclusiveness, to our programme of exhibitions, workshops and events. We also aim to bring innovative perspectives to art through an interdisciplinary approach at the intersection of new technologies and social sciences.

What is your background and what triggered your interest in digital/net art? Could you elaborate on these initial encounters?

N   I've been fascinated with the digital since I was a kid—I was always on the computer, whether inside or outside. In 2013 I realized that I should connect my love for art to my passion for the digital and focus the gallery on whatever is 'digital'. My Master's is about curating the virtual object and the role of the curator within a 'Google Search' visual reference world, which has been my area of interest for the last five years: the non-human curator and the importance of the human hand/rationale in the curatorial process.

R   Being a member of that weird 89plus generation who have known life both with and without social media, smartphones and the Internet, I became interested in the digital in my early teens. I was obsessed with Blingee, MSN Messenger and MySpace, and with trying out AutoCAD and Microsoft Encarta on my dad's desktop computer. I was very fortunate to be able to access technology at a young age, and observing its development over the last couple of decades has been exciting. I started seriously thinking about curating the digital when I began my Master's in curatorial studies. This was back in 2014 when some really exciting artists were coming to the fore and exhibiting in London,

213

like Amalia Ulman, Ryan Trecartin, Sara Ludy and Joey Holder. I remember when I saw *Modern Family* by Ed Fornieles at the Chisenhale, which used the live content of social media profiles to question the value we attach to likes, shares and reposts, and being thrilled to be part of this art world.

> You've been involved in various types of organizations and spaces. Could you share some of your experiences working in these different settings and particular contexts? For example, how does it affect your practice? Are there specific things that work very well in one context but not at all in another?

N   I've only been doing work for arebyte or my own work, which is always related in one way or another to arebyte. At some point people referred to me as arebyte on social media. I found it hard to penetrate the London scene, so it was easier to open my own space, which also allowed me to do whatever I wanted to. From the beginning the main idea was to open up the space so that more artists, curators and organizations can participate in the process. I think it enabled us to really understand the role of art galleries and institutions in general and that whatever we do we are part of a much larger system.

R   Before I joined arebyte I'd curated a couple of shows in the UK but these were all very different. I worked on one of the *Testing Ground* exhibitions at the Zabludowicz, and curated exhibitions and events at The Royal College of Psychiatrists, SE8 Gallery and the Great Central in Leicester, as well as pop-ups in pubs and friends' living rooms. Most of the exhibitions were curated by a group or two people, which I have always found to be better than working alone. There's so much more open dialogue and discussion to be had, which results in better exhibitions. I was also an avid writer, producing and making my own books.

> There has always been a separation between people who stress the technological (material) developments of digital art and those who emphasize the art qualities (content/conceptual). At the same time digital art is also often accompanied by a fair amount of theoretical discussion. How do you position yourself in this discourse?

N & R   Quite simply, we don't. We try not to position ourselves with a specific agenda but rather examine everything on an artist-by-artist basis. We've had projects that rely quite heavily on a theoretical concept, as well as projects where the technology used is the core of the work. For us it's about getting a balance between the two: situating work within a theoretical framework is important, but so is an aptitude for the material or medium each artist works with. We enjoy reading new and old theory but aren't imprisoned by it—it's good to have a grounding, or an anchor, with these things, but it's not imperative to creating good work.

> You organize online and offline exhibitions. Starting with the latter, do you work with certain methods or criteria? For instance, I recall numerous discussions in the past where showing a computer monitor was 'not done', or some curators wouldn't even consider presenting net art in an exhibition at all, while others created entirely new installations based on online work. What are your thoughts/experiences with this?

N & R   Presentation of this kind of work is very fluid, as it follows the media that is used. We like to test the boundaries in terms of the space that this type of work occupies: for Lawrence Lek's show *Nøtel,* we created something akin to a gaming table in the middle of the gallery, with screens rising up out of the floor like totem poles. We've used all types of display devices in other exhibitions, from monitors, to customized computers; we're not concerned with conventions. What matters is that it's right for the exhibition and the artist's work.

> Who do you see as your audience? I guess it changes with each new context but are there also changes (and/or exchanges) that you've noticed over the years, people moving from one place to another, or crossovers from other fields?

N & R   We recently relocated the gallery from Hackney Wick to Canning Town. Our lease in Hackney Wick ended with all the redevelopment of the area but we also felt we'd outgrown the space we had. Our new gallery is four times larger than the old one, with much more visibility and options to create more experimental and ambitious exhibitions. Contrary to what we expected, moving to this new location didn't affect us in terms of our audience, which has actually grown dramatically since we relocated, something we didn't expect to happen that quickly. Art audiences in London are always looking for something new and many are willing to travel beyond the typical art scenes to engage with cultural offerings, which is reassuring given the rising rents of more central areas. We feel there's a shift within the London art scene where new galleries are appearing in relatively unknown parts of town; there's a spirit of spontaneity and assertiveness that appears to be thriving even in uncertain times.

Due to the diversity of the people we work with in our exhibitions, we have audiences from a variety of areas such as music, gaming, science and architecture, which is really inspiring. For our online programme our audiences are from all parts of the world, from Japan to Canada, which reflects the huge potential and span for online work and online artists.

I recently had a few discussions with artists and producers about the usefulness of open source, it seems that although all kinds of codes and suchlike are
available they're hardly ever used, mainly because of the personal approach to
coding and the complexity that derives from such project-based work. What is
your approach to open source in this context?

N   The staff and myself are not coders, but a lot of our artists
are and we like to participate in these discussions. For us open
source is more a state of mind and a value that flows through
our organization in various forms. The idea of being an open
source organization is something we think about more and
more. What this means in practice is being open and accessible
to anyone who contacts us, and allowing others to participate in
our process, by co-programming, for example. We don't have a
wall separating our office from the gallery, which means that the
audience has a direct relationship with us and we with them.

You're one of the curators for arebyte Gallery for which you organize different
types of online exhibitions/projects. Could you explain your approach, also
in relation to the related activities at the gallery? And what is your interest
and perspective when it comes to digital preservation, documentation and
collecting the things you exhibit?

N & R   Working with new media gives us the opportunity to do
things regardless of physical space, which opens up more opportunities to experiment curatorially. This has recently manifested
in a new online programme we launched in early 2019, *arebyte
on screen* (*AOS*). It's similar to an online channel, open to the
public 24/7, and viewable on aos.arebyte.com and via a dedicated
screen in our gallery window in London. The channel show-
cases artists, but also curators, either independent or working
in galleries worldwide, who we invite to experiment with the
platform. *AOS* is a space to show and exhibit new forms of art
and projects, experiment with curatorial work and processes, and
show digital- and media-art related content.

Each year our online and physical art programme features
a mix of UK and international artists and guest curators, enabling
us to contextualize our work internationally and create a dialogue
between London and other art scenes. Since 2017, we've also run
hotel generation, a young graduate development scheme for digital
artists from UK regional cities. The skills-focused programme allows
them to have a sense of place in the London art scene, which is
notoriously difficult to infiltrate, and we hope to equip them with
the expertise to manage sustainable careers. This part of the programme is especially exciting for me as a young curator because I get
to see the next generation of digital artists progressing and gaining

 confidence, as well as invaluable skills and advice, under our care.

We recently went to a symposium at Central Saint Martins on the preservation and archiving of digital work, especially VR and AR. This was really eye opening because many of the panellists had some sort of strategy in terms of archiving, but as yet there's nothing that could be universally adopted. This is especially true of digital preservation, where works can easily be lost or corrupted. At the moment these are institutional tools that aren't suitable for mid-scale organizations like us—not many of us have these specific skills or knowledge and few can afford to hire a specialist to do this kind of work.

As we aren't a commercial gallery this isn't necessarily a huge concern for us yet, but it's something that does concern the artists we work with, especially those who have sold a webpage work, for example. This then opens up questions about responsibility for upkeep, or renewing the domain, all of which changes depending on the collector or artist.

> What do you focus on in your online exhibitions/digital magazine? In the past we've seen examples ranging from lists of links, to commissions, to documentation about a work, to embedding a work in a website? What is your preferred or even ideal 'model'?

N & R   We like to explore whatever is possible, and a lot is possible. Our current online exhibition programme, *AOS*, is a platform dedicated to artist videos, multimedia experiences and curatorial interventions utilizing digital formats to address current political, economic and theoretical discussion. There are three strands, which allows us to experiment in different ways:

> *...by arebyte* which showcases material created by the arebyte team and educational partners, relating to our physical shows in the gallery, as well as earlier screen-based works by alumni artists;
> *...by artists* which is an artist-led curatorial programme, where selected artists present online work and invite their peers to create a succession of content; and
> *...by guest curators*, which invites four curators each year from international digital art galleries, online spaces, biennales and festivals to present online projects and commissions.

As we mentioned, the work is viewable 24/7 both online and via a screen in the gallery window which enables us to bring the virtual into the real, something we consider important. It also questions how audiences consume art now, from 360-degree video walkthroughs to simulated gallery spaces. Audiences want new experiences. This, coupled with the aspect of travel, time and money, means that the gallery's activities reaches audiences further afield, who might not be able to come to see us physically, or have no time to visit galleries during standard opening hours.

AOS follows in the footsteps of our *Storage-un.it* project, which ran from 2015 to 2017 in our storage space in Hackney Wick, and continues our research into online and virtual spaces for curation and artistic production. We've also had other online projects, such as *website seeing* which looked at the way we use the web—the links we click and moving from one website to another as a stream of consciousness—as a curated insight into different ways of experiencing the web.

arebyte is a London-based art organization that supports the development of artists working with digital and emerging artforms. Following the long tradition of artists' experimenting with new technologies, arebyte has led a highly acclaimed pioneering programme since 2013. From web-based work to multimedia installations including virtual and augmented reality, artificial intelligence, computer-generated images, and 3D printing, the gallery commissions new works from emerging, as well as more established artists. It supports multiple voices in digital cultures across the UK and internationally to bring innovative perspectives to art through new technologies.

Nimrod Vardi is the creative director and founder of arebyte (est. 2013), a non-profit digital and media art gallery, and Arbeit Studios (est. 2010), a creative workspace provider with over hundred fifty studios across London. arebyte is dedicated to the exploration of the intersection between art and everything that is digital. In 2017 arebyte moved to a larger site, which allowed for an exciting new programme with more ambitious commissions. Vardi has managed to develop unique and innovative modes of operation, bringing together art and workspaces in an engaging manner. He is currently developing both organizations with a view to establishing larger institutions with international reach.

Rebecca Edwards has been the curator at arebyte since 2016–17, working with emerging media, new technologies and digital culture. She curated arebyte's project space in Clerkenwell throughout 2017 and is currently organizing *hotel generation*, a young artist development programme for the gallery. Rebecca's interests lie in cultivating new curatorial methods spanning physical and digital space, and in artists working at the intersection of technology, online culture and collaboration. She won the NEON Curatorial Award in 2015 and holds an MA in Curating from The Whitechapel Gallery/The Cass.

1   Lawrence Lek & Kode9, *Nøtel*, 2018, installation view. Courtesy of arebyte Gallery. Photo: Luka Radek.

2   Most Dismal Swamp, *Swamp Protocol*, 2019, installation view. Courtesy of arebyte Gallery. Photo: Christopher MacInnes.

3   Pussykrew, *the bliss of metamorphing collapse*, 2019, installation view (part of the exhibition RE-FIGURE GROUND). Courtesy of arebyte Gallery. Photo: Christopher MacInnes.

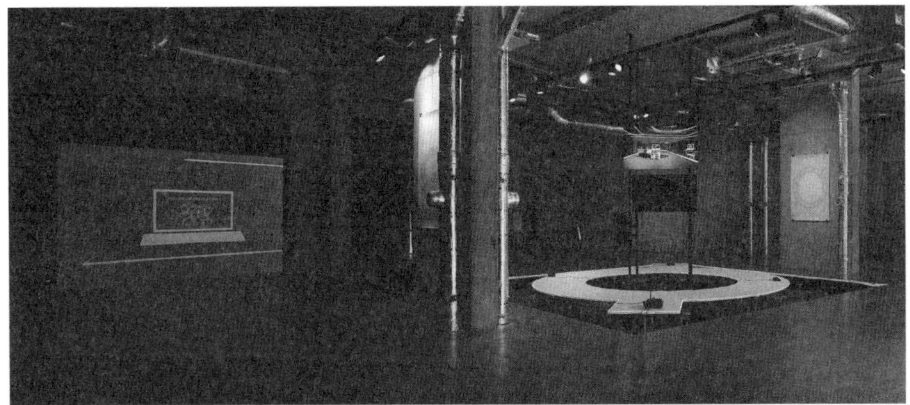

1

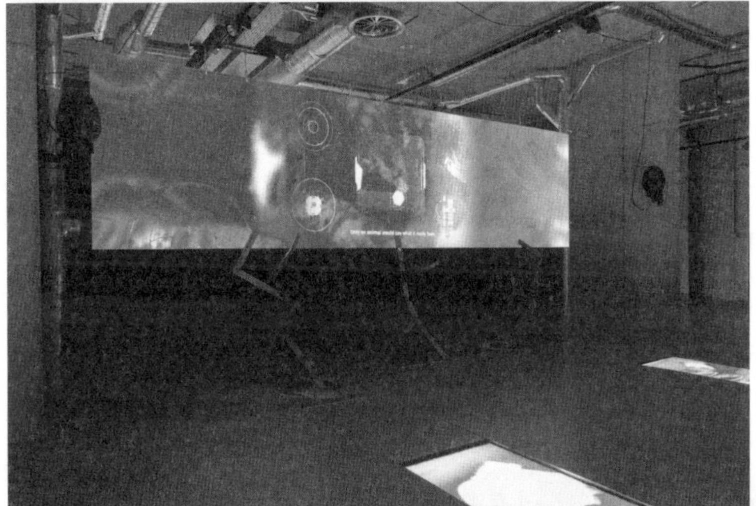

2

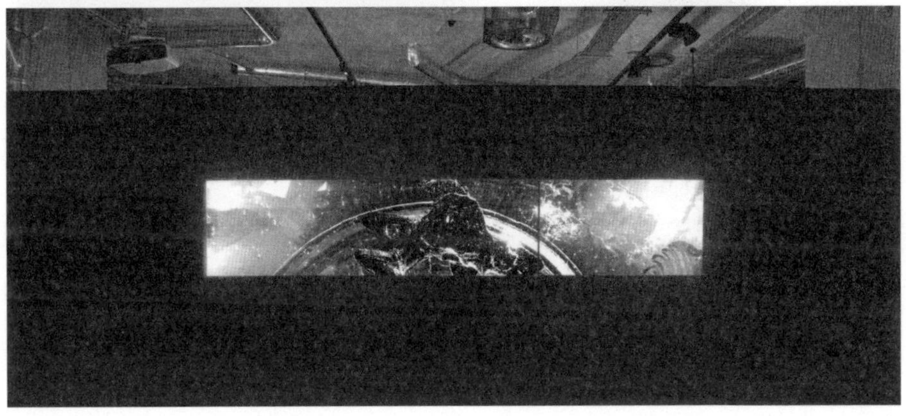

3

Ryder Ripps

INTERVIEWEE: RYDER RIPPS
PROJECT: INTERNET ARCHAEOLOGY, 2009–PRESENT
WEBSITE: *ryder-ripps.com*, *internetarchaeology.org*
DATE: 26 MAY 2019

Can we start by defining the terminology we're using and how you position yourself within existing categories like digital art, new media, net art, contemporary art, or any of the post-arts?

R   It seems as if categories are marketing tools used by people trying to profit financially. I've never been good at doing that aspect of art so I don't think I have much skin in the naming game. I think that art created at a specific time should be relevant to that time, maybe it is no matter what… like if you were cave painting in 2019 that would be a statement.

What is your background and what triggered your interest in digital/net art? Could you elaborate on these initial encounters?

R   *ryder-ripps.com/1999/pages/IMG_7099_jpg.htm*

You've been involved in various types of organizations and spaces. Could you share some of your experiences working in these different settings and particular contexts? For example, how does it affect your practice? Are there specific things that work very well in one context but not at all in another?

R   Working with Rhizome was one of the most awful things that happened to me. They completely shamed me and bullied me without intellectual consideration—they fell into a clickbait trap, like much of the world has. It's a shame that the artist/intellectual class is not impervious to the piling on of virtue signalling and gore fetish.

There has always been a separation between people who stress the technological (material) developments of digital art and those who emphasize the art qualities (content/conceptual). At the same time digital art is also often accompanied by a fair amount of theoretical discussion. How do you position yourself in this discourse?

R   I enjoy art that is thought provoking more than eye candy. I've tried to make that central to my praxis.

You organize online and offline exhibitions. Starting with the latter, do you work with certain methods or criteria? For instance, I recall numerous discussions in the past where showing a computer monitor was 'not done', or some curators wouldn't even consider presenting net art in an exhibition at all, while others created entirely new installations based on online work. What are your thoughts/experiences with this?

R   It's all future landfill, so just do what you need to do to survive in that moment.

223

Who do you see as your audience? I guess it changes with each new context but are there also changes (and/or exchanges) that you've noticed over the years, people moving from one place to another, or crossovers from other fields?

R   Yeah, lost folks.

What do you focus on in your online exhibitions/digital magazine? In the past we've seen examples ranging from lists of links, to commissions, to documentation about a work, to embedding a work in a website? What is your preferred or even ideal 'model'?

R   I don't really do much; I'm just trying to figure out how to survive. I don't get how people do it.

Should digital art enter established museums or organizations or are there better places where it can be preserved and presented? If so, what role should museums play in the future?

R   Yeah, rich people will always control history.

I recently had a few discussions with artists and producers about the usefulness of open source, it seems that although all kinds of codes and suchlike are available they're hardly ever used, mainly because of the personal approach to coding and the complexity that derives from such project-based work. What is your approach to open source in this context?

R   Everything is open source anyway—no matter how hard you try you can't own a thought. All you can do is put a logo on it and pay to advertise that logo.

Until recently in the Netherlands there was always a very good funding system for the arts in general and specifically for digital art. That has since changed, increasing on the one hand the divide between 'traditional' art and digital art, while on the other it generally means looking for money outside the funding system. Could you share some of your experiences working around the globe? How do you and the artists you work with survive?

R   Usually in weird ways, rich parents, suing someone, fucking and/or marrying someone rich (or a gallerist), being related to Nazis, stuff like that.

One of the things that fascinates me about *Internet Archaeology*, a project that 'seeks to explore, recover, archive and showcase the graphic artefacts found within earlier Internet Culture' is that you managed not only to capture a lot of interesting things in collaboration with many others, but that you also insisted on focusing on the image, or 'graphic artefacts'. Could you explain your approach? And what is your interest and perspective when it comes to digital preservation, documentation and collecting?

R   Just like other manmade objects, digital artefacts shape the people who consume them... and oh was I shaped. I thought it was a shame that Yahoo deleted Geocities without any consideration for the cultural significance and love/energy/time that people had put into all the stuff that was made on it—and at a

 time when there were far fewer rules so the range of content was pretty broad. Today the proliferation of online content is beyond exponential, it would be very hard to download and make sense of even an hour of content posted on the Internet today. It's a different world. There should be time to reflect on and preserve the past—although I worry that we are getting to a point where history is as irrelevant as it is overwhelming and will likely be pure fiction soon, rendered in posts.

Internet Archaeology seeks to explore, recover, archive and showcase the graphic artifacts found within earlier Internet Culture. The chief purpose of *Internet Archaeology* is to preserve these artifacts and acknowledge their importance in understanding the beginnings and birth of an Internet Culture. We focus on graphic artifacts only, with the belief that images are most culturally revealing and immediate. Most of the files in our archive are in either JPG or GIF format and are categorized by either still or moving image, they are then arranged in various thematic subcategories. Unlike traditional archaeology, where physical artifacts are unearthed; Internet Archaeology's artifacts are digital, thus more temporal and transient. Yet we believe that these artifacts are no less important than say the cave paintings of Lascaux. They reveal the origins of a now ubiquitous Internet Culture; showing where we have been and how far we have come.

About
Still Images
Moving Images
Collections
Netscrape
Webgrabs
Guest Galleries
.

News

5.2.11 · MAUSOLEUM II · A Holy Ground by Krist Wood

12.10.10 · Now That's What I Call MIDI

07.25.10 · Arran Ridley Guest Gallery Added

12.11.09 · XXX Collection Added

12.2.09 · Y2K Collection Added

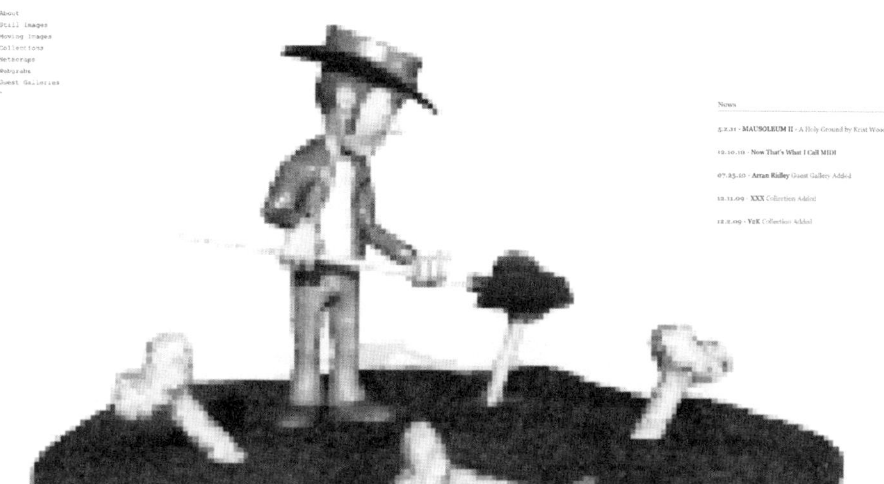

227

Stefan Riebel

INTERVIEWEE: STEFAN RIEBEL
PROJECT: VARIOUS – 700MB GALLERY, 2009–PRESENT
WEBSITE: *stefanriebel.de*, *700mbg.com*
DATE: 8 JULY 2019

Can we start by defining the terminology we're using and how you position yourself within existing categories like digital art, new media, net art, contemporary art, or any of the post-arts?

S   Officially we refer to this platform as a gallery only. The '700MB' in the name 700MB Gallery is the only reference to a digital practice. Internally we think of this as a spatial practice. Among other spaces we develop, curate and operate in, 700MB is a specific space limited to the boundaries of its digital capacity and technology.

What is your background and what triggered your interest in digital/net art? Could you elaborate on these initial encounters?

S   Our backgrounds are in fine arts with a focus on sculptural and performative practices. We share an interest in presentation modes, spatial practices, display design, exhibition choreography, etc. Most of our projects are aimed at investigating ways of presenting art, opening up spaces for artists and experimenting with space. Over time 'space' became our main focus, material and artistic result. (Maybe interesting to see: *Gedanken zur Revolution, Institut für Alles Mögliche, USB-Shuffle-Show.*)

With 700MB we open a specific digital space that is available in unlimited copies, as the compact disc is a mass product—the content is unique each time and refers to the space of 700MB. Besides the digital space there is the collection of discs containing the data, which are objects themselves, that are contained within a bigger storage/gallery if displayed.

You've been involved in various types of organizations and spaces. Could you share some of your experiences working in these different settings and particular contexts? For example, how does it affect your practice? Are there specific things that work very well in one context but not at all in another?

S   I've been involved with several non-commercial project spaces/off spaces in mostly Leipzig and Berlin since 2005. 700MB Gallery is one of many along the way. My practice changed profoundly from creating-space-to-present-art to creating-space-as-artistic-practice/as-an-art-piece. By now I manage about fifty different spaces/settings that together create a conglomerate of contexts and formats that work as a toolkit for presentations, work spaces, social spaces, various kinds of arts, etc. I like to think of this spatial conglomerate/toolkit as an 'unsorted pile', which likewise contains numerous bits and pieces of all sorts that have no specific agency themselves but which

229

can turn into meaningful components or enter into meaningful compositions and relations at any time. Also the 'unsorted pile model' suggests an ongoing process and a radical openness to whatever artworks or spaces or as yet undefined things come along that could settle and become part of it.

> There has always been a separation between people who stress the technological (material) developments of digital art and those who emphasize the art qualities (content/conceptual). At the same time digital art is also often accompanied by a fair amount of theoretical discussion. How do you position yourself in this discourse?

S   I'm having a hard time keeping up with debates and theoretical material, as they seem to develop exponentially. Also as a practicing artist I naturally focus on the content of art and its relation to space and context. Still I wouldn't make a distinct difference between the two. Art can be very enriching, be it digital or analogue, on- or offline, as well as interconnected forms—each form unavoidably transports/speaks through its specific technology and context. I guess the rapid development of technology and media over the past 200 years just makes us aware of that.

> You organize online and offline exhibitions. Starting with the latter, do you work with certain methods or criteria? For instance, I recall numerous discussions in the past where showing a computer monitor was 'not done', or some curators wouldn't even consider presenting net art in an exhibition at all, while others created entirely new installations based on online work. What are your thoughts/experiences with this?

S   I struggle with this constantly and each exhibition and artwork raises new questions about exactly this. We agree on a technological pre-condition though: that all content is performed by its specific material, devices, operations and agents. No video without a data set, storage device, screen, electricity, et cetera, and, equally on the part of the receiver: no video without (human) eyes, body, an understanding of images, an informed reference system, etc. Certain conditions need to be met to make art happen—which parts of a complex (technological) operating system we allow to perform along, highlight, or try to hide, is a negotiation process that needs to address the specific needs of each presentation depending on the presentation and the exhibits. This question becomes concrete to me in our spatial practice in the form of the question: 'When is the space a container for art, when is it the artwork itself, where do the two perspectives intertwine?'

Who do you see as your audience? I guess it changes with each new context but are there also changes (and/or exchanges) that you've noticed over the years, people moving from one place to another, or crossovers from other fields?

S   This is very hard to answer as we honestly set up spaces/exhibitions according to the concepts of the artworks only, without evaluation processes. So potentially anyone and no one. Also as our/my projects are usually very different from one another it seems that they attract a different audience each time.

What do you focus on in your online exhibitions/digital magazine? In the past we've seen examples ranging from lists of links, to commissions, to documentation about a work, to embedding a work in a website? What is your preferred or even ideal 'model'?

S   For 700MB the website functions as a platform that informs about the gallery and its current exhibitions. Fragments from each as well as a brief text refer to the actual shows that are solely on the discs and only accessible through a self-directed way of presentation. The curatorial concept of putting a solo show on a CD is formally very limiting; in return I keep the content that artists can submit very open and without any specific theme.

Should digital art enter established museums or organizations or are there better places where it can be preserved and presented? If so, what role should museums play in the future?

S   The future role of museums is being deeply discussed and rethought, which I believe is a good thing. In terms of digital art and its preservation, museums offer great spaces and infrastructures, and hopefully even better ones in the future. Just like any other artform, the museum context is a good option—museums are good ideas in the first place and sometimes offer interesting ways to see art as well as solutions in terms of preservation and education.

I recently had a few discussions with artists and producers about the usefulness of open source, it seems that although all kinds of codes and suchlike are available they're hardly ever used, mainly because of the personal approach to coding and the complexity that derives from such project-based work. What is your approach to open source in this context?

S   I'm not really into coding but when it comes to political positioning I'm sceptical about open source software. I mainly see them as temporary tools offering short-term solutions to long-term problems.

231

> Until recently in the Netherlands there was always a very good funding
> system for the arts in general and specifically for digital art. That has since
> changed, increasing on the one hand the divide between 'traditional' art and
> digital art, while on the other it generally means looking for money outside
> the funding system. Could you share some of your experiences working
> around the globe? How do you and the artists you work with survive?

S I see the same problems in slightly different shades everywhere—artists struggling for (proper) funding, especially when trying out new, unconventional and experimental ways of creating, presenting or distributing their art. Most people/groups I know just try to survive from one project to the next, constantly apply for funding, constantly work, and are usually stuck in at least one paid job to afford their profession.

Selling solo shows on discs is more a conceptual statement than a serious strategy for making money. With another project, *Institut für Alles Mögliche*, I realized that a residency programme that asks its participants to come up with funding might be a way to delegate this process to artists and associations, but it does have a certain potential for a long-lasting artistic infrastructure and self-sustainability. What I often see are special educational programmes for children and young adults—these seem to provide a stable income for institutions of at least a certain size.

All forms of (proper) funding that I'm aware of are of course either not an option at all, or are in most ways unsatisfying.

> One of the things that struck me about your online exhibitions on 700MB is
> how you assign the components of the artwork/exhibition, some of which can
> be viewed on CD and some on the website, and of course their relationship,
> as well as the economic model you developed to sell the work. Could you
> explain your approach, also perhaps in relation to your other work, *SOA*, for
> instance? And what is your interest and perspective when it comes to digital
> preservation, documentation and collecting?

S The complete exhibitions are presented solely on 700MB compact discs. The website functions as an information platform only and contains fragments from each show/disc as well as a brief text about it. The discs are the gallery space and contain one solo show each, collectible items that might be designed and become an ongoing collectible series. In contrast to most of the other works I produce, the discs are for sale, which highlights the product character even more and suggests the full accessibility of the show—it is purchased and can then be received—a solo show for a solo receiver.

700 Megabyte Gallery initiated by Stefan Riebel and Phillip Sadofsky, operates as a casual gallery but differs in terms of its specific spatial dimensions. 700MBG presents solo exhibitions on compact discs which are partially presented on the gallery's web pages. The project can also be understood as a continuously growing archive for digital art and an art project that questions the boundaries of archiving, transmediation and the accessibility of art.

Stefan Riebel, conceptual artist, lives and works in Athens, Berlin and Leipzig. He has lectured in Media Arts at the Academy of Fine Arts Leipzig, since 2013. Riebel's works operate exclusively in series and focus on non-expressive ways to deal with information, statements and descriptions. His works are poetic, interactive and process-driven and have been presented internationally at conferences, museums and festivals.

1   700MBG, *CD Player*, Karl Heinz Jeron.
2   700MBG, *SINGLE SIGN ON*, Florian Kuhlmann.

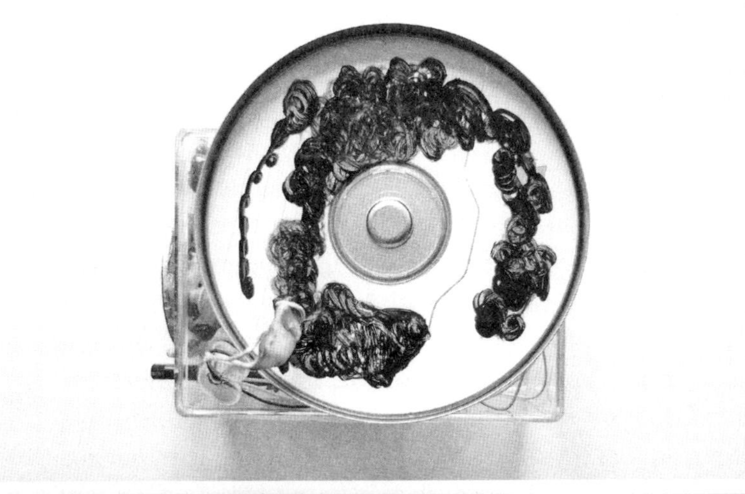

1

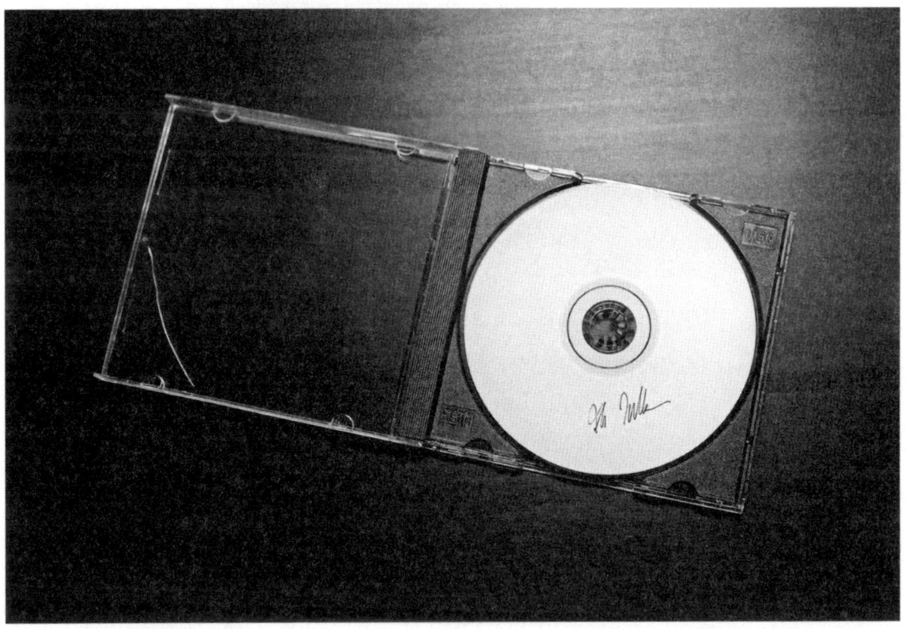

2

235

Pita Arreola-Burns & Elliott Burns

INTERVIEWEES: PITA ARREOLA-BURNS AND ELLIOTT BURNS
PROJECT: OFF SITE PROJECT, 2017–PRESENT
WEBSITE: *offsiteproject.org*
DATE: 15 MAY 2020

Can we start by defining the terminology we're using and how you position yourself within existing categories like digital art, new media, net art, contemporary art, or any of the post-arts?

P & E   As an online gallery, we work with artists across all of these categories. However, we'd describe the focus of the gallery to present Post-Screen Art, which we describe as art that explores the problematization of the physical world in the online. As the Internet has moved from our screens into our subconscious, it has created social, economic and philosophical shifts, as well as material properties.

As for 'post-Internet art', the term has particularly muddled connotations. 2006 is often regarded as a line in the sand, everything to the left being pre-Internet and to the right post-Internet. Suddenly the Internet reached a tipping point, saturating aesthetic production. We've come to think about it in terms of Art Brut and... not Art Brut. It's almost impossible not to be affected by the spatial, cognitive and social transformations brought about by Web 1.0 and Web 2.0, so most artists wittingly or unwittingly fall under the umbrella of being post-Internet, in a similar manner that it was almost impossible not to fall under the influence of 'culture' and therefore escape being branded Art Brut.

As for New Media, all the artists we work with utilize digital and online technologies as a specific medium or within a creative process, including AI, video game software, Google Maps, Virtual and Augmented Reality and social media, to name a few.

To an extent both terms have become catch-alls and it is more meaningful to address the artists we work with by subject than methodology.

What is your background and what triggered your interest in digital/net art? Could you elaborate on these initial encounters?

P & E   Before we began working together we were both focusing on digital art; in fact, when we met at Central Saint Martins in 2015 we both wrote our dissertations on facets of the subject.

E   I played video games excessively growing up and as a teenager spent time in online forums. From 2005 to 2006 I spent a vast number of evenings after school on *TimeSplitters: Future Perfect* and ended up ranking somewhere in the teens of Xbox players. The communities brought together by forums and video games could be uniquely tight, so the aesthetics and cultural contexts inherent to those spaces had a formative effect on me.

Simultaneously, I knew I wanted to go to art school, but it wasn't until much later that I began experiencing Net Art. After my BA, I ended up working on some EC-funded projects linking artists with technologists and was brought into contact with organizations like FoAM in Brussels, Lighthouse in Brighton, and Waag in Amsterdam, among others. That was a crash course that got me on the course to where I am now.

P   Just like Elliott, I grew up playing video games and as a teenager spent most of my time in online forums, MySpace, Tumblr and similar web platforms. For my BA, I studied Design and Visual Communication in Mexico City, where I'm originally from, and I became very interested in online design and started taking classes on HTML and CSS language. I was associate director of a contemporary art gallery for a couple of years and after that, I worked in PR and communications, creating online and offline strategies for different cultural brands. All this experience deeply influenced my interest in the effects that media has in society and especially on the social shifts that were emerging as a consequence of the Internet. I'm especially interested in new art practices as I see them as cultural expressions of our current moment, a way to articulate and engage with what is happening around us, which will be considered in the long term as cultural artefacts that speak of our changing human condition.

> There has always been a separation between people who stress the technological (material) developments of digital art and those who emphasize the art qualities (content/conceptual). At the same time digital art is also often accompanied by a fair amount of theoretical discussion. How do you position yourself in this discourse?

P & E   We wouldn't necessarily distinguish between the technological and aesthetical facets of the work we present. Often the artists and curators we work with, or admire, investigate in parallel technology and its aesthetic values. Technology is both their research subject and medium.

Art history is littered with technological innovations, from new pigments to understanding perspective or even to subject matter taking on symbolic values and becoming a technology like language. The desire for better aesthetic results spurs technology while technological developments seek aesthetic expression to validate themselves; the feedback between them informs greater and more complex theoretical discussion. Subtexts emerge in artistic circles and academia thanks to the interplay between aesthetic and medium.

          We can look back at Net Art and see a period that feels

almost scientific in its approach, like minimalist sculpture, and we love it because it has a digital grain that reminds us of the computer interfaces of our childhoods.

> You organize online and offline exhibitions. Starting with the latter, do you work with certain methods or criteria? For instance, I recall numerous discussions in the past where showing a computer monitor was 'not done', or some curators wouldn't even consider presenting net art in an exhibition at all, while others created entirely new installations based on online work. What are your thoughts/experiences with this?

P & E   Whether working online or offline, we always start by discussing the artists' intentions with them and how they want the work to reach an audience. If the artist is looking for a one-on-one intimate experience on a personal screen, it would be a contradiction to build a large-scale installation.

You have to consider the manner in which you are exporting the artwork between mediums and how this affects the experience and conception of the work. The conditions you set to showcase the piece will influence the audiences' approach to the work. In that way, we are very critical of the experience we want to generate and the message we're projecting, the medium is always part of the message for us.

In regards to placing Net Art within a physical show, you could compare it to a reading room. What makes you want to engage with a book while being in a gallery? Too many books and you're overwhelmed, too few and it looks like an afterthought. The furniture has to feel cohesive, and it has to be comfortable. And you don't want to be too close to the exit.

Context is king. If you're aiming to have an audience sit down with a piece of Net Art then the conditions need to be correct. After all, you're asking them to do something they could do from the comfort of their own homes. The 'do it'/'don't do it' dichotomy isn't so much an issue of curatorial purity but the result of lots of bad and poorly considered attempts. If anything audiences nowadays are more comfortable engaging with screens in public than they were ten years ago.

> Who do you see as your audience, I guess it changes with each new context but are there also changes (and/or exchange) that you've noticed over the years... people moving from one area to another, or crossovers from other fields?

P & E   Without comprehensive analytics of who's visiting the site it can be hard to know who the audience is and how it has changed over the years; unfortunately, we're left with the statistics we draw from Instagram and the anecdotal evidence we gain from seeing who starts following us. It's hard to recall the gradual shifts, but in the last couple of months, the quarantine times, we've seen an increase in new followers, which potentially indicates more art consumers becoming aware of digital arts platforms.

> What do you focus on in your online exhibitions? In the past we've seen examples ranging from lists of links, to commissions, to documentation about a work, to embedding a work in a website? What is your preferred or even ideal model?

P & E   Roughly divided, the homepage exhibitions on *Off Site Project* are solo shows, group exhibitions, or an occasional project we've initiated. In the case of solo exhibitions the model is responsive to the desires of the artist, remodelling the gallery's architecture by switching across templates and amending the CSS coding to make it specifically reflect their needs. Frequently this will come out of extensive email exchanges or Skype/Zoom/Jitsi meetings with both sides sketching options. Sometimes we'll present an option that takes the work in a direction the artists hadn't imagined, and other times they'll ask whether X, Y or Z is possible and we'll go away scratching our heads.

Group shows aren't too dissimilar as we tend to hold back from defining the interface experience until we're narrowing down a final list of participating artists and have a decent understanding of all the requirements of each artwork.

But then on the other hand, the ZIP downloads and Google Maps residency are heavily defined by their format. We're asking the artists to work within a set space to see how they can redefine it. Those limits can be paradoxically productive and there are other models we'd like to explore if we had the time.

> Should digital art enter established museums or organizations or are there better places where it can be preserved and presented? If so, what role should museums play in the future?

P & E   We're no longer talking in terms of 'should'. Museums such as MoMA, New Museum and the V&A have already responded to the challenge and established new departments to begin tackling these issues and we've heard of contemporary art museums such as Tate Modern starting to examine the archival procedures that will need to be established for Net Art. Because museums follow strict guidelines about the collection of artefacts and effectively agree to conserve anything that they acquire, the slow uptake of Net Art acquisitions potentially reflects the myriad complexities of preserving an artform that is essentially performative code.

    What we should ideally be arguing for is a fusion of community care and institutional procedure. Excuse the unfortunate colonial overtones, but it parallels indigenous communities such as Native Americans or Torres Strait Islanders: museums work best when they incorporate tradition into the curatorial job description. Western models of curatorial care have historically ignored the spiritual practices required to care for sacred artefacts to keep them alive rather than letting them die in cabinets. The same can be said with Net Art: it will be best preserved if those with the most relevant skills, community insiders, are present either as advisors to the museum, or are actually given a position.

In the past I've had discussions with artists and producers about the usefulness of open source, it seems that although all kinds of codes are available they are hardly ever used by others mainly because of personal approaches to coding and the complexity resulting from such project-based methodology. What is your approach to open source in this context?

P & E   The level of coding that we engage with on *Off Site Project* isn't necessarily the most sophisticated or complicated, over the past three years we've learned snippets of HTML and CSS code by copy-pasting potential solutions into place and seeing whether they worked or not. Without open source communities we probably wouldn't be where we are and to a similar extent we've been fortunate enough to be friends with some technically proficient artists and creatives who've been able to help us problem-solve and even at times written code to install specific artworks. That ethos has been immensely beneficial and the knowledge we've gained from it is something we've been able to pass on to students we work with.

Until recently in the Netherlands there was always a very good funding system for the arts in general and specifically for digital art. That has since changed, increasing on the one hand the divide between 'traditional' art and digital art, while on the other it generally means looking for money outside the funding system. Could you share some of your experiences working around the globe? How do you and the artists you work with survive?

P & E   We've run *Off Site Project* as an entirely not-for-profit the last three years, with an understanding between us and the artists we've worked with that we'll do everything we can to make sure the effort they put into exhibiting with us will be matched by our efforts. We understand that some people will have reason to criticize this; it's not a position we're comfortable with and it's something we're conscious we have to address.

We couldn't empirically say how the artists we work with survive, though for the most part we imagine it is through a similar combination of full-time, part-time, freelance and contract positions that come together to cover bills, put food on the table, ensure we have a life and can reinvest in our practices. We're lucky that running *Off Site Project* has led to a few paid presentations and panel conversations. Only a few of the artists we work with make pieces to sell; many look to private or public funding to realize their projects, whilst others have started crowdfunding campaigns to help pay for residencies or research trips.

The word 'survive' in your question is already an acknowledgement that this industry is tough and conditions have become increasingly difficult. As a result of quarantine, we've seen the evaporation of zero-hour jobs affecting friends, and those who have been furloughed may not know whether their jobs will exist on the other side.

Cities such as London, which have always profited from a huge influx of creative voices, might see a mass defection, which wouldn't necessarily be a bad thing for the UK.

> You're the initiators of the online platform *Off Site Project*, in which you organize online exhibitions, a residency programme in Google Maps and downloadable ZIP shows. The space you create for your online exhibitions is different and ingenious each time, for example, mimicking ordinary web interfaces of shopping channels or a slightly distorted Mac desktop as the interface for the exhibition. In some cases an artist's personal workplace becomes the work, which can also be downloaded, in a sense bringing the user closer to the creative process of the artwork. So, some of the projects you organize are online for a specific time, while others, particularly the downloadable ZIP shows, can be seen as often and for as long as one likes. Could you discuss your approach and your interest and perspective when it comes to the future of these artworks/practices in terms of digital preservation, documentation and collecting?

P & E   Absolutely, there's a mix of timeframes evoked within the programming of *Off Site Project*. Building the gallery we often thought of it expanding like an IRL space would: you have the main gallery then you open a project space or start a publication series and maybe if you happen to have a spare bedroom available upstairs you invite resident artists.

The homepage exhibitions are exhibited for a set time because we enjoyed the idea that you have to see it while they were open, that they don't simply become archived as a still active space. On a practical side, deinstalling the shows also enabled us to change the entire web design if we wanted to, we could tear down walls and change the architecture without worrying about old shows becoming non-functional. Accordingly, we've had to think about what the best methods of documentation are for digital events; we're still working through that question.

On the other hand, the ZIP downloads have become

comparable to a publication series, so inherent with that form we keep them available and they've become something collectible. Much like most galleries have boxes of old publications in the back room that they struggle to sell.

There's an implication with anything digital that it needs to remain, that it shouldn't disappear, become inaccessible, fall apart or suffer any other natural consequence of time and cell duplication. We wouldn't necessarily subscribe to that, as it will eventually box us into a Derridean archive fever.

Off Site Project is an online curatorial practice founded by Pita Arreola-Burns and Elliott Burns, which hosts a programme of homepage exhibitions, downloadable ZIP shows, and a residency based in Google Maps. Working with a global network of artists, the gallery has explored issues from post-colonialism in Latin America to the increasingly monetized wellness industry, the societal effects of the Internet to the prevalence of conspiratorial thinking, as well as the creative identity of AI minds and our ability to inhabit multiple realities through avatars. Launched in March 2017, the homepage exhibition was the first part of *Off Site Project*'s programme that has to date hosted fifteen solo shows, group exhibitions and projects. Conceived as the equivalent to a 'main gallery', the space is regularly reconfigured and updated with changing templates and revising CSS code.

Pita Arreola-Burns is an independent curator, originally from Mexico City, with nine years of experience working at the forefront of arts and communications within international institutions, including Phillips Auction House and Museo Jumex. She runs *Off Site Project* together with Elliott Burns.

Elliott Burns is Associate Lecturer at the Culture and Enterprise programme of Central Saint Martins in London as well as an exhibition curator and co-founder Off Site Project in London.

1   Alex Anikina, Sarah Derat & Rachel McRae, Sarah Friend, Kelly Ann Gardener, Tamara Kametani, Yoshi Kametani and Simon Weckert, with technical support from Alejandro Ball of Agorama, *screensaver watching you*, 2020, screenshot of exhibition homepage. Courtesy of Off Site Project.

2   Sarah Friend, *Neverending Snake*, 2018, screenshot of artwork subpage. Courtesy of Off Site Project.

< home >
+ exhibition +
[ZIP]
[Google Maps]
< about >
screensaver watching you
(Thursday 16th April - Sunday 19th July 2020)
featuring: Alex Anikina, Sarah Derat & Rachel McRae,
Sarah Friend, Kelly Ann Gardener, Tamara Kametani, Yoshi Kametani
and Simon Weckert.

1

< home >
+ exhibition +
[ZIP]
[Google Maps]
< about >

2

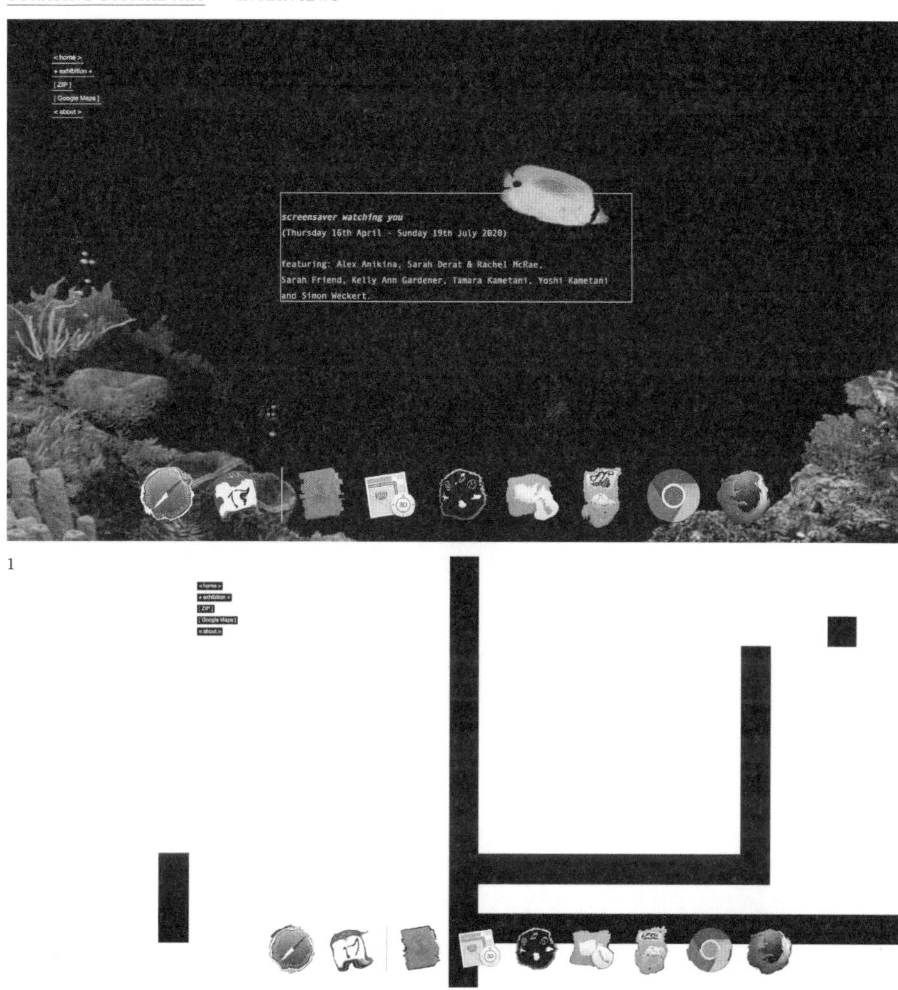

Livia Benedetti & Marcela Vieira

INTERVIEWEES: LIVIA BENEDETTI, MARCELA VIEIRA
PROJECT: AAREA, 2017–PRESENT
WEBSITE: *aarea.co*
DATE: 29 MAY 2020

Can we start by defining the terminology we're using and how you position yourself within existing categories like digital art, new media, net art, contemporary art, or any of the post-arts?

L & M   *aarea* operates at the intersection of contemporary art and the Internet. For the *aarea* platform we commission artworks made for the Internet, mostly by artists who do not work digitally— we're interested in the displacement of their research to this field. Although we're not attached to specific nomenclatures, we tend to use web-based and digital art terminology to designate the commissioned works within the site, but we adapt to other terms as dialogues are established.

What is your background and what triggered your interest in digital/net art? Could you elaborate on these initial encounters?

L   I've been active as a curator in museums and cultural centres since 2007. My background is in visual arts and I've always been interested in institutional critique and art language studies, but hadn't yet worked with the Internet. For me, the creation of *aarea* was an opportunity to rethink models of curatorship and institutions in a very experimental context, modelling new parameters and ways of working. *aarea* also represents an experimental space within the production of the invited artists themselves, as it is generally the first time they've done work on the Internet. As such, the exchange and dialogue with these artists is very intense, they rely on the curatorship to define the implications of this displacement of their practice and it's very valuable to be part of this process with them. For example, it was an immense privilege to have Jac Leirner at *aarea*—in her almost forty-year-long career she'd never made anything for a screen, not even video.

M   I have experience with educational programmes and text editing within cultural institutions, and since 2007 I've also worked professionally as a translator and literary editor (I have a degree in Literature). I am motivated by the opportunity presented by *aarea* to consider the Internet simultaneously as a medium and a means of production. I enjoy the possibility of working with the most varied kinds of artists, as well as the unlimited reach to the most varied audiences. The fact that the works happen online, without the need for physical events, means that we know nothing about the viewers, which gives the project an interesting twist. And it's always surprising to hear

247

the public (until then invisible to us) mentioning a certain work. I'm very interested in the public discussion a work can evoke, be it affective, informal, or theoretical, academic. In this sense, opportunities to discuss a work publicly are always very valid and we've been striving hard in this regard, providing, when possible, occasions for a work to be discussed, often with the artist present.

> There has always been a separation between people who stress the technological (material) developments of digital art and those who emphasize the art qualities (content/conceptual). At the same time digital art is also often accompanied by a fair amount of theoretical discussion. How do you position yourself in this discourse?

L & M   The curatorial line of *aarea* starts from the context of art, not technology—but we see art as a field of knowledge with great transdisciplinary potential, directly linked to its social context. And, in this respect, the Internet has brought about inescapable transformations in the socio-cultural field, and therefore in art. Although always mediated and traversed by technology, as we present one artwork at a time, each project directs *aarea* to specific issues arising from the artists' own research. We've had many different artists dealing with subjects as diverse as image, artificial intelligence, theatre, politics, painting and the Internet itself. Our main interest with *aarea* is to push the barriers that still separate the 'general' art scene from the Internet, departing from the context of the global south but with enough permeability to engage in dialogue with other territories. And we always do this in the company of artists whose works we admire, with resources brought by their artistic thinking.

> You organize online exhibitions and sometimes an offline event. Starting with the latter, do you work with certain methods or criteria? For instance, I recall numerous discussions in the past where showing a computer monitor was 'not done', or some curators wouldn't even consider presenting net art in an exhibition at all, while others created entirely new installations based on online work. What are your thoughts/experiences with this?

L & M   After being exhibited at *aarea*, some of the web-based works we commission become part of exhibitions in physical spaces, but in a different way. Some artists have turned their works into video editions—changing a few details—in order for them to gain autonomy beyond the Internet and be shown at exhibitions. An interesting case was that of artist Cinthia Marcelle, who made a work at *aarea* in 2018 where visitors dialogued through songs; then, in 2019, she returned to *aarea* with another version of this work, this time happening simultaneously on the Internet and in the exhibition space of the CCA Wattis Institute

(San Francisco). There were therefore two ways of accessing the work: the public could participate either via the Internet anywhere in the world or visit the installation (a kind of dancefloor) at CCA Wattis.

> Who do you see as your audience, I guess it changes with each new context but are there also changes (and/or exchange) that you've noticed over the years... people moving from one area to another, or crossovers from other fields?

L & M   So far our audience has been quite specialized, consisting mostly of people interested in art, or working in this field or studying the subject. Some *aarea* projects are able to overcome this barrier when, for example, they're reviewed in major media outlets, which always brings a more diverse audience. We also work with artists who touch on other fields in their research, such as architecture, theatre or technology, and they bring other audiences to *aarea*, which is very welcome.

> What do you focus on in your online exhibitions? In the past we've seen examples ranging from lists of links, to commissions, to documentation about a work, to embedding a work in a website? What is your preferred or even ideal 'model'?

L & M   On the *aarea.co* platform, our exhibition model is very strict: we show one artwork at a time, which occupies the entire site. There's no interference that does not belong to the work, such as a logo, texts, files or links, so the site becomes a different work of art with each edition. All mediation always happens in parallel media, such as social media and the newsletter. Beyond the website, *aarea* works on several types of curatorial projects without using an *a priori* model—we usually observe the particularities of the context in which we're operating, and that can happen in approaches as diverse as an artistic residency, online seminars or projects in the spaces of other institutions.

> Should digital art enter established museums or organizations or are there better places where it can be preserved and presented? If so, what role should museums play in the future?

L & M   As digital art is just one of the many mediums of art, there aren't any reasons why it shouldn't be in museum collections. It seems that interest in collecting digital works is increasing, although slowly, and it is perhaps museums who primarily validate collecting this type of artistic production. We understand that the conservation of these works is quite challenging, because technology changes very quickly, but we've been seeing more and more initiatives of this type from art institutions. They usually create their own conservation and cataloguing parameters for these works, based on the profile of their existing collection and internal guidelines.

Until recently in the Netherlands there was always a very good funding system for the arts in general and specifically for digital art. That has since changed, increasing on the one hand the divide between 'traditional' art and digital art, while on the other it generally means looking for money outside the funding system. Could you share some of your experiences working around the globe? How do you and the artists you work with survive?

L & M   In Brazil, public policy and funding for culture are going from bad to worse, so we knew from the start that *aarea* would be an autonomous project that would rely on the collaboration of a generous network of artists, cultural agents, curators, legal and financial consultants, among others, who are our interlocutors in the project. However, we've managed to make some projects viable through partnering with other institutions, within the country and abroad, as we did with the CCA Wattis Institute, Jeu de Paume, Pivô and Salón Nacional de Artistas de Bogotá, and others. We've also recently developed a patronage programme, with the understanding that, given the almost complete absence of government incentive programme, private initiative is a viable option.

You are the initiators of the online platform *aarea*, where you organize online exhibitions and commission one artist each month to create a new work. Often these artists unfamiliar with the conditions of the web but nevertheless manage to present interesting and innovative ways to either question the space, for instance, Kenneth Goldsmith's *One Square Kilometer (for Walter De Maria)* (a .pdf covering one square kilometer with black rectangles, a homage to De Maria's minimalist and land art projects), or come up with a new twists in their practice, such as the current work *button* by Jac Leirner who's mostly known for her installation work. All the works are only online for a set period and can then be traced through the Facebook or Instagram platform. Could you talk about your approach and also your interest and perspective when it comes to the future of these art works/practices in terms of digital preservation, documentation and collecting?

L & M   These are the questions that have activated us. Currently, the memory of *aarea* has been presented to the public in a series of programmes in which we exhibit and talk about past editions. We're designing a project for our archive and its potential, and are looking at ways of creating a public archive in a more interesting way, for us, than just making a list of past editions available. Although this archive is not yet open to the public, we are dedicated to the preservation and maintenance of our entire collection. We've also talked with some museums about integrating *aarea* works into their collections.

aarea is an online platform founded in 2017 to showcase artworks created specifically for the Internet. *aarea*'s website excludes any fixed elements such as a logo, texts or links that are not a part of the featured artist's work. Each edition presents a single project and the artists are tasked with creating a work whose only vehicle is the Internet, most doing so for the first time. *aarea*'s activities extend beyond its website, and include promoting a broad public programme in partnership with other institutions, and organizing curatorial projects, seminars and talks from a post-digital perspective.

Livia Benedetti is a contemporary art curator, researcher and writer based in São Paulo (Brazil). She co-founded the platform *aarea* in 2017. Since 2007, she has been working as a project curator at the Danish Fotobiennalen, Pivô, Jeu de Paume, CCA Wattis Institute, 45 Salón Nacional de Artistas de Bogotá, and Centro Cultural São Paulo, among others. Her writing has been published in books, catalogues and magazines.

Marcela Vieira is co-founder and curator at the website *aarea* (*aarea.co*) and editor of *Rosa Magazine* (*revistarosa.com*). In addition to her curatorial and edition work, Marcela Vieira also translates (French–Portuguese) and is currently a PhD student at the semiotics and translation programme at the University Paris 8, in co-supervision with the University of São Paulo.

1   Cinthia Marcelle, *A morta*, 2019, installation view. The work happened simultaneously on *aarea* and CCA Wattis Institute. Courtesy of the artist and Vermelho. Photo: Johnna Arnold.

2   Kenneth Goldsmith, Art, *Audiovisual, and Literature in the Digital Age*, 2019, photograph. Performance at the international symposium curated by *aarea* at Sesc São Paulo. Photo: Jean Paz.

3   Jac Leirner, *button*, 2020, online project. Commissioned by *aarea*.

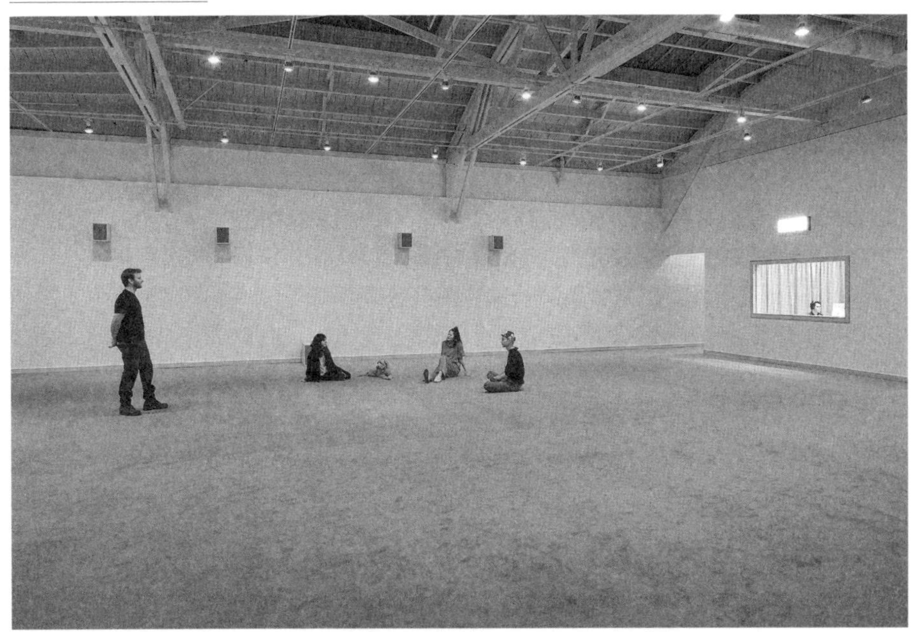

1

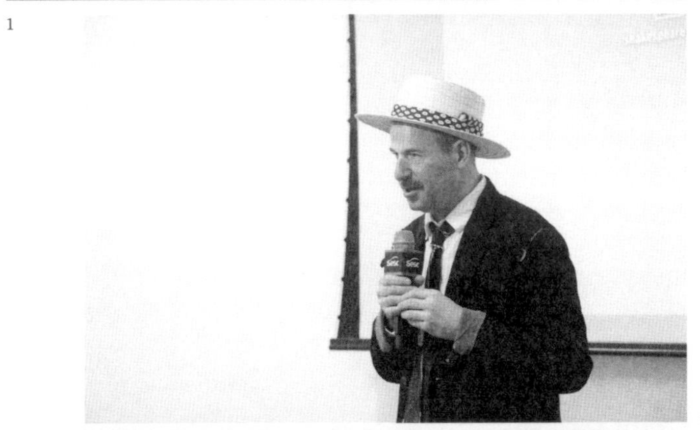

2

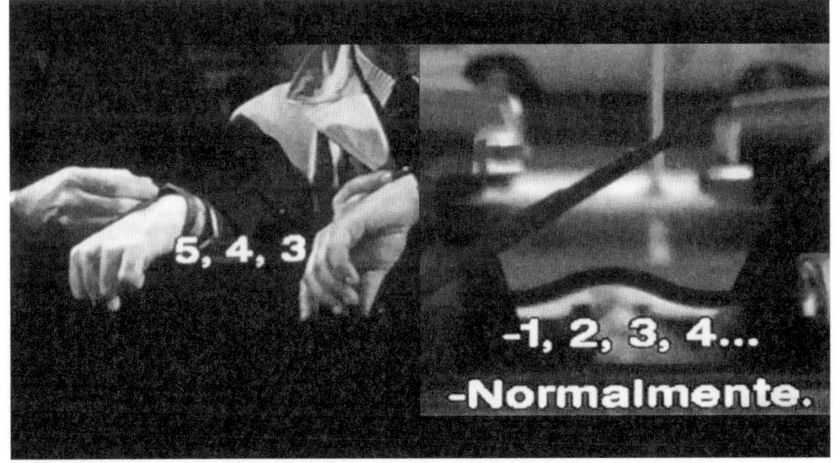

3

Zhang Ga

INTERVIEWEE: ZHANG GA
PROJECT: VARIOUS, WE=LINK: TEN EASY PIECES, ET CETERA, 2020
WEBSITE: *we-link.chronusartcenter.org*
DATE: 1 JUNE 2020

Can we start by defining the terminology we're using and how you position yourself within existing categories like digital art, new media, net art, contemporary art, or any of the post-arts?

Z   When using these terms, I think we first need to distinguish between media-specific practices, such as performance art, installation art, sculpture, painting, digital art, new media, net art, etc., and the general condition in which art is perceived, which falls into contemporary art, or any of the post-arts, etc. By understanding the latter, we can probably better define the former. It's interesting to see that although Jean-François Lyotard in his seminal essay 'The Post Modern Condition: A Report on Knowledge' (1979) explicitly postulated that the unprecedented technological transformation of contemporary society marked the advent of the postmodern epoch, much of his underlining argument about the premise of the technological condition became obscured and sidelined in the cultural and artistic articulation of the postmodern. The artworld's take on the post-modern was very much a post-structuralist proposition spearheaded by Rosalind Krauss and epiphanized in Craig Owens' 'The Allegorical Impulse' (1980). Along that path, the postmodern scenario became the bedrock of a social constructivist agenda of inter-subjective (human as the sole subject *per se*) innuendo. If the postmodern was itself a project of modernity, whose ethical foundation was humanism while its episteme was a Kantian teaching illuminated by Newtonian physics as its understanding of the Real, its apprehension of the material world, then what really constitutes the watershed paradigm shift is the advent of the posthuman via the sirens of the Anthropocene, which Cary Wolf quite elaborately encapsulated:

It comes both before and after humanism: before in the sense that it names the embodiment and embeddedness of the human being in not just its biological but also its technological world, the prosthetic coevolution of the human animal with the technicity of tools and external archival mechanism.... [It] comes after in the sense that it names a historical moment in which the decentering of human by its imbrication in technical, medical, informatic, and economic networks is increasingly impossible to ignore.[39]

255   39   Cary Wolfe, *What is Posthumanism* (Minneapolis: University of Minnesota Press, 2010), p. xv.

In that regard, I consider (new) media art as paradigmatically departing from the convention of contemporary art, which is predominantly predicated on the poststructuralist discourse developed under the postmodern condition. If contemporary art, according to Peter Osborne, is postconceptual art (explicated by postmodern inter-subjectivity as I understand it), then what is to be rehabilitated from the oblivion of the twenty-first century and to be called forward from the shadow of contemporary art is a new art mediated and implicated by posthuman inter-objectivity under the epistemological auspices of a General Ecology (Erich Hörl) in which the Enlightenment subject becomes one instance of the object world.

What is your background and what triggered your interest in digital/net art? Could you elaborate on these initial encounters?

Z   I went to the High School of China Central Academy of Fine Arts in late 1970s. This sort of professional schooling at a young age was a typical Russian Socialist educational model, in which a few out of thousands were selected to receive prestigious training prior to entering college. Then I went to Berlin in the late 1980s to study at the HDK, now UDK (Berlin University of the Arts), and eventually landed in New York in the early 1990s to continue graduate studies at Parsons School of Design. Primarily I was trained as a visual artist. When I came to New York in 1992, it was the early days of the net boom. It was before Mosaic, the first graphic web browser, was invented. But I was able to use telnet to dial into university networks and it fascinated me and prompted me to think about making art beyond traditional means. By the time I did my MFA thesis project I was already working on an installation with Apple computers (sponsored by Apple). I was subsequently quite involved with the New York net art scene, typically the community gathered around the *Thing Net* in the then dilapidated Chelsea. Soon after my graduation, I began teaching at Parsons' newly established Digital Design Department, which was quickly put together to meet the educational vacuum demanded by the encroaching digital era. It was quite a free flow environment with a faculty comprised by critical thinkers, designers, hackers and artists. I was probably one of the few faculty members who came from a Fine Art background. I was interested in the misuse of technology, included art history in my curriculum, and engaged with contemporary art practice. Interestingly enough, my initial encounters with curatorial works were primarily net based; because the Internet at the time presented a utopian possibility to topple the existing institutional infrastructure, everybody was talking about a new art frontier that could rival the established artworld and the institutional hegemony. I initiated Franklin Furnace's Future of the Present artist residency programme at Parsons, which was an attempt to extend performance art into cyberspace, organized a monthly digital salon called Jihui (meaning 'gathering'), which not only received support from Parsons, but also got Rockefeller funding, I organized two conferences *Connectivity and Beyond* (1999) and *Open Source and Proxy* (2000), which were probably the earliest attempts to bring the New York artworld together to discuss the influence of the Internet on art practice in an institutional platform. In fact, my first curatorial project was an online exhibition on the giant screen of the Information Centre at 55 Broad Street in lower Manhattan's Wall Street area. I also began as a consultant for Thundergulch, the Lower Manhattan Cultural Council's (LMCC) new media art initiative and later became the LMCC's director of online media. We incorporated media artists in the Windows on the World residency on the top floor of the World Trade Center before the towers fell. Until the turn of the new millennium, I would often combine making net art, teaching and curating as an integrated practice, but slowly, my focus shifted to only curating as I realized it was cumbersome to be both an artist and a curator, not only in that these two roles are rather different but also I didn't have enough time to do both things equally well.

> There has always been a separation between people who stress the technological (material) developments of digital art and those who emphasize the art qualities (content/conceptual). At the same time digital art is also often accompanied by a fair amount of theoretical discussion. How do you position yourself in this discourse?

Z   This is primarily the new incarnation of the age-old feud between form and content: which one reigns supreme? As modernists championed innovation and while the postmodernist defended re-appropriation and pastiche as hallmarks of a fragmented contemporary, to me, the real problem lies in my proposition in the opening question, that is, form and content are reciprocally entwined, one is made of the other. In particular, as technological media are intrinsically and becoming ever more evidently autopoietic and autonomous, a kind of agential realism as Karen Barad would call it, it is qualitatively different from a medium of signification: images, signs and iconographies, in which they are employed as signifiers (forms) for the signified (content). On the other hand, the theoretical discourses that accompanied media art (I prefer to say media art to any other ways of addressing technology-based art) were in fact attempts to legitimize media art, as it's still quite marginal and sidelined in the mainstream artworld, and contemporary art is heavily contextualized through semiotic and linguistic lenses of post-structuralism. As Arthur Dante so famously said, 'contemporary art is art philosophized'.

But for me, media art follows a different trajectory of intellectual tradition, although one that has been largely overlooked and suppressed by the then postmodern renegades and the now beneficiaries of the institutional establishment, be they museums or academia. Much of my work is trying to advocate a different kind of discourse orientation, that is, to liberate from the conundrum of the many post-arts, as you said in the very beginning, which owed a debt to the humanism of modernity, toward a symbiosis of multitudes of subjecthood, a de-centering of the human for an utopian notion of the pure equality of everything. To that end, media art seems to be the most appropriate candidate.

I think the last paragraph of my curatorial essay for *thingworld*, International Media Art Triennial 2014[40] summarizes my overall agenda.

'The exhibition *thingworld* shows such a promising comingling of a world of actants, as Latour would suggest, of all kinds, animated, alive, present. Technology (as the reciprocal transduction of humanity and technicity) with its initiating motility may be the surprise candidate to turn anthropocentrism on its head: via technical beings physical beings achieve their own vivid presences, their own agency and autopoiesis, their own generativity, thereby evoking a conative penetration for the human being. They act and interact, dialogue and monologue, or chorus in the assemblage of the *thingworld*. In celebration of *thingworld*, an opportunity emerges to reinvigorate the impasse of cultural production that is contingent solely on the premise of a human subject with a much-expanded field of operation; there will be a newfound world of discussions, concerns giving rise to new forms of artistic experimentation and new vocabularies of aesthetic manifestation that resonate with a vision of equity moulded in a renewed political ecology, that is, an "Equality of All Things".'

40   *global.oup.com/academic/product/thingworld-9781781381458?cc=us&lang=en&.*

You organize online and offline exhibitions. Starting with the latter, do you work with certain methods or criteria? For instance, I recall numerous discussions in the past where showing a computer monitor was 'not done', or some curators wouldn't even consider presenting net art in an exhibition at all, while others created entirely new installations based on online work. What are your thoughts/experiences with this?

Z   It depends on how we see net-art. The Internet today is totally a different animal than it was in the 1990s. While many online activities happened in a browser environment back then, today the Internet (network) is ubiquitous and has penetrated everything around us. For that reason, I always believe we can no longer confine the concept of net-art within the boundaries of browser or screen-based experiences. Many artists use the network as the essential mechanism of their installation works in sculptural forms. For example, in the *Datumsoria: the Return of the Real* exhibition,[41] mounted at Chronus Art Center, ZKM and Nam June Paik Art Center, which I curated, we had LIU Xiaodong's robotic painting that drew live traffic data via a webcam from multiple remote locations to instantiate the time-elapsed painting process. The work on view in the gallery was comprised of three large canvases mounted on rusty construction scaffoldings, and a custom-designed robotic painting arm would jitteringly capture the moving targets in real time. Another work by YAN Lei was a 4.5 metre diameter, rotating cylindrical sculpture with over 80 screens of various sizes attached on four levels, the screens displayed images culled from the Internet and processed by an AI program that interpreted the visuals into textual description and averaged the picture into monochrome. Viewers could also upload images directly into the database via mobile devices to activate the aforementioned process. Both works were of monumental physicality and awe-striking visual power, but they were intrinsically network driven and relied on machine or human interaction with the Internet. Of course, browser-based work is still very relevant. For example, in our upcoming exhibition, the inaugural CAFAM Techne Triennial, *Topologies of the Real*, should have opened on the 20th of February 2020, but was delayed due to Covid-19, we will show *Self Portrait* by Olia Lialina, which is a portrait stitched together by drawing segments from three URLs using three alternative browsers to create a triptych presentation. We wanted to use three large vertical LCD displays, leaning diagonally against the wall. Again, the installation

41   *zkm.de/en/exhibition/2017/09/datumsoria-the-return-of-the-real.*

aims to bring about and highlight the inherent logic implicit in this idiosyncratic screen-based work. In general, because browser-centric work is primarily a private viewing or/engaging experience, it would need to adapt to the physical conditions, the flow of people, the ways of interacting in a gallery or museum setting.

> Who do you see as your audience, I guess it changes with each new context but are there also changes (and/or exchange) that you've noticed over the years... people moving from one area to another, or crossovers from other fields?

Z   All exhibitions serve educational purposes to some extent, to inform the public, to say the least, if not to persuade a change of opinion or a worldview. I've very much followed my own convictions when conceiving and planning programmes. Since these exhibitions are media art specific, they also well serve the digitally literate urban population, especially the born-digital generation. Media technologies underlie everyday work and play, politics and economies. I don't specifically intend to cater to a particular demographic or ethnic group in my curatorial works. I think my conceptual framework has been quite consistent along the same evolutionary chain. My goal has always been to advocate for an awareness of the technologically constructed reality and its implications on politics, culture and life in general.

> What do you focus on in your online exhibitions? In the past we've seen examples ranging from lists of links, to commissions, to documentation about a work, to embedding a work in a website? What is your preferred or even ideal 'model'?

Z   For a pure online exhibition such as *We=Link: Ten Easy Pieces*, we explored a collective presentation model, i.e., linking up twelve collaborating institutions to launch the show simultaneously, which seemed quite organic to the medium itself and was logistically also effective and economical, because you don't need to invest much money wise. Since this show is a time-sensitive undertaking and an ad hoc response to the current specific condition, the Covid-19 global pandemic, we commissioned six works in conjunction with a selection of four other works that connected well to the thematic focus. For me, an online work must be network native, i.e., a work cannot exist without the online medium, but not using the net as a presentation or distributing vehicle such as an embedded video, a documentation, etc. All the works in the *We=Link* show were custom-coded, network centric; to me that is the precondition for qualifying as net art or an online work.

Should digital art enter established museums or organizations or are there better places where it can be preserved and presented? If so, what role should museums play in the future?

Z   As a matter of fact, museums have been presenting and collecting 'digital art' for a long time, from MoMA to Tate, from Pompidou to Mori, not to mention the ZKM, whose mission is to acquire, present and preserve 'media art'. It's no longer an issue, except the majority of such works don't enter museum collections under the label of media art/digital art, but rather under the rubric of contemporary art in general. As I mentioned at the beginning, since media art assumes a fundamentally different role under the posthuman condition, it is necessary to demarcate it from traditionally defined contemporary art, which operated primarily under the logic of the post-structuralist discourse within the tradition of the project of modernity.

In the past I've had discussions with artists and producers about the usefulness of open source, it seems that although all kinds of codes are available they are hardly ever used by others mainly because of personal approaches to coding and the complexity resulting from such project-based methodology. What is your approach to open source in this context?

Z   Open source is a very general concept; it simply means you are free to use the codes others have developed, which of course cannot be employed without modification for a specific artwork. In my encounters with artists who are savvy in coding, it's quite common for them to incorporate useful parts from various source codes into their own coding. For example, grafting a special program feature from an open source code library.

Until recently in the Netherlands there was always a very good funding system for the arts in general and specifically for digital art. That has since changed, increasing on the one hand the divide between 'traditional' art and digital art, while on the other it generally means looking for money outside the funding system. Could you share some of your experiences working around the globe? How do you and the artists you work with survive?

Z   Well, I have to say, it's unfortunate that globally the institutional support for media art has dwindled to a new low. The situation has been particularly hard for many European artists, as they have long been used to state support as you mentioned. Since there has traditionally been little governmental support in the US, the shock has been less fatal. Many media artists have a teaching job or some other freelance work to support themselves while pursuing their artistic career. But I do feel the urgency to advocate for media art in the marketplace to promote its collection and distribution. Let's face it, an artform cannot sustain itself if it is solely dependent on government subsidy, but not in the circulation system.

One of the things that fascinates me about *We=Link: Ten Easy Pieces, Et cetera*, which alludes to the American actor Jack Nicholson's iconic movie *Five Easy Pieces* and makes a subtle twist on WeChat, the popular Chinese social media platform, how you are trying—in collaboration with a network of other hosting institutions—to recapitulate the importance of early net art practices. Could you explain the approach and aim? How did the collaboration affect the presentation and perhaps distribution of the works? And what is your interest and perspective when it comes to the future of these art practices in terms of digital preservation, documentation and collecting?

Z   With the doors of the artworld closed, online presentations have already become an institutional standard. Many arts organizations have rushed to present special programmes online in the very brief period since the global lockdown. That is of course very important, but it's one thing to put a picture online and something else entirely to show network-specific art. Net-art had its vibrant, productive and also controversial days in the 1990s when the Internet was a volatile space, and artists were out there inventing their own browsers (Maciej Wisniewski, *Netomatheque*) and trying to disrupt corporate monopolies by creating alternative infrastructures (Paul Garrin, *Name.Space*). I hope net-art revitalizes its critical approach to the network itself at the technical level (ontologically speaking), and re-examines the current predominant mode of adaptation of social media platforms while mobilizing virtual tactility and viscerality. As a matter of fact, I didn't specifically commission for the WeChat platform, but works were required to be compatible with WeChat and any other mobile platforms for the simple reason that most of the Chinese audience essentially use WeChat in their everyday work and play. WeChat is HTML5 compatible, which pretty much allows any dynamic design schemes, whether of the work itself or the exhibition platform. The title, *We=Link: Ten Easy Pieces, Et cetera,* is a word play.

I certainly see many emerging possibilities which expand the horizon of media art practice, and depart from the largely celebrated mode of artmaking on the Internet for quite some time, i.e., using social media platforms as an extension of performative space (e.g., Amalia Ulman and Petra Cortright). For example, Evan Roth's p2p networked video piece elegantly activates the virtual via the physical, Li Weiyi's playful work triggers the computer/mobile phone camera to engage participation; aaajiao's exploration of drawing icons collectively on an endless virtual canvas will eventually be linked with blockchain encryption to establish alternative identities; at first glance Tega and Sam's work seems quite plain, but they are a dynamic aggregation of hundreds and thousands of realtime data streams with a charged political outcry. Of course, you also have the net-art veterans JODI continuing to push the limits of browser-based psycho-visual emotiveness, for example.

The collective launch of the exhibition across continents definitely broadened its accessibility and helped to raise more public awareness. With regards to acquisition, preservation and documentation, I am currently working with ZKM on a large-scale collection, which will include all kinds of technology-based works made since 2000, including net-art in its various embodiments, both online in the browser mode and offline as installations.[42]

42   *zkm.de/en/project/zkm-hong-media-art-collection.*

In February 2020, Chronus Art Center collaborated with Art Center Nabi (Seoul), Rhizome of the New Museum (New York), V2_ Lab for the Unstable Media (Rotterdam), Eyebeam (New York), MU (Eindhoven), Leonardo/ISAST, SETI Institute (Mountain View), LABORATORIA Art & Science Foundation (Moscow), HeK (Basel), Arts at CERN (Geneva) E-flux (New York), to jointly develop the online exhibition *We=Link: Ten Easy Pieces* as a response to the outbreak of the Covid-19 pandemic. *We=Link* has since become a platform for presenting art online.

Zhang Ga is Consulting Curator of CAFA Art Museum, Distinguished Professor and Director of the Center for Art and Technology at China Central Academy of Fine Arts (CAFA). Previously, he was a Professor at the Tsinghua University, and an Associate Professor of Media Art at Parsons School of Design. He has held visiting positions at UCSB, Stanford, MIT, EPFL, CUNY Graduate Center, among others. He has curated numerous exhibitions including Beijing International New Media Art Exhibition and Symposium (2004–2006) and three editions of the Media Art Triennial (National Art Museum of China, 2008–2014). His recent curatorial projects include CAFAM Techne Triennial (CAFA Art Museum, forthcoming), The 6th Guangzhou Triennial (co-curator, Guangdong Art Museum, 2018), *Machines Are Not Alone* (Zagreb Contemporary Art Museum, 2018), and *unREAL: The Algorithmic Present* (co-curator, HeK Basel, 2017). Zhang Ga has spoken widely on media art and culture and his writings and edited books have been published by The MIT Press, *October*, *Flash Art International*, and Liverpool University Press, among others. He has been Director of Chronus Art Center in Shanghai since 2015, and is currently also co-curator of HONG Media Art Collection|ZKM.

Constant Dullaart

INTERVIEWEE: CONSTANT DULLAART
PROJECT: VARIOUS/UPSTREAM.GALLERY, 2020–PRESENT
WEBSITE: *constantdullaart.com*, *upstream.gallery*
DATE: 3 JUNE 2020

Can we start by defining the terminology we're using and how you position yourself within existing categories like digital art, new media, net art, contemporary art, or any of the post-arts?

C   Knowing myself, I would immediately try to escape any definition regarding my artistic position that I would formulate in answer to this question. But perhaps I can avoid talking about my own position, and briefly mention how I regard some of the terms you mentioned. I have a hard time relating to new media because I don't really understand what it means, as any medium can be new. Like the book by !Mediengruppe Bitnik with a javascript injection in the title. And with digital, I always think of the digital watch I got as a kid. So to me the difference between analogue and digital art is the microprocessor, which is hard to avoid in any process today, let alone an artistic process. I tend to use 'net-art' to refer to art that emphasizes the medium-specific materiality of the global computer networked landscape, distributed within it, and often celebrating sentiments referencing ideologies from the 1990s and being able to use a new medium to discuss or celebrate those ideologies, reflecting on the Cold War running independent media, and formal technical values of being able to use the Internet. Radically separating from that, I see 'post-Internet' art as being specifically made for the artworld and industry, and inspired by a cultural transition the Internet enabled post 2006 (when corporations like Google made online publishing easy).

What is your background and what triggered your interest in digital/net art? Could you elaborate on these initial encounters?

C   My mother used to say: 'If there was a way you could study television, you'd be a professor.' She didn't really predict my interest in media criticism, merely belittled me for not studying, while knowing the start and running times of TV shows by heart. When I escaped Dutch suburban hell, and made it to art school, I moved into a place in central Amsterdam without a cable connection and had video tapes filled with hours of TV shows on long play. I also built a TV antenna that spanned an entire floor and more of the house.

At art school I was educated by artists who ran their own local television stations, had been radio pirates, started their own nightclubs and were interested in creating their own audience and/or medium in the 1980's punk movement in Amsterdam.

267

While studying video I had to acquire an expensive camera, lighting, tripods, and other equipment to be able to create content that was ready to be broadcast to a large audience (television in this case). For editing I bought my first computer at the local supermarket (you could buy the first iMac at the Albert Heijn supermarket).

At first the Internet seemed to be an information resource only. Besides some funny URLs from print media, I found most things to be very tedious in comparison to TV, but that all changed as soon as online publishing was simplified by online video and image compression; initially it was small scale on advertising websites, and rapidly moved to video-hosting websites. The amount of content I saw that was made without the expensive camera, lighting, tripods I had and used was revolutionary to me. I saw honest, amateur, non-pretentious content from all over the globe that I liked better than all the content I'd seen at art school combined. As soon as I realized I could make a website in an evening and publish to my own audience within this new vernacular, I was hooked.

> There has always been a separation between people who stress the technological (material) developments of digital art and those who emphasize the art qualities (content/conceptual). At the same time digital art is also often accompanied by a fair amount of theoretical discussion. How do you position yourself in this discourse?

C I am specifically interested in the ways in which the formal values of a medium and it's medium-specific qualities influence how content is created, distributed, consumed and broadcast. Content is mostly interchangeable; it's just the form that changes that helps us relate to the 'seven types of love'; the rest is politics and fashion. It's similar to how Shakespeare's stories can be retold in different languages. How mass-media cultural tropes travel between cultural planes and consumption realms creates a friction akin to hearing a piece of music you already know, orchestrated by different instruments in a new landscape. So perhaps I find myself in the middle, interested in the translation, and how this affects the content. But often the content is arbitrary in my work. So not like the great Conlon Nancarrow, who was interested in the formal possibilities of the player piano, but in translating music that wasn't composed for piano so it could be played on a piano, and enjoying the friction the results create.

You organize online and offline exhibitions. Starting with the latter, do you work with certain methods or criteria? For instance, I recall numerous discussions in the past where showing a computer monitor was 'not done', or some curators wouldn't even consider presenting net art in an exhibition at all, while others created entirely new installations based on online work. What are your thoughts/experiences with this?

C   Chris Coy responded to the group e-mail discussion about Rhizome's archiving of the nastynets website by saying something along the lines of: what we put online was published with the understanding that anyone could download, copy and alter it, so he had no objection to archiving the website with its own context in a new context. I liked that radical notion, and have lived by it ever since. Because I enjoy the friction of translation I tend to enjoy the awkwardness of a physical representation based on an online experience within the realms of a cultural institution, simple and blunt translations emphasizing the difference between the two cultural planes: online and offline.

Who do you see as your audience, I guess it changes with each new context but are there also changes (and/or exchanges) that you've noticed over the years... people moving from one area to another, or crossovers from other fields?

C   This is a very private question, but in principle the audience that understands the cultural references and media-specific values of online or software culture is growing, with more and more people being connected and having a history with the medium or its affiliated hardware and software, which means that there is room for nostalgia and a new cultural understanding of online agency (new generations use the Internet differently each time of course). And more people seem to understand the pleasure derived from referencing this and creating new narratives within or with this.

What do you focus on in your online exhibitions? In the past we've seen examples ranging from lists of links, to commissions, to documentation about a work, to embedding a work in a website? What is your preferred or even ideal model?

C   The new model of showing online works alongside references to offline works in a single website is my all-time favourite. You can hear one work while looking at the next, just as you would in a physical exhibition. You can make relationships between works within the same show, and enjoy a multitude of different media, be it a PDF, a video, a sequence of gifs, a 3D object, 360 image, webgame, etc. Adding the social element of seeing the other visitors represented with a simple dot, and being able to hear the dot when in close proximity (for example when you're looking at the same work), copies social behaviour within an art institution in such a simple and direct way. And I love the friction that this creates.

> Should digital art enter established museums or organizations or are there better places where it can be preserved and presented? If so, what role should museums play in the future?

C   Of course it already has: as art made with the help of microprocessors. As far as I know there aren't any museums devoted only to painting, and for me a museum is a place where shared culture with a defined value for an audience is archived, stored and displayed (in that order). Why this would not include art made with the help of a microprocessor, or which manifests with the networked landscape, is beyond me.

> In the past I've had discussions with artists and producers about the usefulness of open source, it seems that although all kinds of codes are available they are hardly ever used by others mainly because of personal approaches to coding and the complexity resulting from such project-based methodology. What is your approach to open source in this context?

C   Open-core, friends and improvization.

> Until recently in the Netherlands there was always a very good funding system for the arts in general and specifically for digital art. That has since changed, increasing on the one hand the divide between 'traditional' art and digital art, while on the other it generally means looking for money outside the funding system. Could you share some of your experiences working around the globe? How do you and the artists you work with survive?

C   Well most of the people and artists I work with never had the funding opportunities I did, and still have, in the Netherlands. They either live from other jobs such as teaching or programming, management or advertising, and rarely make a living from commercial gallery sales. But I see more people using the Patreon model recently and less people working with crowdfunding solutions for projects. I think there's currently more space for projects with a potential or partial commercial revenue: identifying some of the works for cultural initiatives as startups. Until now I've been lucky enough to cycle between all possible solutions besides the Patreon premium membership model. An additional remark I'd like to make is that I see artists exchanging work, which is something I don't understand. Most of my works are available for free or on request, and those that are for sale were made to help me make rent. Exchanging works with another artist, removes two works from the potential revenue stream. I therefore prefer gifting or buying a work with the revenue from a sale. The idea that an artwork is not immediately a commodity emphasizes the effort needed to have artworks travel as a product, or to be bought. The informal economy that exists between colleagues can mostly do without this, if the exchange of ideas and not the potential value of the commodity is truly of importance.

> You're one of the initiators of the online platform upstream.gallery that launched during the Covid-19 epidemic. For your curated exhibition *The New Outside* you refer to the issue of 'the depiction of this new outside', and while the format stresses the importance and urgency of net art in the current moment, you ask: 'Who will help to redefine this important space to give hope, offer new ways of seeing, reflect, create new worlds, make art?' In what way does *The New Outside* provide an answer and how is it different from the online events you organized or were part of in the past?
> Since you have a long history with online platforms and curation, what is your interest and perspective when it comes to the future of these art practices in terms of digital preservation, documentation and collecting?

C   I spoke with Nieck de Bruijn of Upstream, Jonas Lund and Jan Robert Leegte about the bad online exhibitions we saw as a response to the Covid-19 lockdown, and how easy it would be for us to make a better alternative. We made it happen quickly by using a format I'd already developed in 2011 together with Jonas [editor's note: this format was first applied in *temporarystedelijk.com*, see p. 58]. And I had an interaction idea that I really wanted to try out.

The way that the exhibition provides social feedback by displaying the other visitors, and the feature that allows visitors to actually hear each other (released during the consecutive show), clearly provided a sense of joy during these times of social distancing. People haven't seen each other in a long time and suddenly they're bumping into each other in a virtual gallery. Suddenly the social interaction became more important than the exhibition, which is something that also happens, or used to happen, at a physical exhibition. Within *The New Outside* I am presenting different formal approaches to depicting natural environments and or behaviors online. I am trying to show these formal values as inspiration for future dreams and nostalgia, or the period before social distancing.

Upstream.Gallery: Networks have existed for many decades, yet now is a perfect time to dive into all the great works of art the Internet has to offer. The urgency of this type of art becomes apparent in these times of Covid-19, especially because traditional artworks shown online suffer from the disadvantage that they are reduced to reproductions on a screen. These times demand something different and the artform that is undoubtedly best equipped for these conditions is art made for the Internet. For these exhibitions, no works have to be shipped, no one has to leave their home, and best of all, such works can be experienced in their full glory. The only thing you need is a computer device and an Internet connection. In spring 2020 Upstream and Constant Dullaart decided to develop a new online platform. Joining forces with Jan Robert Leegte, Jonas Lund, and Ties van Asseldonk and Deborah Mora of Interaction Design Artez, the idea manifested as *upstream.gallery*, an online platform for exhibitions developed, curated and participated in by artists and curators who belong to the top of the digital art world. The platform developed independently afterwards and has become its own institutional setting beyond the gallery, developing the interaction technology for future exhibitions, and specifically their openings, as well as creating monthly exhibitions in multiple cities, online.

Constant Dullaart: The fluidity of boundaries between artist and tech communities and questions of authorship, virtuosity, and the performativity of art in a mediated environment, are important aspects in Constant Dullaart's work. He reflects on the broad cultural and social effects of communication and image-processing technologies. Dullaart's work stays firmly yet defiantly within the realm of contemporary art, but from a position profoundly informed by the conditions of new media networks—technical as well as cultural, social, economical and political. Dullaart strives for an honest, respectful, yet unembellished approach to the materials and conditions of the network. At the same time his work is full of humour and critical commentary, and includes websites, performances, routers, installations, start-ups, armies, and manipulated found images, frequently juxtaposing or consolidating technically dichotomized presentation realms. His work is exhibited internationally in museums, galleries and institutions, and Dullaart has curated several online and offline exhibitions and lectured at universities and academies throughout Europe and the United States.

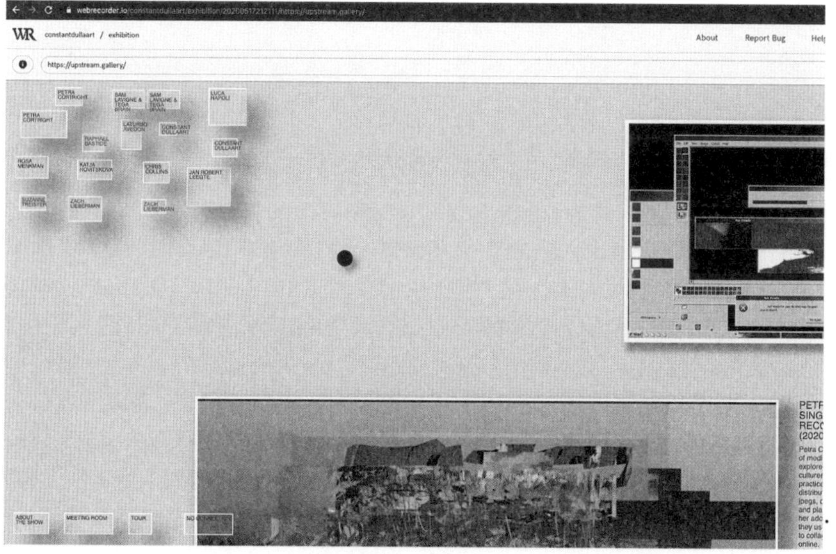

Anika Meier

INTERVIEWEE: ANIKA MEIER
PROJECT: VARIOUS
WEBSITE: *instagram.com/anika*
DATE: 3 JUNE 2020

Can we start by defining the terminology we're using and how you position yourself within existing categories like digital art, new media, net art, contemporary art, or any of the post-arts?

A   I'm interested in art that works with social media. There are many terms such as post-Internet art, social media art, Instagram art, digital art and net art. Do we need all these categories and what is the difference? What would an Instagram artist be for example? Is it someone who does a long-term performance on Instagram like the German artist Andy Kassier, who calls himself a conceptual artist? Or is it someone like Amalia Ulman, who became famous for her performance *Excellences & Perfections* around 2015? Ulman calls herself an artist because she doesn't only make work in relation to Instagram. While these categories might be helpful when describing an artwork they are not appropriate to describe an artist's complete oeuvre because artists don't limit themselves to a social media platform.

Andy Kassier for example created an alter ego on Instagram. In this long-term performance, Kassier's character always shows up where the sun is shining and it's raining money. His hair is on point, a smile is attached to his face, and his shoes and cars gleam. He's never at a loss for a motivational quote that is supposed to help you achieve happiness and success. 'Taking risks and succeeding make you a winning player. Never forget that you could have become a tree instead of a human being. So be happy every second of your life. Just be yourself.' Kassier's character is the personification of the false promise that money, power, and a carefree life are within everyone's reach. He combines critique with a sympathetic attitude towards a generation that always aims farther and higher, wants to get there ever faster, and is choosing #nevernotworking as its mantra even though his jobs often remain somewhat intangible.

In the process, however, Kassier overworked himself. In spring 2019, a burnout drove him into the sea and he disappeared for half a year. Now he—and his character—are practicing self-love and self-care. He no longer lives in the fast lane. Still high above the ground, of course, he is now sitting on a swing in the midst of nature. 'A stable job is a sign of weakness', he once proclaimed. Today, he's on a path of self-discovery through yoga and meditation. He hopes to recalibrate his work–life balance with the help of alternative healing methods. He takes time off to pause and think about things. His mirror reminds him: 'Time to reflect'. Kassier lives in the here and now. Art allows him to maintain a mental equilibrium.

This performance could be called Instagram art. Kassier builds installations for museum and gallery shows that are based on it; he creates an environment for his alter ego such as the living room that was exhibited at the Museum of Fine Arts in Leipzig. This installation could be called 'post-Internet art'. When the artist Marisa Olson coined the term in 2006 she was thinking of art made after the Internet, which means art *in the style of the Internet*. Later, when the art world became interested in the movement, post-Internet art was understood as art that was made to be seen in galleries or museums and at the same time looked good in photos on social media.

A solution could be to use the term 'net art' as an umbrella because the Internet is the common ground and the starting point.

What is your background and what triggered your interest in digital/net art? Could you elaborate on these initial encounters?

A   I studied art history and German literature in Heidelberg and planned to write a PhD about the German poet Stefan George. I lived in Paris for a year after graduating, where I was part of a research group on the topic of silence at Deutsches Forum für Kunstgeschichte. It wasn't as boring as it might sound but it was boring enough for someone who'd moved from a small German town to a big city in France. Everything was new and exciting for me and I wanted to show my family and friends my new life in the big city. That was in 2011, Instagram was new, and I started using it to avoid writing e-mails to my friends every day. Instagram was more interesting than the German poet I was supposed to be reading and writing about daily. Since part of the book I was writing dealt with photos of Stefan George made by artists, I read and learned a lot about photography. I had a feeling that Instagram might be very influential, so I started reading everything on social media and photography and moved on to art and social media when artists became engaged with the platform.

You organize online and offline exhibitions. Starting with the latter, do you work with certain methods or criteria? For instance, I recall numerous discussions in the past where showing a computer monitor was 'not done', or some curators wouldn't even consider presenting net art in an exhibition at all, while others created entirely new installations based on online work. What are your thoughts/experiences with this?

A	There are always people who say that net art doesn't need to be shown in a museum because it was made to be seen on the Internet. This is also what I heard when I curated the group show *Link in Bio: Art After Social Media* at the Museum of Fine Arts in Leipzig. Are only paintings and sculptures worthy of being exhibited in museums? That's why post-Internet art became popular around 2015. Artists created art that was based on the Internet but it looked familiar and could be sold. You don't need to know how code works to understand post-Internet art. You're looking at paintings, sculptures and installations again.

Internet cafés have almost completely disappeared from our cityscapes. Whereas in 2012 only 36% of the German population had a smartphone, 81% had one 2018. Today, the Internet is as close as everyone's pockets. In 2010, however, when German media artist Aram Bartholl developed an exhibition format that transformed an Internet café into an exhibition space for one evening, people were still making regular use of the numerous computers available in such cafés to send e-mails. In Bartholl's *Speed Show*, the same computers display net art—that is, art that uses the Internet as a medium, deals with the genuine properties of the Internet, and addresses its underlying technology.

Anyone can translate the concept of the *Speed Show* into practice. Bartholl's instructions are as follows:

> Go to an Internet café, rent all the computers for one evening, and curate an exhibition on the machines. The works of the participating artists have to be online and are shown in a browser. The use of custom software and offline files is not permitted (browser add-ons are exempted). The Internet café itself must not be changed in any way. The show is open to the public and takes place during the normal hours of the café. Visitors are invited to participate in the exhibition opening, to enjoy the art, and to check their e-mail.

Between 2010 and 2016, 45 *Speed Shows* were held across the globe in cities such as Los Angeles, Lyon, Linz, Hong Kong, Beijing, New York, Toronto, Tel Aviv, Dublin, Vienna, Amsterdam, Milan, and Berlin. In 2019, Bartholl and I reactivated the format in Berlin with the exhibition *Face the Face: A Speed Show on the Post-Digital-Self*. Whereas Internet art came into existence before the general public had access to the web, social media permits a wider audience to encounter Internet art in their everyday lives, whether they are aware of it or not.

For *Link in Bio* Bartholl turned an Internet café into an installation and we curated part two of *Face the Face: A Speed Show on the Post-Digital-Self* together. When it comes to curating museum shows, my criterion is historical relevance, but my focus is on contemporary net art.

Who do you see as your audience, I guess it changes with each new context but are there also changes (and/or exchanges) that you've noticed over the years... people moving from one area to another, or crossovers from other fields?

A   When I curate exhibitions or write texts for newspapers and magazines I don't have a community in mind; I write and curate for everyone who is interested in art. I also keep this in mind when I write exhibition texts: everyone needs to be able to understand the context. The title *Link in Bio* is easy for Instagram users to understand, but it's impossible for someone who isn't active on the platform to know what it means.

What do you focus on in your online exhibitions? In the past we've seen examples ranging from lists of links, to commissions, to documentation about a work, to embedding a work in a website? What is your preferred or even ideal 'model'?

A   So far, I've curated one online exhibition. For me the ideal model is presenting digital art in its genuine environment, the digital realm. With *SURPRISINGLY THIS RATHER WORKS*, curated by gallerist Johann König and myself, KÖNIG GALERIE presents an exhibition of digital art by Manuel Rossner that is both a spatial intervention in and a virtual expansion of the physical gallery. The digital visitor enters the virtual gallery through an app.

SURPRISINGLY THIS RATHER WORKS shows a series of digital objects that form a *parcours*, which the visitor can explore by means of an avatar. Rossner has transformed the Brutalist St. Agnes Church into a gaming environment inspired by the 1990's game show 'American Gladiators' and by 'gyms' that are used for cutting-edge research in artificial intelligence by companies such as OpenAI in San Francisco.

Things that are impossible in physical space become possible in the digital environment. In the latter, a treadmill breaks through the floor and the back wall of the nave of St. Agnes. A huge yellow sculpture sprawls like a plant through the stairwell all the way up to the church tower. An amorphous object made up of blue and pink bubbles spreads out beneath the ceiling of the church. Smooth algorithmic material takes over the austere

 Brutalist building.

Rules that normally apply in exhibition spaces are suspended in this digital environment. Whereas visitors are typically warned not to touch the artwork, they are now asked to 'please interact'. Using the navigation on their smartphone displays, visitors steer the avatar through the gallery with the commands 'Walk', 'Jump', and 'Look'. Accordingly, the avatar runs and jumps over large boulders that lead up to the ceiling of the nave, where two more objects need to be traversed before it enters the amorphous sculpture. Another jump—and the avatar runs on, into the blue bubbles, up an enormous yellow sculpture, turning round and round, ascending ever higher until it reaches the very top. After yet another leap, the avatar returns to the floor of the nave, where the digital visitor can explore paintings and sculptures by Rossner. The invitation to interact with these works of art also means that the visitor is allowed to knock them over.

In the digital realm, the boundaries between painting and sculpture begin to blur. Rossner explains his work process as follows: 'A controller that passes the position of my hand in 3D space on to the computer converts my movements into lines, which in turn are transformed into volumes.' Rossner thus creates objects that are, at one and the same time, both paintings and sculptures.

> Should digital art enter established museums or organizations or are there better places where it can be preserved and presented? If so, what role should museums play in the future?

A   The role of museums and institutions is to show art that is relevant for the history of art and for our time. Museums have to keep their audience in mind if they want to be relevant in the future. The younger generation grows up on social media, they are used to scrolling through photos and videos and interacting with art and artists online. This is what Johann and I kept in mind when we were working with Manuel on his solo show. We asked ourselves, what can art be in the digital age? How can it be experienced? Museums need to understand that their audience is used to interacting with art. Digital art can fulfill these needs because things that are impossible in a white cube in a museum can be realized in the digital realm.

> Until recently in the Netherlands there was always a very good funding system for the arts in general and specifically for digital art. That has since changed, increasing on the one hand the divide between 'traditional' art and digital art, while on the other it generally means looking for money outside the funding system. Could you share some of your experiences working around the globe? How do you and the artists you work with survive?

A   The role of the artist has changed in the digital age. Artists who have grown up on social media are artists and digital creatives. Most of them have a large following on Instagram. They know for example how to make AR filters or how to come up with a communication strategy. Brands hire them to create content, to build filters and websites or to plan a communication strategy. They don't need to sell art for a living, which doesn't mean that they don't sell art. Imagine an artist whose project is a long-term performance on Instagram living from his or her art—it would be almost impossible. Artists have learned that they have skills that are still rare these days. For example, Johanna Jaskowska, who created the famous Beauty3000 AR filter, works with brands like Burberry and musicians like Billie Eilish and Lady Gaga.

You break with the suggestion that photography on Instagram is merely about getting likes and how such platforms can actually still complement the traditional publication of photography. Could you explain your approach, also in relation to your other work as a curator (for instance of the exhibitions *Virtual Normality: NetzkünstlerInnen 2.0* and *Link in Bio: Art After Social Media*)?

A   Artists and photographer who think about photography in the digital age don't necessarily take photos themselves or make new photographs. One of the chapters in *Link in Bio* was about photography in the age of social media. On social media such as Instagram and Tumblr, images never appear in isolation but, rather, refer to each other in 'curated' accounts. With hashtags such as #thattoweragain, users react to each other and make it clear that they're aware that Berlin's Television Tower is a frequent motif. Binschtok reclaims her autonomy as a photographer by creating her own networks of images. For the series *Cluster* (2014), she uses a photograph from her archive as her point of departure. Using image search on the Internet, she found pictures that resembled her original photograph in terms of form, colour, and structure. Binschtok then re-photographed the found materials and arranged them in clusters. She responds to visual practices that are widespread in the era of digital media. As in music, an original is followed by numerous cover versions, but there are no longer any clues as to where the original came from.

On social media, photographs are not objects in their own right but, rather, a way to communicate experiences. German artist Hannah Sophie Dunkelberg also turns photographs into objects, in the literal sense of the word. She scans her analogue photos and assembles them into collages, which then serve as the surfaces of her sculptures. In nature water droplets on leaves reflect their surroundings. Dunkelberg directly prints the outside world onto the leaf as a three-dimensional object. In the exhibition space, fallen leaves lie next to life buoys: just as in the past, photography has to do with remembrance and offers something to hold on to.

Roland Barthes once wrote that photographs produce death while trying to preserve life. In a similar vein, Susan Sontag remarked that the link between photography and death haunts all photographs of people. Today, people write happy autobiographies with the images they post on social media. As if on stage, they perform perfection and success. The moment is shared with friends and followers. After 24 hours, the past disappears from Stories on Instagram.

Critics complain that the visual waste on social media knows no bounds. Dunkelberg references a piece of furniture that was popular in the nineteenth century, during a time when photography had just been invented but already provoked feelings of discomfort and excess. Her couch for fainting provides a place where one can recover from a dizzy spell.

> What is your interest and perspective when it comes to digital preservation, documentation and collecting the things you exhibit—both online and offline, and/or how they influence each other?

A   I don't collect art because I prefer my walls to be empty.

Anika Meier, author and curator, studied art history and German literature in Heidelberg and Paris. She writes a column on art and social media for the magazine *Monopol*, and her texts have appeared in *Die Zeit, Frankfurter Allgemeine Zeitung, Die Welt, Spiegel Online, Kunstforum, Numéro Berlin, der Freitag, Tagesspiegel*, and *Mindstate Malibu*, among others. Her most recent exhibitions include the exhibition series *The Artist is Online* curated with Johann König at KÖNIG GALERIE and KÖNIG DIGITAL. The first exhibition in this series was the digital show *Surprisingly This Rather Works* with Manuel Rossner (2020). Other exhibitions include *Link in Bio: Art after Social Media* (2019–2020) and *Virtual Normality*. She co-edited the catalogue accompanying *Women Net Artists 2.0* (2018) at the Museum of Fine Arts in Leipzig with Alfred Weidinger (published by the Verlag für moderne Kunst).

1   Manuel Rossner, *Surprisingly This Rather Works*, 2020, exhibition view.
2   Manuel Rossner, *Surprisingly Surprisingly*, 2020, light. Courtesy of the artist and König Galerie, Berlin.

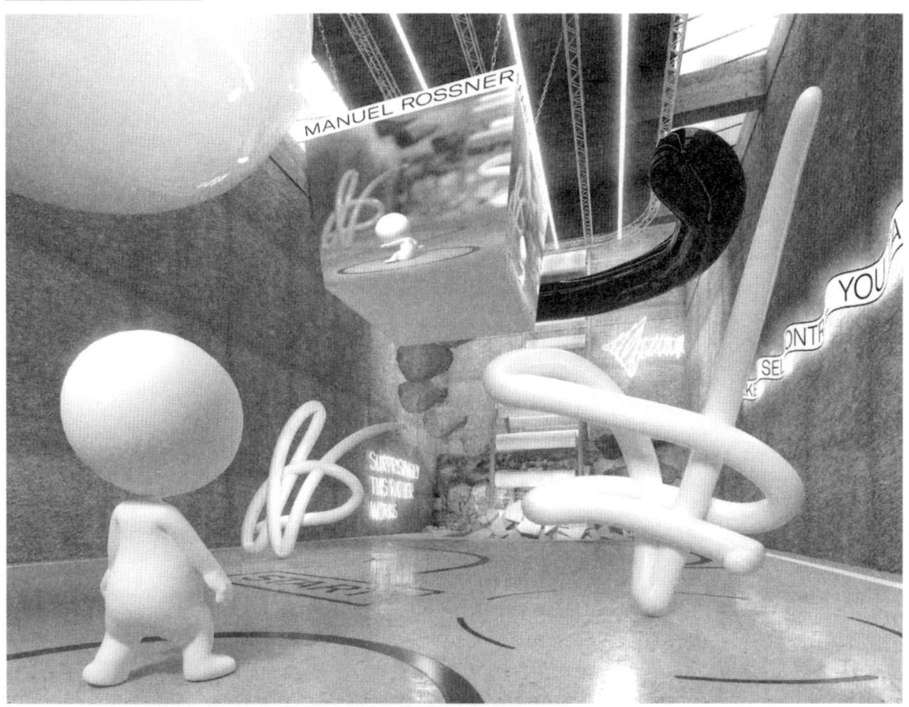

1

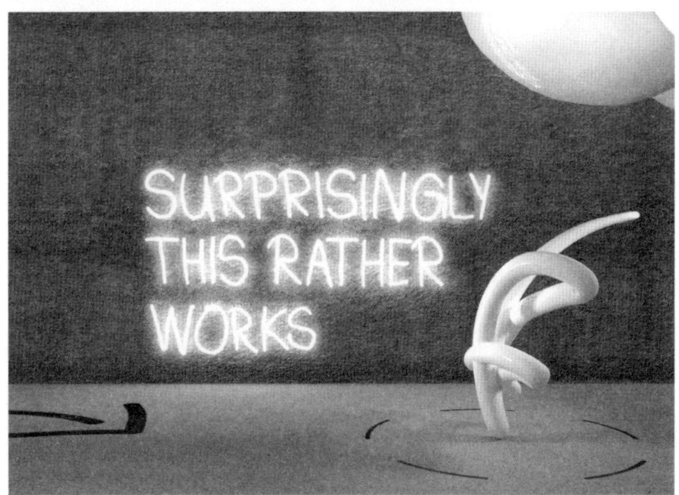

2

Marco De Mutiis, Katrina Sluis & Jon Uriarte

INTERVIEWEE: MARCO DE MUTIIS, KATRINA SLUIS, JON URIARTE
PROJECT: VARIOUS – YOU MUST NOT CALL IT PHOTOGRAPHY IF THIS EXPRESSION HURTS YOU, 2019–PRESENT
WEBSITE: *youmustnotcallit.photography*
DATE: 8 JUNE 2020

Can we start by defining the terminology we're using and how you position yourself within existing categories like digital art, new media, net art, contemporary art, or any of the post-arts?

K   When Jon, Marco and I started our collaboration, we were all dealing with the somewhat perplexing experience of working as digital curators within different European photographic institutions. There was something amusing and paradoxical about championing digital practices within organizations whose mission it is to uphold medium specificity. Of course, these disciplinary boundaries are in themselves very interesting to probe and observe, and reveal much about circuits of cultural value. Photography, as a technology of reproduction, fought long and hard to be regarded as 'art'. In Britain, the Tate only deemed it necessary to appoint its first photography curator in 2009—by that point, post-photographic discourse was already two decades old. This project of legitimation has resulted in a denial of the bastardized, vernacular, ubiquitous messiness of photographic culture—which is precisely the sort of chaos we want to insert into cultural institutions! So this gives you a flavour of our inherited positions—before we even get to the slippery taxonomies of digital art. Speaking for myself, the context of working within The Photographers' Gallery has liberated me from defending any cultural practice as 'art' (or its new media sub-brands), since photography is both *art* and *not-art*—and its role as not-art is arguably the more interesting.

What is your background and what triggered your interest in digital/net art? Could you elaborate on these initial encounters?

K   I grew up in Sydney, and my first experience of network culture was when I started hanging out on a local BBS and different MUDs as a teenager. I went on to art school in the 1990s when Australia was an important hub of media art practice, and was exposed to the work of Mongrel, Stelarc, Sandy Stone, McKenzie Wark. During that period I also worked on the CompuServe Pacific helpdesk, so I was very immersed in the technical and cultural aspects of the early net. However, it took me a long time to connect these various spheres of my life and interests, as I was devoted to painting as an undergrad! I defected to the Photomedia workshop, and after graduation escaped to the UK where I ended up in a media sociology department teaching photography and digital art. This framing shifted my practice tremendously, and by the mid 2000s I started fusing photography theory with software studies in my writing about the networked image.

J   My parents bought a Fujitsu computer when I was a kid in the 1980s. Even though their jobs were not particularly related to computers and they didn't know much about them, they thought that it would be good for us to become familiar with the technology. When I later studied first sound, then film and finally photography I always ended up connecting those interests with the digital in one way or another. Digital photography started to be commercially available when I was majoring, but the school where I studied forced the students to make photographs using only black and white film for the first two years. I was only allowed to make digital photos and use Photoshop in the third year. However, I managed to make my final project using appropriation and digital post-production. My frustration about the traditional and conservative standards of photography in Spain during the 1990s and the joy and new possibilities that digital technologies offered inspired me to keep on following that path.

M   I've always tinkered with computers, but it's only when I moved to China in my twenties that I felt computational technologies were part of contemporary culture. I often felt suffocated by outdated ideas of what is allowed in the museum growing up in Italy, a country that comes with such heavy historical baggage and where the past seems to smother everything. I remember arriving at the School of Creative Media in Hong Kong to attend my MFA studies and feeling finally part of an international community of artists and scholars who critically and playfully engaged with technology and digital tools to express themselves and address social and political issues. My experience in Asia was also very formative in helping me to think outside of Western traditions and disciplinary boundaries. Moving back to Europe to work for a photography museum made me realize how much the institutional walls complicated a more fluid approach to and understanding of photographic and visual cultures.

> You've been involved in various types of organizations and spaces. Could you share some of your experiences working in these different settings and particular contexts? For example, how does it affect your practice? Are there specific things that work very well in one context but not at all in another?

K   As Marco notes I think the limitations of institutions and their unrealized potential has been the dominant context of our work, both collectively and as individuals. Many of the artists we work with in our respective institutions will be familiar to those engaged with new media art; however, their work is unknown and yet potentially transformative for the photographic community. At the same time, at The Photographers' Gallery I was interested in moving beyond the artist as a privileged site of knowledge, in order to engage with a variety of practitioners—from computer scientists to cat photographers—as active agents in the production of visual culture. Photography provides a less intimidating, banal and unassuming cover from which to operate—and allowed us incredible scope to experiment, whether it's commissioning Jonas Lund to transform a floor of the Gallery into a propaganda office in an attempt to reverse Brexit, or our endeavour to exhibit the fourteen million images of the computer vision dataset ImageNet on our media wall in 2019.

> There has always been a separation between people who stress the technological (material) developments of digital art and those who emphasize the art qualities (content/conceptual). At the same time digital art is also often accompanied by a fair amount of theoretical discussion. How do you position yourself in this discourse?

K   I don't think the material and conceptual can be disconnected—can they? On the one hand, I share Geert Lovink and Alexander Galloway's frustration with 'vapour theory', which ignores the material conditions of networks and protocols in favour of grand theorizations of 'the digital'. At the same time, I also have a healthy scepticism for contemporary art, its practices and discourses. Given my background, I'm very much drawn to artists and scholars who approach the material technical conditions through which art and culture is reproduced as profoundly political.

J   I agree with Katrina that both need to be connected; the technical conditions as well as the art discourses where the artistic practices take place should be related and very well balanced. If I had to choose between a technically poor artwork with a strong idea and a spectacular material development, I'd definitely go for the first one, most probably because I'd connect the second one to the logic of the neo-capitalist branding of the latest technological development, where seemingly innocuous and useful tools hide potentially harmful intentions.

M   Yes, both are essentially intertwined. While there is definitely a tension between the two, I personally feel that the divide lies more in what is accepted within the art discourse and what is excluded—like Katrina was hinting in her remark. Net art and new media art initially became isolated art worlds and self-sufficient systems, yet they are organically so much part of many other art worlds and contribute to the discourse of so many other disciplines. Similarly, photography and digital art have so much to 'learn' from each other, and they share both the technical and conceptual aspects.

> Who do you see as your audience? I guess it changes with each new context but is there also a change (and/or exchanges) that you've noticed over the years, people moving from one place to another, or crossovers from other fields?

J   Given my photographic background and the institutions where I've worked (Foto Colectania/TPG) my core audience has been mainly people interested in photography. However, as most of my curatorial practice has been related to the digital and I've always sought to connect photography with other mediums, there's also always been an audience from new media arts, computer science, net art, digital arts and so on. As the digital has become much more present in our everyday lives, I've also seen a growing interest from photography and art students over the last few years.

K   It's worth noting that the establishment of a digital programme at The Photographers' Gallery in 2012 was informed by a desire to reach new audiences. This has since become something of a mantra of UK arts policy framework where 'the digital' is mobilized as a solution for transmitting art to new audience segments. My own approach has been to develop projects that draw upon the knowledge of our audiences, who are not passive consumers of an art experience but actively engaged in producing photographic culture. This has been reflected in a series of *Media Wall* projects, including *Born in 1987: The Animated GIF* (2012), *d(^_^)b* (2015) and *For the LOL of Cats: Felines, Photographers and the Web* (2012), which was produced in collaboration with many online curators of cat photography. When we decided to throw a *25th Birthday Party for Photoshop*, we had 750 visitors, including many local Soho post-production workers who were drawn in by the promise of RGB cocktails, a cut-and-paste live Photoshop studio and a live Photoshop Battle. A very different crowd of Instagram hipsters and older 'photo daddies' were seduced by our *Hyperanalogue Geekender* which offered a more palatable steampunk vision of art and technology. Of course, our collective work as *YMNCIPITEHY (You Must Not Call It Photography If This Expression Hurts You)* exploits audiences in different ways—drawing on their frustrations and expertise to co-author a new manifesto of photography, collected via focus group or e-questionnaire, and dutifully distributed on Twitter by a photo manifesto bot.

M   Looking back, I definitely think there's more interest and activities on the part of museums to tackle many of the issues that relate to contemporary digital technologies in the context of photography. However, we should be careful not to succumb to the tyranny of the audience, in the way that more and more cultural institutions segment and target their content to follow the metrics of neoliberal market strategies. I think museums and programmes can shape their audience, rather than offering content in response to what they imagine their viewers want. It's also very important to take into consideration audiences who remain more invisible to the traditional metrics used to measure the success of exhibitions (e.g., ticket sales). With the Fotomuseum's blog *Still Searching* we have attracted a community of scholars and people interested in the discourse around photography, with an impact on an international audience who might range from photography lovers to artists, from university students to curators. I think The Photographers' Gallery *Unthinking Photography* platform is another great example of what the online museum could offer and how it can create platforms that facilitate the transmission of knowledge to a diverse audience from different places and backgrounds.

> What do you focus on in your online exhibition/project(s)? In the past we've seen examples ranging from lists of links, to commissions, to documentation about a work, to embedding a work in a website? What is your preferred or even ideal 'model'?

K   Working within a cultural organization, the online space becomes very contested, as it's usually the domain of the communications and marketing team, who are under incredible pressure to convert online traffic into physical audiences. Corporate web servers are tightly controlled, and administered by expensive external web developers who are rarely sympathetic to the installation of unauthorized scripts. So this becomes a boring, yet important factor limiting the format and scale of online projects. For a long-term project like *Unthinking Photography*, it made sense to escape these battles and establish a satellite website where we had the freedom to experiment with different formats and (crucially) potentially fail. Other projects, such as Sebastian Schmieg's commission *Decision Space* (2016), required major strategic manoeuvring and an excellent working relationship with the artist to realize it as a site-specific online project. *Decision Space* ultimately turned all the visitors to The Photographers' Gallery website into clickworkers who classified the platform's visual content, producing a new dataset for machine vision in the process. Working in collaboration with Jon and Marco as *YMNCIPITEHY*, it's been liberating to be able to focus less on logistics and more on the subversive possibilities of different formats, both online and offline.

M	In our *SITUATIONS* programme at Fotomuseum Winterthur, we've tried to play a lot with the specificity of the online platform and of the physical space, sometimes showing works that had complementary parts on both sides. I enjoy ephemeral online projects which connect to the performative side of the Internet, but institutionally I think online platforms have a great advantage compared to exhibitions in physical spaces in terms of temporality and knowledge transfer. We often preserve and host documentations and links and bibliographies online, allowing content to be experienced long after the exhibition experience is available.

> Should digital art enter established museums or organizations or are there better places where it can be preserved and presented? If so, what role should museums play in the future?

M	I definitely think digital art should be preserved by museums, although a shift in both the infrastructure and the mindset of such institutions is still largely absent. Also, collecting culturally relevant digital works might be more problematic in terms of authorship rather than solely because of technical concerns. The ways museum collections and archives work are structured around very different parameters—think editions, copyright, value, insurance—that are hard to apply when preserving and presenting memes and gifs, which defy scarcity and authorship through their circulatory power and cultural impact. My wish is for museums to support external initiatives. Instead of seeing *Know Your Meme* being acquired by Cheezburger Network and *Giphy* by Facebook, I would love to see support and assistance from major cultural institutions, while respecting the unique role these individuals and small organizations are playing outside of the museum.

> One of your recent projects is *You Must Not Call It Photography If This Expression Hurts You*, which you mention can take the form of a (subverted) manifesto, a map, a guidebook, group therapy and aims to disrupt, provoke, and parasitically infiltrate the traditional photographic discourse and propose alternative approaches that are critical, playful and sincere. Could you explain your approach?

J	The manifesto and the events that we've done with *YMNCIPITEHY* are playful and provocative responses to the traditional understanding and practice of photography. When

I was working on *DONE* with Foto Colectania in Barcelona, I felt quite isolated in my curatorial approach to visual networked culture. Even if I was following an international scene with which I could feel somehow connected, it was formed mainly by artists or artists/curators working independently abroad and not specifically within photography. There were not, and still aren't, many photo curators working at photography institutions with whom a wider critical point of view on the medium in relation to the digital can be discussed. *YMNCIPITEHY* became a place to share frustrations, provocations, jokes and critical thoughts; maybe first as a therapy between peers that would then also be shared with an audience to enlist them in the cause :)

K   There is no doubt the project was born out of isolation and frustration with our organizational silos. Our collaboration is underpinned by a deep mutual fascination with the conceptual richness of approaching art, media and technology through the lens of post-photography. In addition to being artists and curators, all three of us work as educators—and I would argue that *YMNCIPITEHY* is underpinned by a desire to make quite complex ideas and practices accessible to the wider community. Our humour and the formats we adopt is, in part, a reaction to the very male, heroic and insular discourse of photography that museums have historically propagated. On the one hand, running a 'Who did it better in Google Street View' championship at Paris Photo is a hilarious thought experiment. In reality, it offered an opportunity to playfully engage with the politics of Google Street View photography, and introduce the work of numerous practitioners to an audience who had never encountered this genre before.

M   I definitely think *YMNCIPITEHY* was—and still is—very therapeutic for the three of us, but it was also conceived as a way to infiltrate the photographic world with our reflections, questions and topics. We play a lot, but our topics are very relevant—and I think it can also be a strategy to include more people in these discussions. We might do quiz shows where we ask the audience to identify which cat photo is not computer generated, or sell iPhone covers with a screenshot of Wikipedia's list of death by selfies, but we are also smuggling these issues into museum and photography festivals. Also, our first edition of Roland Barthes condoms sold out incredibly fast at Arles Photography festival, and as a pleasing by-product we've prevented many traditional photographers from procreating.

What is your interest and perspective when it comes to digital preservation, documentation and collecting the things you exhibit—both online and offline, and/or how they influence each other?

M   Fotomuseum Winterthur is a small to medium sized museum, so we're interested in experimenting with collecting and preserving works that are of a digital or hybrid nature. We've done this with a number of works, and always in discussion with the artist. We've collected born digital artworks like desktop wallpapers, 360° videos and custom applications, online specific generative artworks, and 3D models. We have a digital infrastructure for long-term preservation, but we're also aware that some works might inevitably suffer in the long run, so I'm thinking more about the documentation and contextualization of the works, but it's really a work in progress at the moment.

You Must Not Call It Photography If This Expression Hurts You [beta] is a collective initiative that aims to disrupt, provoke, and parasitically infiltrate the traditional photographic discourse and propose alternative approaches that are critical, playful and sincere. It is a work-in-progress that can take the form of a (subverted) manifesto, a map, a guidebook, or group therapy.

Marco De Mutiis works as Digital Curator at Fotomuseum Winterthur, where he leads and co-curates the experimental exhibition format and research lab *SITUATIONS*, which explores the changing role of photography in contemporary digital and networked cultures. He co-created *Screen Walks*, a series of live streams with artists using the screen as their medium. He is currently part of an SNF-funded research project titled *Post-Photography* at the Lucerne University of Applied Sciences and Arts, and is a PhD researcher at the Centre for the Study of the Networked Image at London South Bank University.

Katrina Sluis is Head of Photography and Media Arts at the School of Art and Design, Australian National University; and a founding Co-Director of the Centre for the Study of the Networked Image, London South Bank University. Prior to this she was Senior Curator (Digital Programmes) at The Photographers' Gallery where she developed projects on machine vision, synthetic imaging, posthuman photography and speculative photographic education.

Jon Uriarte is curator of Digital Programmes at The Photographers' Gallery in London and curator of Getxophoto International Image Festival, in Getxo, Spain. He previously curated *DONE*, a programme on digital online photography launched by Foto Colectania, in Barcelona. He has been a guest researcher at MACBA's Study Centre, and was a digital photography consultant to the Landscape Observatory of Catalonia during the development of their Online Image Archive. He has curated group and solo exhibitions as a co-founder of Widephoto, an independent platform which organized workshops, performances and self-publishing related events in partnership with different institutions. He regularly guest lectures and runs photography, film and design workshops at universities.

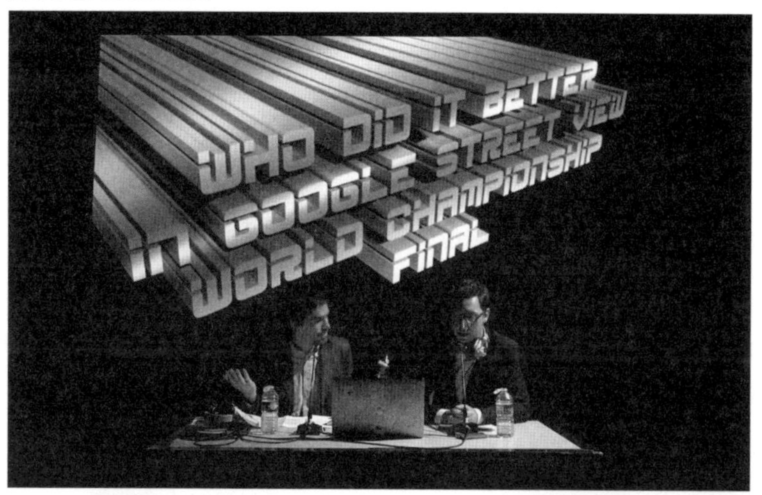
WHO DID IT BETTER
IN GOOGLE STREET VIEW
WORLD CHAMPIONSHIP
FINAL

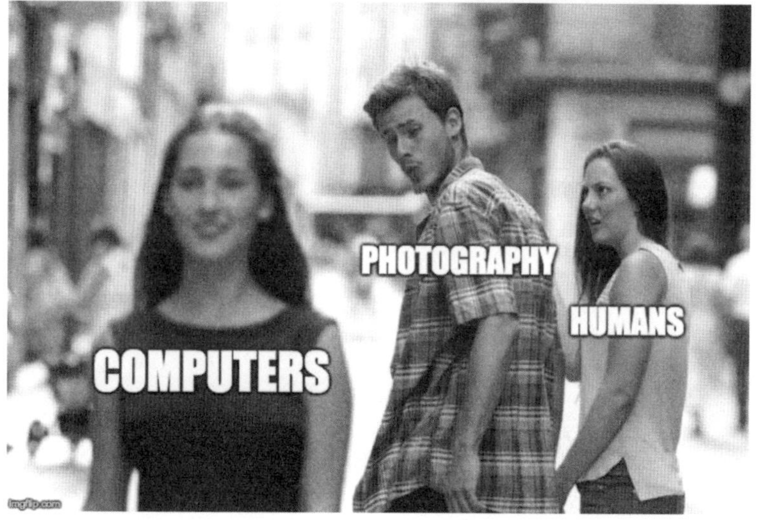
PHOTOGRAPHY
HUMANS
COMPUTERS
imgflip.com

The Broken Timeline

Marialaura Ghidini, Gaia Tedone
& Annet Dekker

The Broken Timeline (TBT) presents historical exhibition projects that were curated online. Inevitably partial and subjective, TBT burrows back in time to present a lineage of web-based curatorial projects that are too often unseen, neglected or ignored by the mainstream artworlds and their discourses. Confronted with a wide range of practices, TBT formulated the following criteria:

- Prioritize projects that are web-specific, for instance, which propose intricate navigation or interaction modes, or misuse existing platforms;

- Disregard exhibitions that follow the conventional logic of 'vitrine', archival repository or straightforward display, and instead focus on attempts that challenge how online art is experienced;

- Exclude collaborative projects that resemble artworks, even though the boundary is often fuzzy;

- List organizations engaged in a series of curatorial projects by the organization's name rather than as individual projects.

TBT is broken for a number of reasons. Firstly, because of the limits of our particular experience, geographical knowledge and network. Secondly, many links to historical projects don't function anymore and users are redirected to '404 Not Found' messages. While some projects were meant to be visible only for a specific period, most cease to exist after a while because they're no longer maintained or updated and, more generally, due to technological obsolescence, which condenses the endurance of online content to the 'survival of the fittest'. Thirdly, the role of the curator or, curating as a practice, has become fragmented. The complex relation between human behaviour and machinic processes is deeply embedded within the continuously evolving socio-technical ecosystem. In such an environment it is not always clear who or what propels a project that reshapes the function, tasks and values of curating. For this reason, a historical-technical timeline complements TBT, which charts some of the most significant web and Internet developments that influenced the aesthetic, spatial and temporal conditions of curating online. Finally, TBT is a response to as much as it is a reflection of the gaps between different curatorial discourses, primarily between (new) media curating and contemporary art curating. Underlying this 'curatorial digital divide' is a different notion the role of technology plays when it comes to art and online curatorial practice. Thus, broken means you're not always in control.

In a sense, the year 2020 has become exemplary of this divide. As a result of the global pandemic and its local lockdowns an unprecedented migration took place in which museums and galleries—compensating for the lack of access to their physical spaces—started organizing their activities online. The move resulted in an overabundance of online exhibitions, virtual tours of collections, and talks that were live-streamed on social media platforms. Yet, in the midst of this frantic transition, a number of art and curatorial projects that had engaged with the web conceptually and curatorially in recent years, decided to pause their activities. This discord underscores the opposing views on how art (or curating) on the web, and more generally technology, is understood: as a tool to mimic the practices and dynamics of the white cube, or as an ecosystem in which cultural, economic, social and technical dimensions converge and hence changes the definitions of art and curating.

TBT emphasizes how the web is not only a tool or a medium, but a socio-technical culture that has enriched and transformed curatorial and art practices with new ways of creating and co-creating, sharing and viewing, questioning traditional concepts and notions of authenticity, authorship, ownership, and relations between curators, artists, institutions and audience members. As such, it presents examples of how curating on the web is an evolving practice and an endless space in which critical questions are posed about the rules of curating and the environment where it is taking place, with the aim of reinventing those very rules and modes of practice. While TBT is another attempt at narrowing the divide, it merely presents a sliver of the scope and the potential of curating on the web.

An extended version of The Broken Timeline can be found on *valiz-makingpublic.net*.

1982
- Smiley emoticon
- Minitel launches

1983
- ARPANET (TPC/IP)

1984
- Apple Desk Accessories
- Electronic Mall marketplace launches

1985
- NASA Ames VIEW headset

1986
- Public registration starts for Domain Name System of the Internet

1989
- Zip file format
- SimCities release

1990
- HTTP protocol
- HTML
- Archie

1991
- WWW PUBLIC
- Sega VR headset
- Gopher
- The Thing

1992
- Phrase 'surfing the internet' becomes common
- The Virtual Fixtures platform by the United States Air Force

BAD INFORMATION
people.well.com/user/jmalloy/badinfo/bad.html
1986–1990
Curator: Judy Malloy

ART COM ELECTRONIC NETWORK (ACEN)
people.well.com/user/couey/artcom/leonardo91.html
1986–1990
Curators: Carl Loeffler and Ted Truck

1993

- Mosaic Netscape browser

1994

- Yahoo
- links.net (first blog)
- QR codes
- PlayStation
- Web Banner
- Julie Martin creates first 'Augmented Reality Theater production', 'Dancing in Cyberspace'
- The Palace

1995

- Amazon
- eBay
- craigslist
- Explorer browser
- GeoCities
- Adobe Shockwave
- mp3
- Nintendo's Virtual Boy console
- The terms 'telecommuting' and 'telework' become popular in the USA

C@C-NAVIGATOR
🔗 *artnetweb.com*
1993–1997
Curators: Remo Campopiano and
Robbin Murphy

MOCA.VIRTUAL.MUSEUM
🔗 *moca.virtual.museum*
1993–
Curators: Don Archer and Bob Dodson

ÄDA 'WEB
🔗 *www.adaweb.com*
1994–1998
Curators: John Borthwick and
Benjamin Weil
☆ äda 'web combined different curatorial
functions to provide a multifunctional
space consisting of chats, commissions,
exhibitions, and e-commerce. It
provided an intricate navigation system
to negotiate while merging online and
offline spaces.

PLEXUS: OMNIZONE
🔗 *plexus.org*
1994–1998
Curators: Yu Yeon Kim and Stephen
Pusey

LIN HSIN HSIN ART MUSEUM
🔗 *www.lhham.com.sg*
1994–
Curator: Lin Hsin Hsin

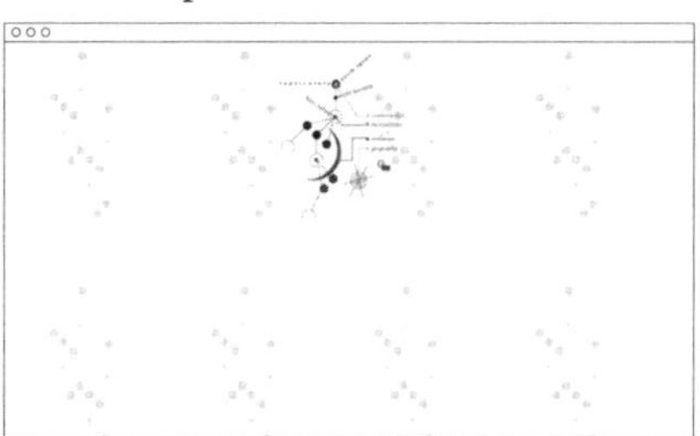

HELL.COM
🔗 *hell.com*
1995–2009
Curator: Kenneth Aronson

SITO
🔗 *www.sito.org/help/00/00.html*
1995–2019
Curator: Ed Stastny

DIA ART - WEB PROJECTS
🔗 *www.diaart.org/artist_web_projects*
1995–
Curators: Lynne Cooke and Sarah
Tucker

HYPER-X ONLINE GALLERY
🔗 *www.altx.com/hyperx*
1995–2007
Curators: Marisa Olson and Abe
Linkoln

XCULT
🔗 *xcult.org*
1995–2016
Curator: Reinhard Storz

PARALLEL
🔗 *va.com.au/parallel/x1/index.html*
1995
Curators: Virtual Artists and Hewson/
Walker

1996

- JAVA
- browsers war, The Internet Archive was founded
- IndiaMART marketplace launches
- Netscape proposed frames in HTML 3.0

1997

- Netflix
- AOL
- Microsoft Agent
- Dreamweaver
- Microsoft Active Desktop
- 'Weblog' coined by J. Berger

1998

- Google
- PayPal
- XML
- Open Diary
- Popup Ads

REFRESH
🔗 *nettime.org/Lists-Archives/
nettime-l-9610/msg00000.html*
1996
Curators: Alexei Shulgin, Vuk Ćosić,
Andreas Broeckmann

WHY NOT SNEEZE?
🔗 *nondes.home.xs4all.nl/sneeze/frame
.html*
1996–2000
Curators: Michael Gibbs and Brigitte
van der Sande

CYBERATLAS
🔗 *jonippolito.net/cyberatlas/cyberatlas_
archive/intro/ca-f.html*
1996–1998
Curator: Jon Ippolito

TURBULENCE
🔗 *turbulence.org/organization*
1996–2016
Curators: Helen Thorington and
Jo-Anne Green

CYBERPOWPOW
🔗 *turbulence.org/organization*
1996–2004
Curator: Skawennati Tricia Fragnito

DOCUMENTA X
🔗 *www.documenta12.de/archiv/dx/
english/frm_home.htm*
1997
Curator: Simon Lamunière

STIR-FRY
🔗 *adaweb.walkerart.org/context/stir-fry*
1997
Curator: Barbara London

GALLERY9
🔗 *gallery9.walkerart.org*
1997–2003
Curator: Steve Dietz

ALTX: DIGITAL STUDIES: BEING IN CYBERSPACE
🔗 *altx.com/ds*
1997–?
Curators: Mark Amerika and Alex
Galloway

BEYOND INTERFACE: NET ART AND ART ON THE NET
🔗 *gallery9.walkerart.org/midevent.html*
1998
Curator: Steve Deitz

INTERNYET
🔗 *www.moma.org/interactives/
projects/1998/internyet*
1998
Curator: Barbara London

SPLASHBACK: RHIZOME'S SPLASH PAGES
🔗 *rhizome.org/editorial/2009/apr/14/
splashback-rhizomes-splash-
pages-1998-2002*
1998–2002
Curator: Brian Droitcour

DESKTOPIS
🔗 *www.easylife.org/desktop/desktop_is
.html*
1998
Curator: Alexei Shulgin
☆ DesktopIS was a participatory project
in which the web as a culture, i.e.
a space for work and leisure, was
initiated by its users, thus providing
a window to desktop aesthetics and
creative organization.

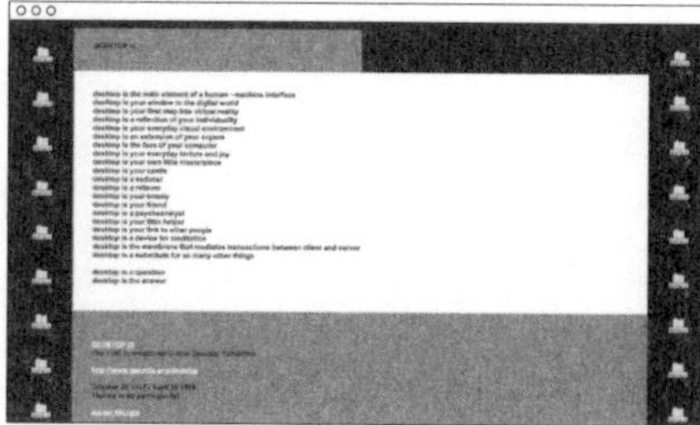

1999

- Napster
- Blogger
- RSS Web 2.0 (by Darcy DiNucci)
- Alibaba.com marketplace launches
- Amazon patents its 1-Click service

2000

- HTTPS protocol
- Microsoft Office Assistant
- Google AdWords
- dot.com bubble
- Walmart marketplace launches

VIRTUAL WORLDS: CHELSEA IN ACTIVE WORLDS

timeline.manetas.com/situations/virtualworlds
1998–2001
Curators: Miltos Manetas and Andreas Angelidakis with Ginger Freeman

---

ARTCART

artcart.de
1999–2000
Curator: Mario Hergueta

IMPAKT ONLINE

www.impakt.nl/online
1999–2013
Curators: various (a.o. Martijn van Boven, Annet Dekker, Wander Eikelboom, Deanna Herst, Derek Holzer, Sabine Niederer)

ART.TELEPORTACIA

art.teleportacia.org
1999–
Curator: Olia Lialina

☆ Art.Teleportacia addresses the aesthetic and cultural value of net art by highlighting the location bar as an intrinsic part of the work, thereby rethinking collection and exhibition methods and offering an alternative archival model based on appropriation and versioning.

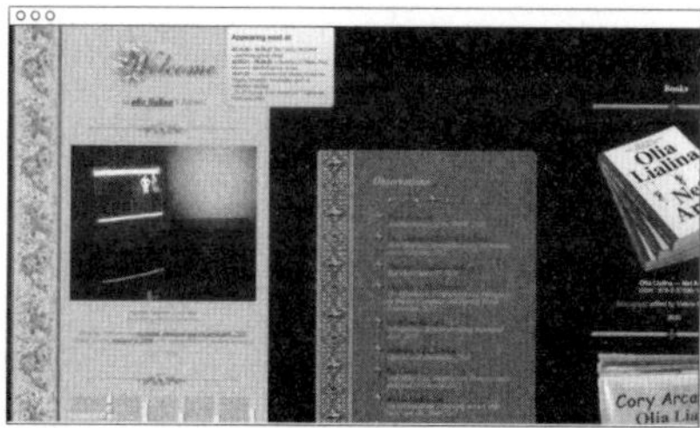

THROUGH THE LOOKING GLASS

www.voyd.com/ttlg
2000
Curator: Patrick Lichty

WHITNEY 2000 BIENNIAL

whitney.org/exhibitions/the-biennial
2000
Curators: Maxwell Anderson (museum director) and other curators

ART ENTERTAINMENT NETWORK

aen.walkerart.org
2000
Curators: Steve Dietz and designed by Vivien Selbo

NETART: VERNACULARS

ww.closky.info/?p=1629
2000–2001
Curators: Alison Gingeras and Jean-Noël Lafargue

JAVA MUSEUM

www.javamuseum.org
2000–2005
Curator: Wilfried Agricola de Cologne

E.SPACE SFMOMA

web.archive.org/web/20020408152231/http://www.sfmoma.org/espace/espace_overview.html
2000–2009
Curators: Aaron Betsky, Benjamin Weil, Joseph Rosa and Helen Hilton Raiser

2001

- Wikipedia
- Wayback Machine
- The Smiley Company developed The Smiley Dictionary

2002

- Skype
- Onion Tor Browser
- WebMuseum

TATE'S NETART PROJECTS

🔗 *www2.tate.org.uk/intermediaart/ archive/net_art_date.shtm*
2000–2011
Curators: Honor Hagar and Kelli Dipple

THE IDEA [INDIAN DOCUMENTARY OF ELECTRONIC ARTS]

🔗 *www.shankarbaba.com/the-idea.html*
2000–2004
Curator: Shankar Barua

IGALERIE: MUDAM

🔗 *https://ww.closky.info/?p=1628*
2000–2006
Curators: Claude Closky, with Simon Lamunière, Jean-Charles Massera and Benjamin Weil (editorial committe)

KOREA WEB ART FESTIVAL

🔗 *www.koreawebart.org/2001/Home .html*
2001
Curator: YOUNG-HAE CHANG HEAVY INDUSTRIES

ALT.INTERFACE

🔗 *archive.rhizome.org:8080/exhibition/ interface*
2001–2003
Curator: Rhizome

WHITNEY ARTPORT

🔗 *www.whitney.org/exhibitions/artport/ commissions*
2001
Curator: Christiane Paul

THE INTERFACE ZONE

🔗 *sarai.net/about-us/spaces*
2001–2009
Curator: Sarai Media Lab

WHITNEY 2002 BIENNIAL

🔗 *whitney.org/www/2002biennial/index .shtml*
2002
Curators: Lawrence Rinder, Chrissie Iles, Christiane Paul

WHITNEY BIENNIAL

🔗 *www.whitneybiennial.com*
2002
Curators: Miltos Maneta and Patrick Lichty

DAY JOBS

🔗 *http://web.archive.org/ web/20090429064435/http://www. newlangtonarts.org/view_event .php?category= Network&archive =&&eventId=35*
2002
Curator: Richard Rinehart

TRANSLOCATIONS

🔗 *latitudes.walkerart.org/translocations/ index.html*
2002–2003
Curator: Steve Dietz

WEBMUSEUM

🔗 *www.ibiblio.org/wm*
2002–2007
Curator: Nicolas Pioch

MIX-M

🔗 *www.mix-m.org*
2002–2008
Curators: Simon Lamuniere and fabric (architecture)

WEB BIENNIAL

🔗 *www.webbiennial.org/wb14.html*
2002–2014
Curator: Genco Gulan (founder)

2003

- WordPress
- Blogger
- MySpace
- 4Chan
- SecondLife
- Safari browser
- Google ADsense
- ITunes
- Del.icio.us
- EyeToy for the PlayStation 2
- Google AdSense
- The Pirate Bay

2004

- Facebook
- Orkut (India and Brazil) by Google
- Flickr
- 'blog' word of the year in Marriam-Webster dictionary
- 'Web 2.0' coined by Tim O'Ralley
- 11.4 million users of Facebook in a year

2005

- YouTube
- Adobe Flash
- Infinite Scroll JavaScript plugin
- Reddit
- Renren
- Apple Dashboard
- Kurator
- Criteo SA launches

NEEN WORLD
sites.rhizome.org/anthology/afterneen.html
2002
Curator: Miltos Manetas

NET.NARRATIVE
web.archive.org/web/20080418015346/http://www.sfcamerawork.org/past_exhibits/netnarrative.html
2002
Curator: Marisa Olson

THE KINGDOM OF PIRACY
v2.nl/archive/works/kingdom-of-piracy
2002–2003
Curators: Yukiko Shikata, Armin Medosch and Shu Lea Cheang

VIRTUAL TRANSFER
www.archimuse.com/publishing/ichim03/014C.pdf
2002–2004
Curators: Harald Kraemer and Konrad Jaggi

LOW LEVEL ALL-STARS
archive.rhizome.org:8080/exhibition/Low_Level_All_Stars/
2003
Curators: Radical Software and Beige Records

PACKET
web.archive.org/web/20051214121328/http://newlangtonarts.org/list_events.php?category=network&archive=1&
2003–2005
Curator: Richard Rinehart

WIDTH: 700PX
700gallery.tumblr.com/info
2003–2014
Curator: Levi Bruce

RUNME.ORG
runme.org
2003–
Curators: Amy Alexander, Olga Goriunova, Alex McLean and Alexei Shulgin

INSPECTOR LONDON
www.kathrinkur.com/inspector-london/info.html
2004
Curator: Kathrine Kur

M+K::YA HEARD: SOUNDS FROM THE RHIZOME ARTBASE
archive.rhizome.org/exhibition/ya_heard
2004
Curators: mendi & keith obadike

NO/COPY/RIGHT
no-org.net/no/copy/right/
2004
Curators: Sala-Manca Group and Matvey (no-org.net)

NET ART'S CYBORG[FEMINIST]S, PUNKS, AND MANIFESTOS
archive.rhizome.org/exhibition/cyborg/essay.html
2005
Curator: Marina Grzinic

RAIDERS OF THE LOST ARTBASE
archive.rhizome.org/exhibition/raiders
2005
Curator: Michael Connor

BINARYKATWALK
binarykatwalk.net
2005
Curators: Jeremy Hight and Sindee Nakatani

2006

- Twitter
- Wix
- Cloud computing popularised
- Adblock
- 'Surf Clubs'
- Google as a verb is introduced by Merriam-Webster

2007

- Tumblr
- iPhone
- AppleTV
- Google Street View
- Bitstrips
- 'Like' Button on Facebook
- FFFFOUND!
- Blingee
- Facebook's Beacon
- Gridr
- 'Hashtag' word coined by Chris Messina
- Flipkart marketplace launches in India

EBAYADAY

exstrange.com/relatives/ebayaday/
2006
Curators: Rebekah Modrak, Aaron Ahuvia and Zack Denfeld

TIME SHARES

archive.rhizome.org/exhibition/ timeshares/professionalsurfer.php
2006
Curator: Lauren Cornell

VICTIMS' SYNDROM

victims.labforculture.org
2007
Curator: Ana Peraica

TAGGALLERY

web.archive.org/web/20150913151707/ http://cont3xt.net/blog/?p=268
2007–2010
Curators: cont3xt.net (Sabine Hochrieser, Michael Kargl, Birgit Rinagl, Franz Thalmair)

☆ TAGallery used tagging and linking as a curatorial method to emphasize contextual meaning and broaden the act of selection. They also explored what it means to curate links or representations of artworks online, playing with semantically dense exhibition titles.

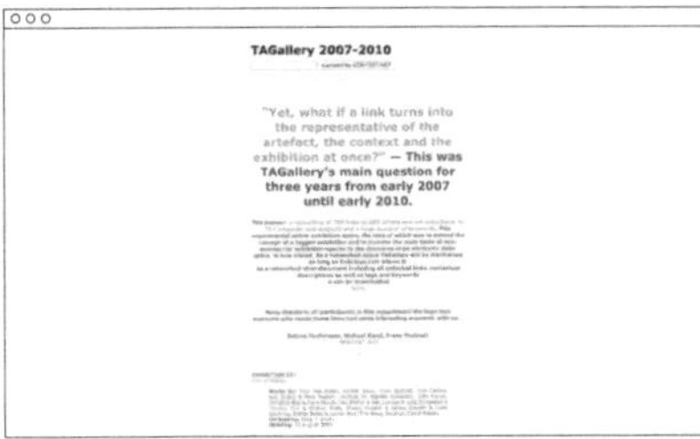

TEMPORÄRE KUNSTHALLE BERLIN SECOND LIFE

slurl.com/secondlife/Pixel%20 Art/127/138/32
2007
Designer: Krischanitz ZT GmbH

BLOGUMENTA

noemalab.eu/memo/blogumenta
2007–?
Curator: Robert Labossiere

CURATINGYOUTUBE

www.curatingyoutube.net
2007–
Curator: Sakrowski

☆ CuratingYouTube, and particularly GRIDR, reconsidered the idea of broadcasting by appropriating the rules of YouTube. While emphasizing amateur curating, it questioned users' relationships with the web as a social and archival space.

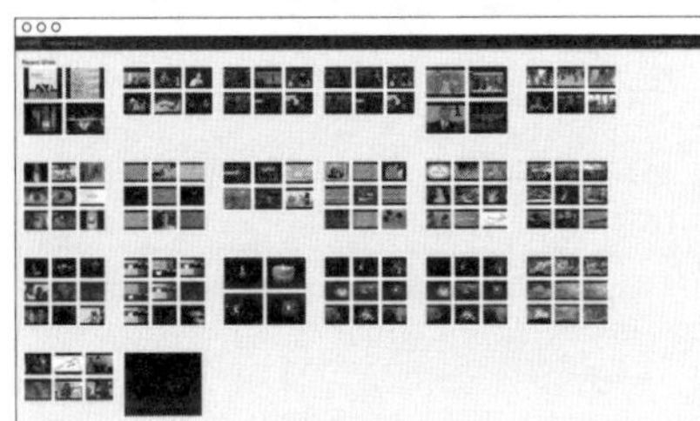

ESPACE VIRTUEL

espacevirtuel.jeudepaume.org
2007–
Curators: various

2008

- Bitcoin
- Blockchain
- Apple Store
- Android Market
- Facebook Chat
- Tor browser
- Airbnb
- Google Lively
- GitHub
- DuckDuckGo web browser
- PayPal Credit is acquired by eBay

2009

- WhatsApp
- Uber
- Kickstarter
- Push notifications
- Sina Weibo
- 'Prosumer' word coined
- Minecraft release
- World Wide Web Foundation

MONTAGE: UNMONUMENTAL ONLINE
🔗 *archive.rhizome.org/exhibition/montage/08_fei.php*
2008
Curators: Lauren Cornell and Marisa Olson

CLUB INTERNET
clubinternet.org
2008–2009
Curator: Harm van den Dorpel

NETESCOPIO. NEW ART VIEWER OF THE MEIAC
🔗 *netescopio.meiac.es/en/index.php*
2008–
Curator: Gustavo Romano

NOBELPRIZE.NO
🔗 *web.archive.org/web/20120304230937/http://www.nobelprize.no/about.html*
2008
Curators: Alejandra Salinas and Aeron Bergman

PROBE
🔗 *www.projectprobe.net*
2008–2017
Curator: Suze May Sho

XYM.NO
xym.no
2008–2011
Curators: Yngve Holen and Marlie Mul
Design with Per Törnberg and Joel Galvez
☆ xym.no played with the native currency of the Symbol public blockchain (xym is the core value transfer mechanism for the blockchain) by foregrounding the download and its format restrictions and highlighting the temporality, and thus the sustainability, of digital art.

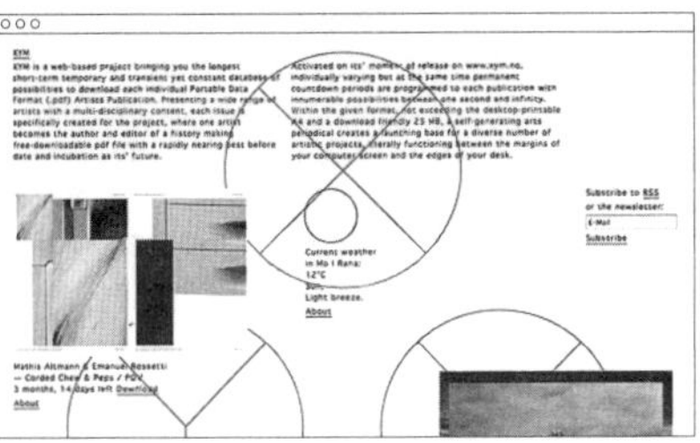

DELICIOUS CONTEMPORARY SEMANTICS
🔗 *www.constantdullaart.com/arti.html*
2009
Curator: Constant Dullaart

BEAM ME UP
🔗 *beam-me.net*
2009–2010
Curator: Reinhard Storz

JSTCHILLIN.ORG
🔗 *jstchillin.org/schedule*
2009–2011
Curators: Parker Ito and Caitlin Denny

OR-BITS.COM
🔗 *www.or-bits.com/index.php*
2009–2015
Curator: Marialaura Ghidini

MYBIENNIALISBETTERTHANYOURS
http://mybiennialisbetterthanyours.com/
2009
Curator: Tolga Taluy

PADIGLIONE INTERNET
🔗 *timeline.manetas.com/situations/internetpavilion/*
2009–2015
Curator: Miltos Manetas

700MGB
🔗 *www.700mbg.com*
2009–
Curators: Phillip Sadofsky and Stefan Riebel

2010

- Instagram
- Pinterest
- Google Maps
- Siri
- LibreOffice
- Microsoft's Kinect for Xbox 360
- 'App' word of the year in Marriam-Webster dictionary
- First purchase Bitcoin
- European Union launches three antitrust investigations into Google for violating the EU's competition laws
- Android becomes most popular smartphone operating system
- Groupon marketplace launches

2011

- iMessage
- iPhone Siri
- Twitch.tv
- Google Wallet
- Minecraft
- Alipay designs a QR code payment method
- Google Art Project
- The term 'Postinternet' was coined by Marisa Olson
- The Xiaomi Mi1 smartphone is announced

IN.F3XXX10N.US
🔗 *joncates.blogspot.com/2010/07/
inf3xx10nus.html*
2010
Curator: jonCates and Jake Elliott

THE GALLERY SPACE
🔗 *http://thegalleryspace.info*
2010
Curator: Louis Doulas

TEMPORARYSTEDELIJK.COM
🔗 *temporarystedelijk.com*
2010–2012
Curators: Kalle Mattsson and Amber
van den Eeden
☆ *Temporary Stedelijk* was both a critique
of the institutional art world who ignored emerging local artists and digital
art and an experiment in using iFrames
to embed multiple elements, websites
and contextual information, therefore
addressing what it means to curate
Internet art in an online environment.

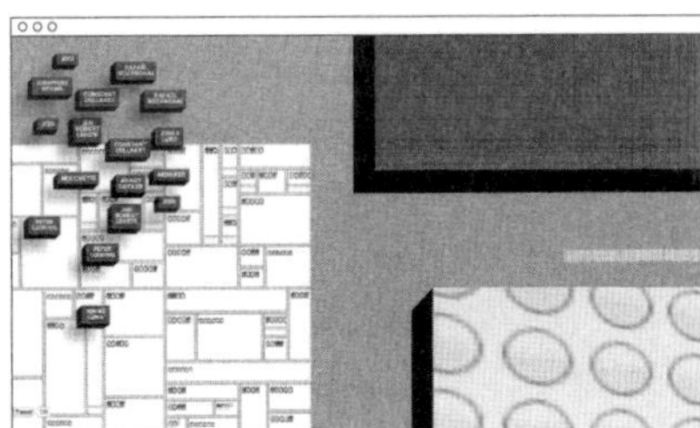

STATE
🔗 *thestate.tumblr.com*
2010–2011
Curator: ?

NETARTWORKS (SKOR)
🔗 *aaaan.net/netartworks-identity-works*
2010–2012
Curator: Annet Dekker

LEA (NEW) MEDIA EXHIBITIONS
🔗 *www.leoalmanac.org/category/
exhibitions*
2010–2013
Curators: various

CHRYSTAL GALLERY
🔗 *chrystalgallery.info*
2010–2015
Curator: Timur Si-Qin

PARALLELOGRAMS
🔗 *www.parallelograms.info/about.html*
2010–2015
Curators: Leah Beeferman and
Matthew Harvey

DUMP.FM
🔗 *dump.fm*
2010–2017
Curators: Ryder Ripps in collaboration
with Scott Ostler and Tim Baker

STUFFINABLANK
🔗 *www.stuffinablank.com/index.html*
2010–2020
Curator: Pedro Torres

A CLOCK THAT RUNS ON MUD
🔗 *www.neromagazine.it/a_clock_that_
runs_on_mud/-/*
2011
Curator: Jennifer Teets

ART MICRO-PATRONAGE
🔗 *artmicropatronage.org/about#*
2011–2012
Curators: The Present Group (Eleanor
Hanson Wise and Oliver Wise)

BUBBLEBYTE
🔗 *www.bubblebyte.org/about*
2011–2013
Curators: Attilia Fattori Franchini,
Rhys Coren and Paul Flannery

ANI GIF
🔗 *ani-gif.com/about*
2011–2014
Curators: Kyra Rehn and Sarah Caluag

2012

- Medium
- Google Drive
- Zoom
- Stop Online Piracy Act - SOPA (USA)
- The term 'new aesthetics' was coined by James Bridle
- 'meme' is Merriam-Webster's Words of the Year

KLAUSGALLERY.NET

www.klausgallery.net/ebooks/about.html
2011–2017
Curators: Klaus von Nichtssagend Gallery and Paul Pescador

FELT

news.feltzine.us
2011–
Curators: Mark Sabb and Devon Moore

THE WIDGET ART GALLERY (WAG)

the-widget-art-gallery.blogspot.com
2011–
Curator: Chiara Passa

☆ The Widget Art Gallery responded to the boom in app development and usage and the increasing use of smartphones to access the web. In response to users' intimate relationship with their smartphones the project proposed the smartphone as a gallery that could be kept in your pocket, thus bypassing the commercial gallery system.

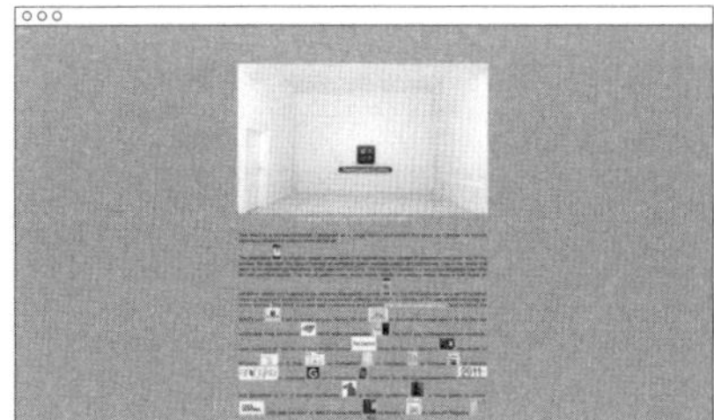

SPAMM (SUPER MODERN ART MUSEUM)

spamm.fr/about
2011–
Curator: various (a.o. Systaime)

☆ SPAMM, the SuPer Modern Art Museum, shows the eclectic panorama of digital creation while merging web and physical spaces. Based on decentralised princples, curated by various people, using open calls and unconventional categorisation, the project challenges the many gatekeeping mechanisms of traditional practices.

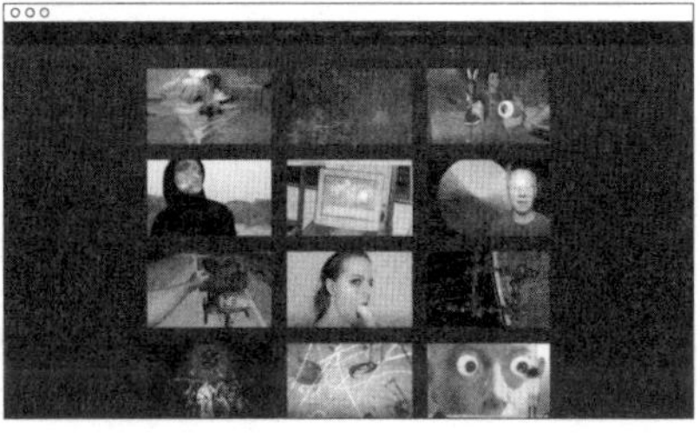

LAFIAC.COM

lafiac.com
2011–?
Curators: Florent di Bartolo, Julien Levesque and Margherita Balzerani

PRINT FICTION

www.printfiction.net
2012
Curator: Michael Alfred

DALLAS BIENNIAL DB12: VOLUME 1 – 4

dallasbiennial.org/db-12/
2012
Curators: Jesse Morgan Barnett and Michael Mazurek

UNLIMITEDGTI

unlimitedgti.com/messestand%20steph.html
2012
Curator: Yves Scherer

SLEEPING UPRIGHT

sleepingupright.com
2012
Curator: Candice Jacobs

DOMAIN GALLERY

www.domain-gallery.net
2012–2013
Curator: Manuel Fernández

GALLERY ONLINE

www.facebook.com/GalleryOnline
gallery0nline.wordpress.com
2012–2017
Curators: Ronen Shai & Thomas Cheneseau

2013

- Deliveroo
- Google Hangouts
- Telegram
- Slack
- Facebook begins letting users sponsor posts

FIELD BROADCAST
🔗 *www.fieldbroadcast.org*
2012–2013
Curators: Rebecca Birch and Rob Smith
☆ FieldBroadcast popped up unexpectantly on users' computer screens as a moment of disruption of daily routines. It was engaged in rethinking the relationship between and online behaviours of its audience and art on the web, as well as the complex relationship between art, work and leisure via users' computer screens.

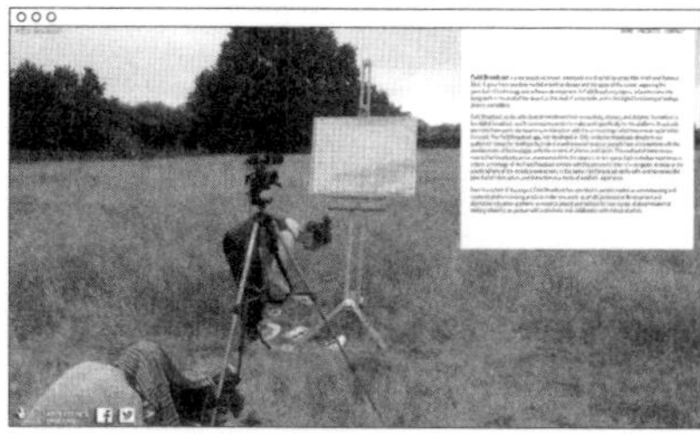

GENERATION WORKS
🔗 *generationworks.me*
2012–2013
Curator: Jasper Spicero

FIRST LOOK: NEW ART ONLINE
🔗 *www.newmuseum.org/exhibitions/online*
2012
Curator: Lauren Cornell

THE DOWNLOAD
🔗 *rhizome.org/download/#works*
2012–2018
Curator: Zoë Salditch

FLOAT GALLERY
🔗 *float.gallery*
2012–
Curator: Manual Rossner

LEGION TV: ONLINE
🔗 *legion-tv.com/online*
2012–2017
Curators: Kiera Blakey and Matthew Hughes

NET.SPECIFIC
🔗 *netspecific.net/en/netspecific*
2012–2015

IDLE SCREENINGS
🔗 *idlescreenings.com*
2012–
Curator: Mitch Trale

SCREEN SAVER GALLERY
🔗 *screensaver.metazoa.org*
2012–
Curator: Mary Meixner

ESPACIO BYTE
🔗 *www.espaciobyte.org/ien*
2012–
Curator: Enrique Salmoiraghi

MON3Y AS AN 3RROR | MON3Y.US
🔗 *www.mon3y.us*
2013
Curator: Vasily Zaitsev

WELCOME SCREEN
🔗 *www.picuki.com/profile/welcomescreengallery*
2013–2015
Curator: Michael Pybus

NEVERLAND SPACE
🔗 *neverlandspace.com*
2013–2017
Curator: Y7K

AOYS (ART ON YOUR SCREEN)
🔗 *aoys.zkm.de*
2013–2016
Curators: Matthias Kampmann, Margit Rosen (2013–2015), Janine Burger, Caroline Clausnitzer (2014–2016)

V4ULT
🔗 *www.facebook.com/V4ULT-506458162754140/*
2013–2016
Curators: Anna Mikkola and Hanne Lippard

2014

- Amazon Alexa
- Signal
- PlayStation VR
- Microsoft Cortana
- Bitmoji
- HTML5
- UBlock Origin
- Apple Pay
- NSA Facial Recognition Project
- Facebook purchases Oculus VR

BEAUTIFUL INTERFACES: THE DEEP IN THE VOID

miyovanstenis.com/blog/beautiful-interfaces-the-deep-in-the-void/
2013
Curator: Miyö Van Stenis

Beautiful Interfaces wanted to turn the public's attention away from the 'surface web' to the Tor network, also known as the dark web. At the core of the project was an interest in exploring the limitations of the interface and the networked infrastructure of Tor.

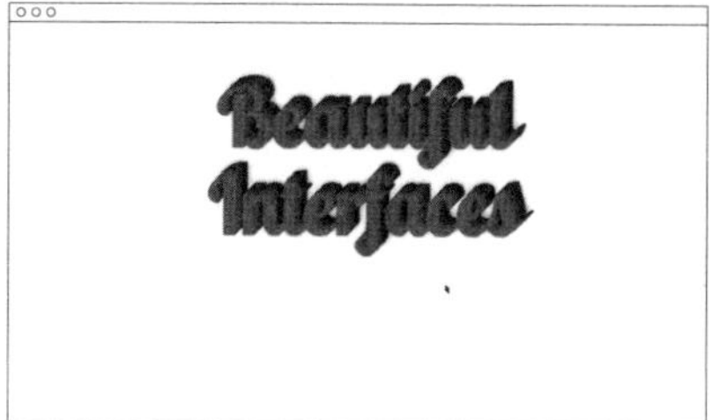

PROPRIOCEPTION

proprioception.in
2013–
Curator: Charu Maithani

THE WRONG NEW DIGITAL ART BIENNALE

biennale.thewrong.org
2013–
Curator: David Quiles

DECENTER: AN EXHIBITION ON THE CENTENARY OF THE 1913 ARMORY SHOW

www.decenterarmory.com
2013
Curators: Andrianna Campbell and Daniel S. Palmer

DESKTOP RESIDENCY

www.desktopresidency.com
2013–
Curators: John Henry Newton and Barnaby Page

PANTHER MODERN

panthermodern.org
2013–2017
Curator: LaTurbo Avedon

FIFTEEN STARS

fifteenstars.com
2013
Curator: Brian Droitcour

YOUNG INTERNET BASED ARTISTS

younginternetbasedartists.com
2013
Curator: Anthony Antonellis

FLATNESS.EU

archive.flatness.eu
2013
Curator: Shama Khanna

BITRATES : GIFBITES

gifbites.com/exhibition
2014
Curator: Daniel Rourke

YOU MIGHT BE A DOG

ymbad.hotglue.me/#about
2014
Curator: Teresa Dillon in collaboration with LEAP

COSMOS CARL

cosmoscarl.com
2014
Curators: Frederique Pissuise and Saemundur Thor Helgason

63RD - 77TH STEPS

www.63rd77thsteps.com/about.html
2014–2019
Curator: Fabio Santacroce

OPENING TIMES – DIGITAL ART COMMISSIONS

otdac.org
2014–2017
Curators: Rhys Coren, Paul Flannery, Attilia Fattori Franchini, Dave Hoyland, Tim Steer

DOT DASH 3

www.dotdash3.com
2014–
Curator: ?

2015

- Windows Holographic and the HoloLens augmented reality headsets
- Ethereum
- Google's Android Pay
- Mass-production of 'Smart TVs'
- Deep Dream Generator

EXHIBITION KICKSTARTER
www.kickstarter.com/projects/ksouth/exhibition-kickstarter
2014
Curator: Krystal South
☆ Exhibition Kickstarter used the commercial platform Kickstarter to create an exhibition format to sell specific editioned artworks and in return discussed artistic practices, labour and commerce by tweaking the rules of the platform.

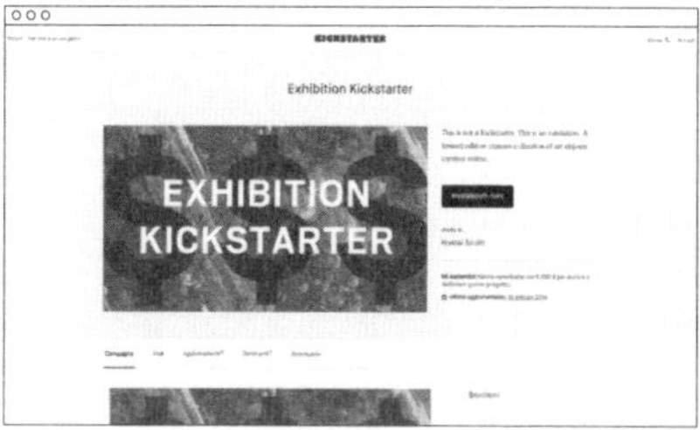

DESKTOP SHOW
www.enardediosrodriguez.com/wp/curatorial/#desktop1
2014–2015
Curator: Enar de Dios Rodríguez

COINTEMPORARY
cointemporary.com
2014–2016
Curators: Andy Boot and Valentine Ruhry

HTTP://WWW.O-U-T-O-F-O-F-F-I-C-E.COM/
www.o-u-t-o-f-o-f-f-i-c-e.com
2014–2016
Curator: Matthew Britton

TITLE DATE DURATION
clok.uclan.ac.uk/18360/
2014–2017
Curators: Maeve Rendle and Noel Clueit

LINK CABINET
linkcabinet.eu
2014–2019
Curator: Matteo Cremonesi for Link Art Centre

0000FF
www.facebook.com/h0000ff
2014–
Curator: Georges Jacotey

UNFOLD
unfold.thevolumeproject.com
2015–2017
Curator: Sara Giannini

/PERFORMING THE TEXT
newhive.com/kerry/tag/performingthetext
2015
Curator: Kerry Doran

DIMODA
ymbad.hotglue.me/#about
2015–
Curators: Alfredo Salazar-Caro and William Richard Robertson

NEW SCENARIO
newscenario.net
2015–
Curators: Paul Barsch and Tilman Hornig
☆ New Scenario uses a documentary format to create an imaginative and immersive space to showcase inaccessible art exhibitions. In the process it questions the space of art viewing, re-evaluates documentation practices and stresses the importance of context.

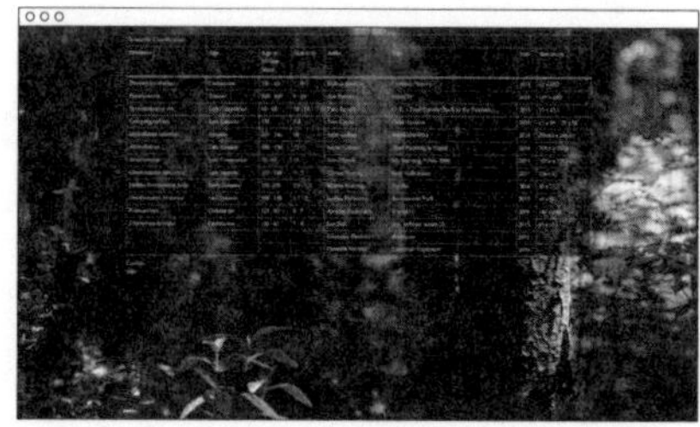

2016

- Google Assistant
- Snapchat
- DAO
- Webrecorder
- Brave browser
- Pokémon Go mobile game
- European Union introduces the General Data Protection Regulation (GDPR)

BODY ANXIETY
bodyanxiety.com/about
2015
Curators: Leah Schrager and Jennifer Chan

ÅZONE FUTURES MARKET
azone.guggenheim.org
2015
Curators: Troy Conrad Therrien and Ashley Mendelsohn

DE:FORMAL
www.deformal.com
2015–
Curators: Vincent CY Chen and Wednesday Kim

OPEN SPACE
openspace.sfmoma.org/category/project-space/
2015–?
Curators: Claudia La Rocco and Bosco Hernández

THIS ROOM IS TOO DARK FOR A FRIEND
www.doggerland.info/digitalprojects
2016
Curators: Emily Pope and Doggerland

LIAUX
liaux.org
2016–2019
Curator: Francesca Verga

I.O.U.A.E
www.instagram.com/i.o.u.a.e/?hl=en
2016–2020
Curator: Stacey Davidson

#NFCDAB
nfcwproject.tumblr.com
2016–
Curator: Dominik Podsiadly

ANTI-MATERIA
anti-materia.org
2016–
Curator: Doreen A. Rios

LOCAL HOST
www.localhost.gallery/index.php/about/
2016–
Curator: Drew Nikonowicz

SKELF
skelf.org.uk/index.html
2016–
Curator: ?

THIS IS PUBLIC SPACE
www.upprojects.com/projects/this-is-public-space/
2016–
Curator: UP Projects

GALERIE GALERIE
www.galeriegalerieweb.com
2016–
Curators: Gabrielle Bernatchez (web integration), Marie-Charlotte Castonguay-Harvey (development and administration), Sophie Latouche (programming)

INTERNET MOON GALLERY
www.internetmoongallery.com/home.html
2016–
Curator: Manuel Minch

ISTHISIT?
www.isthisitisthisit.com
2016–
Curator: Bob Bicknell-Knight

NET ART ANTHOLOGY
anthology.rhizome.org
2016–2019
Curator: Rhizome

2017

- TikTok
- Beaker browser
- Amazon Cash opens in USA and Canada

#EXSTRANGE

🔗 *exstrange.com*
2017
Curators: Marialaura Ghidini and Rebekah Modrak

☆ exstrange listed artworks on eBay to foster accidental encounters and exchanges with the 'stranger's. It tested the limits of eBay as a platform for online curation by experimenting with its digital tools for data aggregation and collection creation, partnering with its search algorithm Cassini.

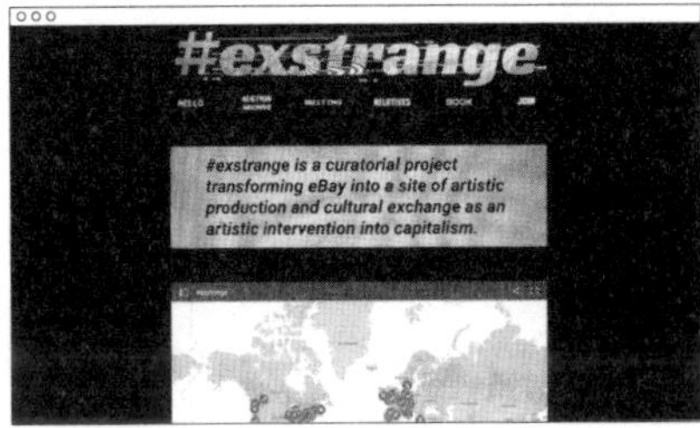

UNAUTHORIZED SFMOMA

🔗 *sfmoma.show/#*
2017
Curators: Enar de Dios Rodríguez in collaboration with Lasse Scherffig and Ana María Montenegro Jaramillo

SUPER-INFORMATION-HIGH-MARKET

🔗 *super-information-high-market.com*
2017
Curator: Florian Kuhlmann

UNSOLICITED EXHIBITION

🔗 *unsolicited.website/Unsolicited_exhibition-Catalogue.pdf*
2017
Curator: Enar de Dios Rodríguez

#MEMEPROPAGANDA (OR #MEMEMANIFESTO)

🔗 *memepropaganda.clusterduck.space*
2017
Curator: Clusterduck

ONSCROLL - INSTAGRAM

🔗 *www.instagram.com/exhibit_onscroll*
2017
Curators: Kert Viiart and Kristina Õllek

PAPER-THIN

🔗 *www.paper-thin.org*
2017–2018
Curators: Daniel Alexander Smith and Cameron Buckley

INTERNET FAME

🔗 *clusterduck.space/internet-fame.html*
2017–2018
Curators: Clusterduck and panke.gallery

X-TEMPORARY

🔗 *x-temporary.org/index.html*
2017–2018
Curators: Marenka Krasomil in collaboration with Miriam LaRosa of curatingthecontemporary

A V D

🔗 */a-v-d.xyz*
2017–?
Curators: various

THE RECOMBINANTS

🔗 *www.neddam.info/madja-e-g-online-curator/*
2017–2019
Curator: Madja Edelstein-Gomez

☆ The Recombinants explored the notion of machine curation as a critique of the power of the uber or star-curator. While the format followed the conventional model of an open call, a database and a final presentation, a chain of digital participation is also set in motion in which every user becomes a recombinant.

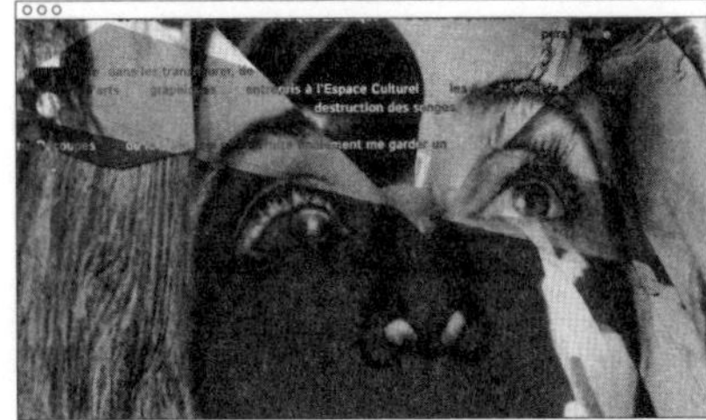

PIYENJI STICKER GALLERY

🔗 *piyenji.com*
2017–
Curator: Hello Velocity

2018

- Mozilla Hubs
- Google Duplex
- Parler
- Facebook–Cambridge Analytica data scandal
- Google announces that its Chrome browser would mark HTTP sites as 'Not Secure'
- Google Chrome announces it may start using link shorteners for all URLs
- Amazon Go store opens in Seatttle
- Flipkart is acquired by Walmart

GREEN CUBE GALLERY
🔗 *greencube.gallery/info/about*
2017–
Curators: Guido Segni and Matìas Ezequiel Reyes
☆ Green Cube Gallery promotes art that functions as a collection of events. Moving seamlessly between virtual and physical spaces, they reflect on the current state of digital technology, questioning labour and other services of the e-economy, for whom IRL and URL can easily be exchanged.

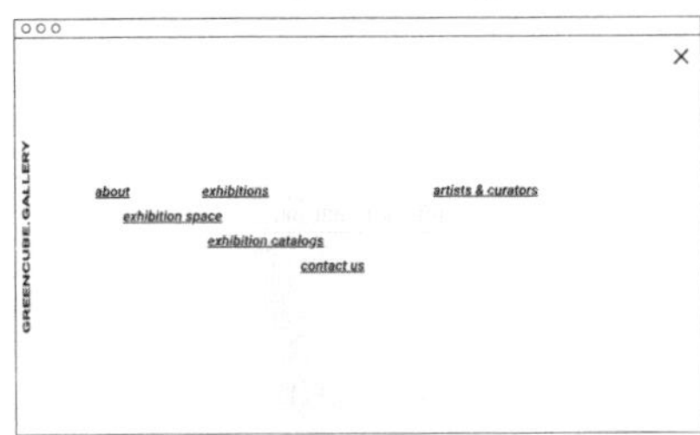

OFF SITE PROJECT
🔗 *www.offsiteproject.org*
2017–
Curators: Pita Arreola-Burns and Elliott Burns

DEEP DIVE
🔗 *www.itskindof.com/info.html*
2017–
Curators: Corey Bartle-Sanderson and Steven Gee

AAREA
🔗 *www.aarea.co*
2017–
Curators: Livia Benedetti and Marcela Vieira

MOR, MUSEUM OF OTHER REALITIES
🔗 *www.museumor.com*
2017–
Curators: Colin Northway and Robin Stethem

FIRST LOOK: ARTISTS' VR
🔗 *www.newmuseum.org/exhibitions/view/artists-vr*
2017
Curator: Rhizome

THE ZIUM GARDEN
🔗 *theziumsociety.itch.io/the-zium-garden*
2017–
Curator: Michael Berto

JUST BROWSING
🔗 *iamjustbrowsing.com*
2018
Curators: Joanne McNeil and Nicole Antebi

MUST SEE
🔗 *thehmm.nl/dossier/dossier-0-archive*
2018–2020
Curators: various

EXTERNAL PAGES
🔗 *externalpages.org*
2018–
Curator: Ana Meisel

FLOATING SWARM
🔗 *floating-swarm.hashbase.io*
2018–
Curators: Raphaël Bastide

LIKELIKE3D
🔗 *likelike.org/shows*
2018–
Curator: Paolo Pedercini

DIGITAL ARTIST RESIDENCY (DAR)
🔗 *digitalartistresidency.org*
2018–
Curator: Tom Milnes

YPUCCKO GALLERY
🔗 *ypuccko.net*
2018–
Curator: Nico Lillo

2019

- Google Art Zoom
- AR integrated in the browser
- Adobe Shockwave discontinued
- USA's Do Not Track Act

2020

- Versatile Video Coding (VVC) is finalised
- Amazon Luna gaming platform
- Clubhouse invite-only app
- Adobe announced it will no longer update or maintain Flash
- Hospitality industry uses QR codes en-masse across the globe
- 'Covid-19' contact-tracing apps
- India bans TikTok and 58 other Chinese apps
- The 'new normal'

THE WHITE PAGE GALLERY/S
www.whitepagegallery.network
2019–?
Curators: Anna Utopia Giordano, Zsolt
Mesterhazy, Domenico Barra

FOOTNOTES ON EQUALITY
footnotesonequality.eu
2019
Curators: Alejandra Benítez Silva,
Tegiye Birey, Zerrin Cengiz, Barbara
Grabher, Lieke Hettinga, Wilmarie R.
Pérez, Raluca Pinzari, Sara Verderi

GOING AWAY.TV
www.goingaway.tv
2019–
Curators: Marc Blazel and Alexander
Harding with arebyte for The Wrong

THE NEXT BIENNIAL SHOULD BE CURATED BY
A MACHINE
whitney.org/artport-commissions/the-next-biennial/index.html
2019–2021
Curators: UBERMORGEN, Leonardo
Impett, Joasia Krysa, Christiane Paul

AREBYTE ON SCREEN (AOS)
www.arebyte.com/aos
2019–
Curators: various

EMOTIONAL INTERFACES
emotional-interfaces.com
2019–
Curators: Virginie Tan and Astrid
Lours-Riou

CAFÉ INTERNET
cafeinternet.github.io/taller-xyz
2019–
Curator: Wilmer Rodriguez

GALLERY GALLERY
www.gallerygallery.space/en/about-us
2019–
Curators: Albena Baeva and Rene
Beekman

LE GRAND TRAMPOLAGE
mythical-institution.org/an-outlook/le-grand-trampolage/curatorial.html
2019
Curator: Jan Berger

BIENNALE.NO
biennale.no
2020–2021
Curators: Bjørn Magnhildøen and Zsolt
Mesterhazy (Noemata)

TIME OUT OF JOINT
fjroxjgxhmd2ymp2.onion
2020–2021
Curators: Eva and Franco Mattes

YEREVAN BIENNIAL DIGITAL EXHIBITION
yerevanbiennial.org/digital-exhibition
2020–2021
Curator: Lorenzo Fusi

SPECTER
specter.world
2020–
Curators: Agnes Momirski and Georgia
Kareola

WELL NOW WHAT THE FUCK
wellnow.wtf
2020
Curators: Faith Holland, Lorna Mills,
and Wade Wallerstein

FINAL HOT DESERT
www.instagram.com/finalhotdesert
2020–
Curator: Ben Sang

INTER.ARCHIVE
inter-archive.oncurating-space.org
2020–
Curators: Giovanna Bragaglia, Miwa
Negoro and Camille Regli

N MENOS 1
www.nmenos1.xyz/public
2020–
Curators: Juan Covelli and Lina Useche

KOENIG GALLERY
www.koeniggalerie.com/ exhibitions/28709/surprisingly-this-rather-works/
2020
Curator: Anika Meier/König Gallery

POST HOC, AN ONLINE ART SHOW
nickm.com/post/2020/05/post-hoc-an-online-art-show/
2020
Curator: Nick Montfort

FLOW OUT
www.isthisitisthisit.com/flow-out-1
2020
Curators: Collective Çukurcuma (Naz Cuguoğlu, Mine Kaplangı)

END DEMO
epoch.gallery
2020–
Curator: EPOCH Gallery

DO NOT LINK
donotlink.org/index2020.html
2020
Curators: Dirk Paesmans and Bob Bicknell-Knight

FESTIVAL, ACCÈS)S(CULTURES ÉLECTRONIQUE
xx.acces-s.org
2020
Curator: Thomas Cheneseau

UPSTREAM.GALLERY
upstream.gallery
2020–
Curators: various

COME CLOSER PT.1
online.officeimpart.com
2020–
Curators: various (interface by Constant Dullaart)

TECH OF THE SACRED
sacred.display.cz/en
2020
Curators: Lukáš Likavčan and Display – Association for Research and Collective Practice

WE=LINK: 十个小品 TEN EASY PIECES
we-link.chronusartcenter.org
2020
Curator: Zhang Ga i.c.w. others

WORLD WIDE WEBB
webb.game
2020
Curators: Anika Meier and Thomas Webb

STICK.T.ME
netzkunst.berlin/stm/
2020
Curator: Zentrum für Netzkunst

HEK NET WORKS
www.hek.ch/en/program/events-en/ event/hek-net-works-iocose-moving-tasks-forward.html
2020–
Curators: various

ART AT A TIME LIKE THIS
artatatimelikethis.com
2020–
Curators: Barbara Pollack and Anne Verhallen

NEXTMUSEUM.IO
nextmuseum.io
2020–
Curators: various

INBTWN - IN BETWEEN
www.inbtwn.it/index.html
2020–
Curator: Claudia D'Alonzo

FOAM TALENT I DIGITAL
talent.foam.org
2020–
Curator: Foam

REAL-TIME CONSTRAINTS
www.arebyte.com/real-time-constraints
2020
Curators: Rebecca Edwards and Luba Elliott

SILICON VALET
www.siliconvalet.org
2020
Curators: Faith Holland, Lorna Mills,
Wade Wallerstein

VOUS ÊTES ICI
hubs.mozilla.com/VnMK4vT/vous-etes-ici
2020
Curator: Valentin Godard

ARTE-19 - VIRUS VIRTUAL REALITY GAMES
arte19vvr.games
2020–
Curators: various (Arte-19 VVR /
Fusolab)

TRANSMISSIONS
www.twitch.tv/transmissions2020
2020
Curators: Anne Duffau, Hana Noorali
and Tai Shani

THE ARCHIVE TO COME
www.carlagannis.com
2020
Curators: Clark Buckner and Carla
Gannis

THE MUSEUM OF CONTEMPORARY ART
KITTENGALE (MOCAK)
www.juliamaiuri.com/mocak
2020–
Curators: Julia Maiuri and Joolz, her
avatar within the game

NEW ART CITY
newart.city
2020–
Curators: d0n.xyz, Martin Mudenda
Bbela, Christina Lelon, Benny Lichtner
and Sammie Veeler

THE ART HAPPENS HERE
www.annkakultys.com/online/statement/
2020–?
Curator: Annka Kultys

LOST IN A GARDEN OF CLOUDS
cloud.radical-openness.org/lost.html
2020
Curators: Davide Bevilacqua, Us(c)hi
Reiter in collaboration with AMRO
Community Members

THIRD SPACE NETWORK
thirdspacenetwork.com/about
2020–
Curator: Randal Packer

SCREEN WALKS
screenwalks.com
2020–
Curators: Jon Uriarte, Marco De Mutiis
☆ Screen Walks investigates the screen
as medium, creating new social spaces
of interaction by emphasising the
connections between curating, research
and presentation and blurring the
distinctions between a desktop tour, a
workshop and web distribution.

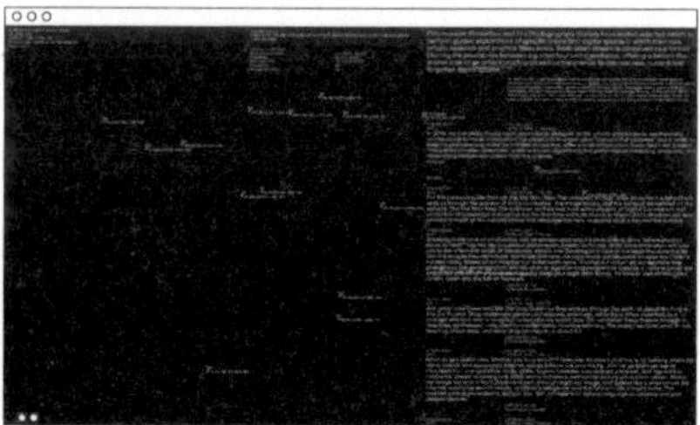

FITART
apps.apple.com/app/id1515130239
2020–
Curators: Nina Roehrs and Damjanski
☆ FitArt responds to the massification
of apps and the way they shape social
behaviour and personal interaction.
It does this by experimenting with
in-app series to test the boundaries of
what is conventionally considered to be
'art' and an 'exhibition space', thereby
developing a new set of aesthetics.

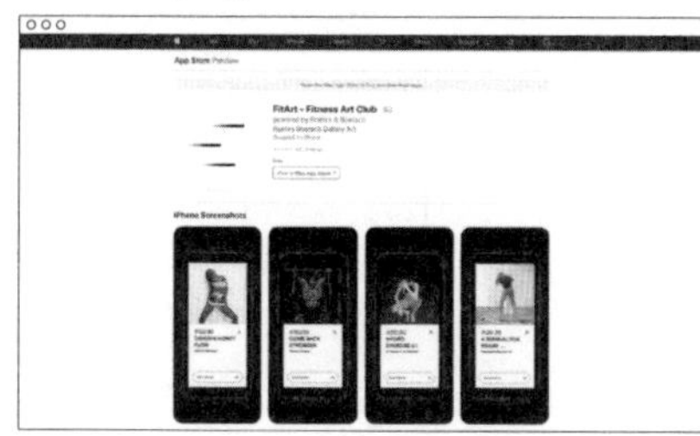

2021

- Signal sees 7.5 million dowloads in 4 days after WhatsApp says it will share data with Facebook
- DarkMarket has been taken offline by a Europol-coordinated international operation
- Alphabet Workers Union was founded with over 700 members

E-XHIBITION
www.andypicci.com/e-xhibition
2020
Curator: Andy Picci

VIRTUAL FACTORY
virtual-factory.co.uk/#
2020–
Curator: Manchester International Festival

ART IS STILL HERE: A HYPOTHETICAL SHOW FOR A CLOSED MUSEUM
www.mwoods.org/Art-Is-Still-Here-A-Hypothetical-Show-for-a-Closed-Museum
2020–?
Curator: Victor Wang

ART HOMEPAGE FAIR
arthomepagefair.net
2021–
Curators: exonemo and IDPW (I.D. Password, affectionately known as 'I pass')

STUDIO VISIT
5e.centre.ch/en/works/?id=454
2021
Curator: Domenico Quaranta

LE BIENNALI INVISIBILI
lebiennaliinvisibili.org
2021
Curator: Alfons Hug

CIVA
civa.at
2021–
Curators: Eva Fischer, Martina Menegon and Angie Shahira Pohl

ERGO PROXY - MUESTRA VIRTUAL
uca.edu.ar/es/pabellon-de-bellas-artes/ergo-proxy
2021–
Curator: Merlina Rañi

SYNTHETIC CORPO-REALITY
hubs.mozilla.com/MS8EuTz/meet-digital-culture-center
2021
Curator: Julie Walsh

Index

0–9

6th Guangzhou Triennial, CN   264

20 Bedford Place, Brighton UK   75, 80

37PK, Haarlem NL   110, 113, 114

45 Salón Nacional de Artistas de Bogotá, CO   127

319 Scholes, New York US   23, 39, 44

430-500 nm   186

700 MB Gallery   229, 231, 232, 234

A

A Foundation, Liverpool UK   80

A morta   252

Aarea   9, 247–250, 252

Accademia di Belle Arti di Carrara, IT   44

Acosta, Helena   145, 147

AFK (Stichting Amsterdams Fonds voor de Kunst), Amsterdam NL   156

Agorama   244

AHRC (Arts and Humanities Council), UK 56, 101

All My Messages   134

All that is Solid Melts Into Clouds   106

Altmann, Kari   67

Altri tempi, altri miti   44

American Mountains   119

Anamorvista   80

Anikina, Alex   244

AOS (arebyte on screen)   216–218

Appendix Project Space, Portland US   68

Apple   112, 256

Arbeit Studios, London UK   220

Arcadia Missa, London UK   9, 50, 52, 54–56

Arcangel, Cory   135

Archive 2020   9

Are.na   26

arebyte Gallery, London UK   9, 213, 214, 216, 217, 220

Arles Photography festival, FR   291

Arnold, Johanna   252

Arreola-Burns, Pita   9, 33, 244

Art.Teleportacia   118, 124

Arti et Amicitiae, Amsterdam NL   23

Arts Council England   54, 80, 101

Asseldonk, Ties van   272

Austin, Evelyn   9, 158

Avedon, LaTurbo   9, 166

B

BAK, Utrecht NL   56

Baker, Tim   23

Ball, Alejandro   244

Baltan Laboratories, Eindhoven NL   10

Banner Repeater, London UK   122

Barad, Karen   257

Barsch, Paul   9, 203, 210

Barthes, Roland   281, 291

Bartholl, Aram   277, 278

BB5000   210

Beautiful Interfaces   145, 147, 149, 150

Beijing International New Media Art   264

Benedetti, Livia   9, 252

Benetton, Niccolò   95

Berlin Biennale, DE   72, 210

Berlin, Zentrum der Netzkunst – damals und heute   17, 176

Bernartova, Jana   186

Bewersdorf, Kevin   44

Bicknell-Knight, Bob   9, 142

Big Sausage Pizza 1   56

Bin Laden, Osama   97

Binschtok, Viktoria   280

Bitforms Gallery, New York US   109

Bits of Freedom   153, 158

BODY HOLES   208, 210

Boerdam, Elki   157

Boven, Martijn van   155

Brighton Photo Fringe festival, UK   80

Bruijn, Nieck de   271

Bubblebyte   40, 68

Buffalo Bill Gates   64

Bule, Violette   145

Bunting, Heath   118, 153

Burns, Elliott   244

button   250, 252

BYOB (Bring Your Own Beamer)   146

C

C(h)roma Show   119, 130

C@C (Computer-Aided-Curating)   16–18

CAFA (China Central Academy of Fine Arts), Beijing CN   256, 264

CAFAM Techne Triennial, Beijing CN   259, 264

Camberwell College of Arts, London UK   56, 142

Cambridge University, UK   142

Caroline in the Gallery   56

Cascella, Daniela   118

CCA Wattis Institute, San Francisco US   248–250, 252

CD Player   234

Central Saint Martins College of Art and Design (CSM), London UK   49, 56, 217, 237, 244

Centre for the Study of Existential Risk, Cambridge UK   106, 136, 294

Centre Pompidou, Paris FR   261

Chan, Jennifer   53, 56

Childish Gambino (Donald Glover)   154

Chisenhale Gallery, London UK   214

Chronus Art Center, Shanghai CN   259, 264

Cirio, Paolo   118

Clark, Tom   9, 56

Club Internet   22, 40

Club Rothko   164

(c)merry   180, 186

CO-OP   102, 103, 106

Collect the WWWorld. The Artist as Archivist in the Internet Age   38–40, 43, 44

Collecting the Web   104

Committed Suicide   84

Connor, Katy   77

Cook, Sarah   26

Cornell, Lauren   66

Cortright, Petra   67, 139, 262
Ćosić, Vuk   109, 145
Cosmos Carl   136
Coy, Chris   269
Creative Industries Fund   158
Critchley, Emma   80
CRUMB (University of Sunderland), UK   130
CUNY Graduate Center (City University of New York), US   264
Curated By, Vienna AT   56
CuratingYouTube   176
Cyphoria   44

D

Dammbeck, Lutz   203
Dante, Arthur   258
Data Centers Grand Tour (This Data Belongs Here)   80
Datumsoria: the Return of the Real   259
David Roberts Art Foundation, London UK   56
David, Catherine   98
De Maria, Walter   250
De Mutiis, Marco   286, 290
De Roze Tanker, Amsterdam NL   154
Decision Space   289
Deli.near.info   23
Delicious Contemporary Semantics   23, 41
DeOrigenBelico   146
Derat, Sarah   244
Digital R&D Fund for the Arts, UK   101
digital3mpire   197, 199
Discipula   95, 106
Discord   11
Dismantling the Simulation   145, 150
Dissociations   23
Doctorow, Cory   41
Documenta X   98
Domanović, Aleksandra   25, 96
DONE   291, 294
Dorpel, Harm van den   22, 23, 40, 67
Drage, Matt   52
Dresden Art Academy, DE   203

Dullaart, Constant   9, 22–24, 64, 67, 77, 79, 80, 124, 133, 153, 174, 180, 272, 273
DUMP.FM IRL   23
Dunkelberg, Hannah Sophie   280, 281
Duty Free   135

E

e-PERMANENT   75, 77–80
E-Werk, Berlin DE   170
eBay   26, 27, 97, 100, 122, 126–128, 130, 192
Edelstein-Gomez, Madja   9, 28, 31, 83, 84, 88, 92
Edwards, Rebecca   220
Eeden, Amber van den   9, 64
Eilish, Billie   280
Elastobabe   210
Electronic Superhighway   99
EPFL (École polytechnique fédérale de Lausanne), CH   264
European Graduate School   67
Excellences & Perfections   275
Exercise in Hopeless Nostalgia: World Wide Web   33
#exstrange   97, 100, 120, 122, 125–128, 130

F

Face the Face: A Speed Show on the Post-Digital-Self   277, 278
Facebook   25, 26, 69, 134, 147, 156, 158, 190, 250, 290
FAMU, Prague CZ   180
Farinati, Lucia   118
Farkas, Rózsa   9, 56
Fear of Content   210
First Real Net Art Gallery   18, 118
FoAM, Brussels BE   238
Fondazione La Quadriennale di Roma, IT   44
Fornieles, Ed   214
Foto Colectania, Barcelona ES   288, 291, 294

Fotomuseum Winterthur, DE   290, 292, 294
Freaks   150
FREE   96
Friend, Sarah   244
Friese, Holger   172, 175
Fuller, Matthew   99
Furnace, Franklin   257
FutureSonic   153

G

Ga, Zhang   9, 264
Gallaway, Cheryl   75, 80
Galloway, Alexander   287
Gardener, Kelly Ann   244
Garrin, Paul   262
Gedanken zur Revolution   229
GeoCities   122
George, Stefan   276
Gerrit Rietveld Academie, Amsterdam NL   64
Getxophoto International Image Festival, Gexto ES   294
Ghidini, Marialaura   9, 21, 24, 97, 100
Giphy   290
god and bodies   84
Goldsmith, Kenneth   250, 252
Goldsmiths, University of London, UK   56, 142
Golem/s   84
Google   27, 48, 52, 77, 103, 134, 148, 156, 158, 205, 213, 237, 240, 242, 244, 267, 291
Google Will Eat Itself   118
Goriunova, Olga   29
GOTOIO   119
Grand Union, Birmingham UK   118, 119, 122
Great Central, Leicester UK   214
Groenendijk, Stefan   114
Ground Zero Earth   136
Group Etcetera   96
Grubinger, Eva   16–18
Guez, Emmanuel   83

H

Haehnel, Stefan   210
Hall, Todrick   33
Halter, Ed   23

Haraway, Donna   161
HDK (UDK Berlin University of the Arts), DE   256
HeK (House of Electronic Arts), Basel CH   19, 44, 264
Hendricks, Manique   9, 114
Hendriks, Martijn   96
Here We Go Again   137
Hermstedt, Heidelberg DE   170
Hershman Leeson, Lynn   84, 118
Hirsch, Ann   47, 48, 56
Höflich, Ruth   80
Holder, Joey   214
Honert, Martin   203
Hope   139
Hörl, Erich   256
Hornig, Tilman   9, 210
Howard, Lindsay   23
Huber, Hans Dieter   172, 175
Hyperemployment   44

I

ICA (Institute of Contemporary Arts), London UK   56
iMessage   156
Impakt, Utrecht NL   101
InExchange   50
Information Center, New York US   257
Instagram   26, 33, 111, 123, 147, 155, 156, 190, 239, 250, 275, 276, 278, 280, 281, 288
Institut für alles Mögliche   229, 232
Interaction Design ArtEZ, Arnhem NL   272
Internet Archaeology   39, 40, 224, 226
Internet Ecology   192, 194
INTIMIDAD ROMERO   150
isthisit?   134, 136, 139, 142

J

Jan Hus Foundation, Brno CZ   184
Jansen, Ward   155
Jaskowska, Johanna   280

JavaScript   148, 149, 267
Javůrek, Tomáš   180, 186
Jeron, Karl Heinz   234
Jeu de Paume, Paris FR   250, 252
Jitsi   240
JODI.org   37, 139, 170
Judd, Donald   111
Julia Stoschek Collection, Düsseldorf DE   137
Just Chilling 40

K

Kametani, Tamara   244
Kametani, Yoshi   244
Kard, Kamilia   44
Kassier, Andy   275, 276
Kaulmann, Thomax   17
Kayak Libre   119
Keil, Morag   137
Keller, Daniel   176
Kelton, Tara   123
Kernohan, Woodrow   76
KHM (Academy of Media Arts), Cologne DE   197
Kholeif, Omar   99
Klap, Roosje   155
Know Your Meme   290
Kode9   220
Kohout, Martin   180
KÖNIG GALERIE, Berlin DE   278, 282
König, Johann   278, 282
Kraupa-Tuskany Zeidler, Berlin DE   72
Krauss, Rosalind   255
Kruger, Barbara   84
Krysa, Joasia   28
Kuhlmann, Florian   9, 200, 234

L

Lady Gaga   280
Lambert, Steve   96
Landman, Joris   157
Laric, Oliver   25, 69
Last Real Net Art Museum   18, 20, 21
Lazzarini, Francesca   95, 106
Legrady, George   67
Lei, Yan   259
Leirner, Jac   247, 250, 252
Lek, Lawrence   215, 220
Leonardo da Vinci   41, 42

Lialina, Olia   18–20, 109, 118, 153, 259
Lighthouse, Brighton UK   238
LIMA Art Institute, Amsterdam NL   114, 154
Link Art Center, Brescia IT   42, 44
Link in Bio: Art after Social Media   277, 278, 280, 282
Linux   112
LMCC (Lower Manhattan Cultural Council), New York US   257
London South Bank University, UK   106, 294
Lorusso, Silvio   80
Loshadka   22
Lovink, Geert   96, 287
Lucerne University, CH   106, 294
Lucky PDF   68
Ludovico, Alessandro   118
Ludy, Sara   214
Luksch, Manu   119
Lund, Jonas   64, 271, 272, 287
Lundahl & Seitl   119
Lyotard, Jean-François   255

M

MACBA (Museu d'Art Contemporani de Barcelona), ES   294
Machines Are Not Alone   264
Maduro, Nicolas   145
Malevich, Kazimir   23
Malraux, André   19
Manovich, Lev   120
Manzano, Alexia   176
Marcelle, Cinthia   248, 252
Masaryk University, Brno CZ   186
Mattes, Eva and Franco   44
Mattson, Kalle   9
Mauro-Flude, Nancy   77
MayDayRooms, London UK   55
MBCBFTW   18, 19
McCarthy, Diana   29
McNeil, Joanna   17
McRae, Rachel   244

Media Art Triennial, National Art Museum of China, Beijing CN   258, 264
Media Wall   288
Mediamatic, Amsterdam NL   67, 158
!Mediengruppe Bitnik   267
Meier, Anika   9, 33
Meixnerová, Marie (Mary Meixner)   9, 186
Metamoderne   199
Metronom, Modena IT   102
MFG Paltrinieri   95
Michela Rizzo Gallery, Venice IT   102
Michigan University, Ann Arbor US   128
Miles, Jonathan   50
MINI Museum of XXI Century Art   43
MIT (Massachusetts Institute of Technology), Cambridge US   56, 264
MLZ Art Dep, Trieste IT   102, 103, 106
Modern Family   214
Modrak, Rebekah   97, 100, 120, 126
MoMA (Museum of Modern Art), New York US   72, 240, 261
Mongrel   285
Moody, Tom   25
Mora, Deborah   272
Mori, Tokyo JP   261
Morkevicius, Visvaldas   176
Mosaic   256
Most Dismal Swamp   220
Mousavi, Laura   9, 80
MU, Eindhoven NL   19, 154, 264
Museum of Fine Arts, Leipzig DE   276, 277, 282
Museum of London, UK   104
Must See   156
My Boyfriend Came Back From The War   18

N

Nake, Frieder   67
Nam June Paik Art Center, Yongin KR   259

Nancarrow, Conlon   268
Nasty Nets   22
National Centre of Biological Sciences, Bangalore IN   119
National Portrait Gallery, Washington DC., US   137
Neddam, Martine   29, 83
Netart-datenbank.org   170, 172, 176
Netartdatabase   126
netpoineers 1.0   176
Neverending Snake   244
Neverending Story   70
New Museum, New York US   96, 240, 264
New Scenario   9, 31, 139, 203, 204, 206–208, 210
Nicholson, Jack   262
NON, Düsseldorf DE   200
Nøtel   215, 220
Novitskova, Katja   9, 72

O

O'Doherty, Brian   119
Off Site Project   9, 33, 240–242, 244
OKONOstudio, Murcia ES   44
Olson, Marisa   25, 47, 276
(On) Accordance   122
On the Upgrade   120
Open Codes   98
Open Office: And Lore, Arcadia Missa   52, 56
OpenAI, San Francisco US   278
or-bits.com   40, 97, 118, 120–124, 126, 130
Osborne, Peter   256
Ostler, Scott   23
Out of Caste   84, 85
Owens, Craig   255

P

PAF Festival, Olomouc CZ   180, 182, 186
Paglen, Trevor   96
Palazzo delle Esposizioni, Rome IT   44
panke.gallery, Berlin DE   17, 170, 172, 174–176
Panther Modern   164, 166
Paris Photo, FR   291

Parsons School of Design, New York US   256, 264
Patel, Mukul   119
Pattison, Yuri   80
Paz, Jean   252
Permanent Gallery, Brighton UK   76, 78, 80
Picasso, Pablo   90
Pisuisse, Frederique   103
Pivô, São Paulo BR   250, 252
Playlist: Playing Music, Games, Art   43
Plohman, Angela   9
Podsiadly, Dominik   186
POIUYT   95, 97, 100, 102, 104, 106
POIUYT: Point Zero Critical Practices in Contemporary Italian Photography   103, 106
!POP!: points of reference   119
Post Internet Survival Guide   70, 72
Post-Photography   294
Price, Elizabeth   77
Priglinger, Christoph   25
Project Native Informant, London UK   137
Pussykrew   166, 220

Q

Quaranta, Domenico   9, 10, 25, 31, 44

R

Radek, Luca   220
Rafman, Jon   96
RE-FIGURE GROUND   220
Re-Materialising Feminism   56
readme.html   118
Reas, Casey   67
Refresh!   40
Rehearsals in Instability   56
Reisman, Leah   16
Revolver Publishing   72
Rhizome   83, 101, 124, 223, 264, 269
Riebel, Stefan   9, 234
Rihanna   69
Rijksakademie van beeldende kunsten, Amsterdam NL   72

Ripps, Ryder   9, 23, 39, 44, 100
Rossner, Manuel   278, 279, 282
Roth, Evan   44, 262
router.gallery   174, 175
Royal College of Art, London UK   50
Royal College of Psychiatrists, London UK   214
Rozendaal, Rafaël   111
Rubens, Peter Paul   41
Runme   124

S

Saaze, Vivian van   16
Sadofsky, Phillip   234
Sakrowski   9, 124, 180, 186
Sambini, Alessandro   95, 97, 106
Sandberg Instituut, Amsterdam NL   67, 72
Santilli, Simone   95
Sanz, Carolina   145
Schmieg, Sebastian   289
Schnitzer, Georg   25
School of Art and Design, National University of Australia, Canberra AU   294
School of Creative Media, Hong Kong CN   286
Screen Walks   294
screensaver watching you   244
ScreenSaverGallery   180, 182, 184, 186
SE8 Gallery, London UK   214
Search Engine   118, 119, 130
Second Life   11, 161
#selfie   186
Semiconductor   80
Shakespeare, William   268
Sherman, Cindy   84
Shulgin, Alexei   145
Silicon Plateau   120, 123, 130
Singer, R.   186
SINGLE SIGN ON   234
SITUATIONS   290, 294
Skype   11, 240
Sluis, Katrina   9, 12, 33

Smerdel, Mirko   95
SOA   232
Soda, Molly   137
Solmi, Federico   44
Somrová, Anita   186
Sontag, Susan   161, 281
Sound Threshold   118
SPAMM (SuPer Art Modern Museum)   191, 192, 194
Spazio Contemporanea, Brescia IT   44
Speck, Hendrik   67
Speed Show   277, 278
Srishti Institute of Art, Design and Technology, Bangalore IN   117, 130
Stanford University, US   264
Stedelijk Museum Amsterdam, NL   59, 61, 64
Stelarc   285
Steyerl, Hito   135
Stimuleringsfonds Creatieve Industrie, Rotterdam NL   156
Stolk, Lilian   9
Stone, Sandy   285
Studio , Prague CZ   186
SuperCentral   22
Surprisingly Surprisingly   282
Surprisingly This Rather Works   282
Sutter, Loïq   150
Swamp Protocol   220
Systaime (a.k.a. Michaël Borras)   9, 194
Szűcsová, Monika   186

T

T.A.J. Residency & SKE Projects, Bangalore IN   118
TAG Gallery   40, 124
Tanini, Tommaso   95
Tate Modern, London UK   142, 240, 261, 285
Teachers College, Columbia University, New York US   182
Teams   11
Tedone, Gaia   9, 12, 27, 106
Temporary Stedelijk   64
Testing Ground   214

The Artist is Online   282
The bliss of metamorphing collapse   220
The Cool Couple   95, 106
The Curated Web   112–114
The Death of the URL   133
The Hmm   9, 154, 156, 158
The New Outside   271
The Others   44
The Photographers Gallery, London UK 285, 287–289, 294
The Posthuman Era Became a Girl at the South London Gallery   56
The Recombinants   28, 29, 83, 86–88, 91, 92
The Rose Goldsen Archive of New Media Art, Cornell University, Ithaca US   124
The Wrong Bienniale   147, 149, 150
The Wrong Router   150
The Yes Men   96
This is America   154
Thundergulch   257
Topologies of the Real   259
Tor Browser   149, 150
Towner Art Gallery, Eastbourne UK   99
Transmediale Festival, Berlin DE   68, 101, 170, 176
Trecartin, Ryan   69
Trnková, Barbora   180, 186
Troemel, Brad   100
True To You When I Punch You   210
TU Berlin, DE   176
Tumblr   22, 26, 41, 100, 109–114, 203, 238, 280
Turbulence   124, 125
Twitch   11
Twixt Two Worlds   99
Tyżlik-Carver, Magda   28

U

UAL (University of the Arts London), UK   56
UBERMORGEN   118
UCSB (University of California Santa Barbara), US   264
Uffizi Museum, Florence IT   33

Ullman, Ellen   125
Ulman, Amalia   135, 214, 262, 275
Un-published Outsourced 122
University of Amsterdam, NL   109
University of São Paulo, BR   252
University Paris 8, FR   252
Unknown Cloud 119
Unseen 2017 106
Unseen Photo Fair, Amsterdam NL   102, 103
Unthinking Photography 289
UPOL (Palacký University), Olomouc CZ   186
Upstream.Gallery, Amsterdam NL   271, 272
Uriarte, Jon   9
USB-Shuffle-Show 229

V

V&A (Victoria and Albert Museum), London UK   240
Van Abbemuseum, Eindhoven NL   10
Van Stenis, Miyö   9, 130
Vardi, Nimrod   9, 220
Venice Biennale, IT   72
Vermelho   252
Vieira, Marcela   9, 252
Vigipirate Quadcopter Drone 148
Virtual Normality: NetzkünstlerInnen 2.0 280, 282
VVORK   25, 124

W

Waag, Amsterdam NL   238
Wark, McKenzie   285
Ways of Living 56
We=Link: Ten Easy Pieces 260, 262, 264
Webb, Thomas   33
Weckert, Simon   244
Weidinger, Alfred   282
Weiyi, Li   262
Wharton, Glenn   16, 17

Whereby   11
Whitechapel Gallery, London UK   99, 220
Whitneybiennial.com 40
Willumeit, Lars   102, 106
Windows   112, 257
Wisniewski, Maciej   262
Wolfe, Cary   255
Women Net Artists 2.0 282
Women on Waves   158
Wooldridge, Duncan   103
Wordpress   22, 25
World Wide Web   18, 113

X

Xiaodong, Liu   259

Y

You Must Not Call It Photography If This Expression Hurts You [beta] (YMNCIPITEHY) 9, 288, 290
YouTube   11, 25, 26, 43, 77, 102, 103, 106, 149, 154, 174, 191, 192

Z

Zabludowicz Collection, London UK   214
ZHdK (Zürcher Hochschule der Künste), CH   56
Žižek, Slavoj   161
ZKM (Zentrum für Kunst und Medien), Karlsruhe DE   98, 259, 261, 263, 264
ZKM | Hong Media Art collection   264
Zombectro   83
Zoom   11, 240
Zoonosis Project 145

Colophon

EDITOR
Annet Dekker

AUTHORS
Pita Arreola-Burns
Evelyn Austin
LaTurbo Avedon
Paul Barsch
Livia Benedetti
Bob Bicknell-Knight
Elliott Burns
Tom Clark
Marco De Mutiis
Constant Dullaart
Madja Edelstein-Gomez
Rebecca Edwards
Amber van den Eeden
Rózsa Farkas
Marialaura Ghidini
Manique Hendricks
Tilman Hornig
Florian Kuhlmann
Kalle Mattsson
Anika Meier
Marie Meixnerová
Laura Mousavi
Katja Novitskova
Domenico Quaranta
Stefan Riebel
Ryder Ripps
Sakrowski
Katrina Sluis
Lilian Stolk
Systaime
Gaia Tedone
Jon Uriarte
Miyö Van Stenis
Nimrod Vardi
Marcela Vieira
Zhang Ga

COPY-EDITING
Mark Poysden

PROOFREADING
Els Brinkman

INDEX
Elke Stevens

GRAPHIC DESIGN
Irene Stracuzzi, *irenestracuzzi.com*

TYPEFACES
STIX Two Text, Suisse Int'l

PAPER INSIDE
EOS 2.0 90 g/m²

PAPER COVER:
Munken Lynx Rough 300 g/m²

LITHOGRAPHY AND PRINTING
Wilco Art Books, Amersfoort

PUBLISHER
Pia Pol, Astrid Vorstermans,
Valiz, Amsterdam

Amsterdam, 2021
Valiz, Amsterdam, *www.valiz.nl*

This publication has been printed on FSC-certified paper by an FSC-certified printer. The FSC, Forest Stewardship Council promotes environmentally appropriate, socially beneficial, and economically viable management of the world's forests.
fsc.org

This publication was made possible through the generous support of:

**creative
industries
fund NL**

Prins Bernhard Cultuurfonds, NL

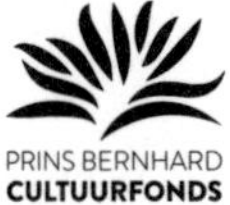

PRINS BERNHARD
CULTUURFONDS

The editors and the publisher have made every effort to secure permission to reproduce the listed material, texts and illustrations. We apologize for any inadvert errors or omissions. Parties who nevertheless believe they can claim specific legal rights are invited to contact the publisher. *info@valiz.nl*

INTERNATIONAL DISTRIBUTION

BE/NL/LU: Centraal Boekhuis, *www.centraal.boekhuis.nl*

GB/IE: Anagram Books, *www.anagrambooks.com*

Europe (excl GB/IE)/Asia: Idea Books, *www.ideabooks.nl*

Australia: Perimeter, *www.perimeterdistribution.com*

USA, Canada, Latin-America: D.A.P., *www.artbook.com*

INDIVIDUAL ORDERS
www.valiz.nl; *info@valiz.nl*

ISBN 978-94-93246-01-0
Printed and bound in the EU

Making Public Series

The series *Making Public* investigates 'the public', the civil domain where space, knowledge, values and commodities are shared. What does this notion of 'public' mean? How does this domain change under the influence of technological, political and social tendencies? Where are the boundaries of 'the public' and how are they determined? What forms of responsibility and solidarity does 'the public' invoke? And how do artists and culture critics shape the debate on these issues?

From 2021 onwards the series is designed by Irene Stracuzzi.

2017   **Authenticity?: Observations and Artistic Strategies in the Post-Digital Age**
Barbara Cueto, Bas Hendrikx (eds.)
Contributors: Erika Balsom, Franco 'Bifo' Berardi, Jazmina Figueroa, Bas
Hendrikx & Barbara Cueto, Holly Herndon & Mat Dryhurst, Rob Horning,
David Joselit, Oliver Laric, Timotheus Vermeulen, Beny Wagner
With Impakt Foundation
Designed by Template, Lasse van den Bosch Christensen & Marlon Harder
ISBN 978-94-92095-23-7

2017   **Being Public: How Art Creates the Public**
Jeroen Boomgaard, Rogier Brom (eds.)
Contributors: Barbara Alves, Jeroen Boomgaard, Rogier Brom, Anke Coumans,
Florian Cramer, Eva Fotiadi, Maaike Lauwaert, Gabriel Lester, Steven ten Thije
With LAPS / Rietveld Academie
Designed by Template, Lasse van den Bosch Christensen & Marlon Harder
ISBN 978-94-92095-28-2

2017   **Compassion: A paradox in Art and Society**
Jeroen Boomgaard, Rini Hurkmans, Judith Westerveld (eds.)
Contributors: Jesse Ahlers, Nick Aikens, Sarah van Binsbergen, Jeroen
Boomgaard, Pascal Gielen, Rini Hurkmans, Susan Neiman, Leonhard de Paepe,
Judith Westerveld
With LAPS / Rietveld Academie
Designed by Template, Lasse van den Bosch Christensen & Marlon Harder
ISBN 978-94-92095-29-9

2017   **Lost and Living (in) Archives: Collectively Shaping New Memories**
Annet Dekker (ed.)
Contributors: Babak Afrassiabi, Dušan Barok, Tina Bastajian, Nanna Bonde
Thylstrup, Özge Çelikaslan, Annet Dekker, Olia Lialina, Manu Luksch, Nicolas
Malevé, Aymeric Mansoux, Michael Murtaugh, Josien Pieterse, Ellef Prestsæter,
Robert Sakrowski, Stef Scagliola, Katrina Sluis, Femke Snelting, Igor Štromajer,
Nasrin Tabatabai
With Piet Zwart Institute
Designed by Template, Lasse van den Bosch Christensen & Marlon Harder
ISBN 978-94-92095-26-8